Book History through Postcolonial Eyes

This surprising study draws together the disparate fields of postcolonial theory and book history in a challenging and illuminating way.

Robert Fraser proposes that we now look beyond the traditional methods of the Anglo-European bibliographic paradigm, and learn to appreciate instead the diversity of shapes that verbal expression has assumed across different societies. This change of attitude will encourage students and researchers to question developmentally conceived models of communication, and move instead to a re-formulation of just what is meant by a book, an author, a text.

Fraser illustrates his combined approach with comparative case studies of print, script and speech cultures in South Asia and Africa, before panning out to examine conflicts and paradoxes arising in parallel contexts. The re-orientation of approach and the freshness of view offered by this volume will foster understanding and creative collaboration between scholars of different outlooks, while offering a radical critique to those identified in its concluding section as purveyors of global literary power.

Robert Fraser has published books on Proust, J. G. Frazer, Ben Okri, African poetry and postcolonial fiction. He is co-editor with Mary Hammond of the two-volume *Books Without Borders* (2008), and also enjoys a parallel career as a biographer. Professor of English at the Open University, he is Fellow of the Royal Society of Literature and of the Royal Asiatic Society.

Also by Robert Fraser

Proust and the Victorians: the lamp of memory

The Making of *The Golden Bough*: the origins and growth
of an argument

Lifting the Sentence: a poetics of postcolonial fiction

Victorian Quest Romance: Stevenson, Haggard, Kipling
and Conan Doyle

West African Poetry: a critical history

The Chameleon Poet: a life of George Barker

The Novels of Ayi Kwei Armah

Ben Okri: towards the invisible city

As editor

Sir James Frazer and the Literary Imagination

The Golden Bough: a new abridgement

The Collected Poems of George Barker

The Selected Poems of George Barker

This Island Place

The Book in the World: readers, writers and publishers
(with Susheila Nasta)

Books without Borders, Volume 1: The cross-national
dimension in print culture
(with Mary Hammond)

Books without Borders, Volume 2: Perspectives from
South Asia
(with Mary Hammond)

Book History through Postcolonial Eyes

Rewriting the script

Robert Fraser

Routledge
Taylor & Francis Group

LONDON AND NEW YORK

For David Daiches (1912–2005) and
A. Norman Jeffares (1920–2005)
In memoriam

First published 2008
by Routledge
2 Park Square, Milton Park, Abingdon, Oxon. OX14 4RN

Simultaneously published in the USA and Canada
by Routledge
270 Madison Ave, New York, NY 10016

Routledge is an imprint of the Taylor & Francis Group, an informa business

© 2008 Robert Fraser

Typeset in Baskerville by
Bookcraft Limited, Stroud, Gloucestershire
Printed and bound in Great Britain by
CPI Antony Rowe, Chippenham, Wiltshire

British Library Cataloguing in Publication Data
A catalogue record for this book is available from the British Library

Library of Congress Cataloging in Publication Data
Fraser, Robert, 1947–
Book history through postcolonial eyes : re-writing the script / Robert Fraser.
    p. cm.
Includes bibliographical references and index.
1. Books—South Asia—History. 2. Books—Africa—History. 3. Printing—South
Asia—History. 4. Printing—Africa—History. 5. Written communication—South
Asia—History. 6. Written communication—Africa—History. 7. Book industries
and trade—South Asia—History. 8. Book industries and trade—Africa—History.
9. Transmission of texts. 10. Oral tradition. I. Title.
Z8.S64F73 2008
002.0954—dc22   2008002020

ISBN10: 0-415-40293-X (hbk)
ISBN10: 0-415-40294-8 (pbk)
ISBN10: 0-203-88811-1 (ebk)

ISBN13: 978-0-415-40293-4 (hbk)
ISBN13: 978-0-415-40294-1 (pbk)
ISBN13: 978-0-203-88811-7 (ebk)

Contents

Illustrations

Preface

No one person can – or will soon – write a comprehensive history of the book from a postcolonial point of view. The subject is too protean, the readjustments required too radical for this moment in time. What I have attempted to do in this modest volume is to set a course by which others may later choose to steer. To adapt a title of Kant's, I have tried to provide my readers – specialists, students and freelance scholars – with a Prolegomenon to Any Future Set of Histories of Textual Transmission in the pre-imperial, imperial and post-imperial worlds – and principally those of Africa and South Asia.

Some preliminary remarks are in order. I am concerned here with the book in the broadest meaning of the term, especially in so far as it draws on the parallel communicative modes of spoken expression and script. The phenomenon of hypertext lies largely outside my scope, though I have tried to keep it in mind as a field of contemporary comparison. Throughout I have endeavoured none the less to avoid privileging the print medium above others: much of my argument, indeed, concerns the parity between different communicative regimes. I have also tried to avoid over-privileging literary works in the narrow sense above other sorts of book, and works in English above those in other – specifically indigenous – languages. The result – though I hope concise – is a comparative study with a fairly broad sweep. In it, I should add, the term postcolonial refers to the historical vantage point from which the material is regarded rather than to a period under particular consideration, still less to an ideology of redress.

Though my examples are selective, and mostly drawn from two distinct geographical regions, it should be obvious that I am conducting an argument potentially of far wider application. Here then is an essay in method that derives its justification from a plea of necessity. Though the subject of book history enjoys diverse roots – several French, some British and American – its main guiding lights have to date been drawn from half a millennium's experience of print culture in the West. Admittedly, over the last few years, the discipline has demonstrated a cautious willingness to peer beyond this spacious lair. Hitherto, however, it has principally conducted this inquiry with outdated – and fairly parochial – equipment. Properly to account for the origins, development and proliferation of verbal diffusion in a global environment we require a number of drastic readjustments of vision, entailing for example a radical questioning of what we *mean* by a book, or indeed by a text. We will also need a broader approach to issues such as production, distribution, exchange, readership, audience and verbal authority than any so far espoused.

I have an ulterior motive, which is to explain book history to postcolonial theorists, and postcoloniality to book historians: two groups whose mutual incompatibility remains a scandal among the nations. In effecting this introduction, I hope I will be forgiven for explaining the basic assumptions of each specialism to the other in what may sometimes appear over-zealous terms. Despite my presumption, my hope is that – somewhere between the lofts of literary theory and the vaults of book history – my theme will find its allotted place.

Acknowledgements

The Arts and Humanities Research Board (now Council) of the British Academy funded much of the preparatory work for this book, and during it I enjoyed a Senior Research Fellowship at the Open University in England and residencies at a number of overseas departments: The University of Delhi, Jadavpur University in Kolkata and the University of Legon in Accra. I would like to record my appreciation for their attentiveness to Dr Graham Shaw and his staff at the Asian and African Studies Reading Room in the British Library; to Susannah Rayner and the staff of the manuscripts section of the library of the School of Oriental and African Studies in the University of London; Martin Maw of the Oxford University Press; Sheila Noble and the staff of the archives at Edinburgh University Library; and Sue Mills of the Angus Library at Regent's Park College, Oxford. Further thanks are due to the personnel of the following collections: the National Archives in Delhi; Delhi University Library; the Asiatic Society in Kolkata; the National Library of India; the National Collection of English Literary Manuscripts in Grahamstown, South Africa; the Cory Library at Rhodes University; the National Library of South Africa, Cape Town; the Centre for the Book, Cape Town; the library of Rhodes House, Oxford; the Balme Library at the University of Ghana, Legon, and the National Archives of Ghana both in Accra and Cape Coast.

I would like to thank Priya Joshi for permission to reproduce Figure 3.1, which derives from her book *In Another Country*, and Jason Glavy for the use of his online version of Kisimi Kasara's Mende script in Figure 4.1, and Simon Ager, who produced the chart for Figure 4.1 and kindly made the files available for printing purposes. The title page of *A Grammar of the Bengal Language*, issued in Calcutta in 1778 by Nathaniel Halhed and others, is reproduced as Figure 1.1 by permission of the British Library. I salute my friends Suman Gupta and Tapan Basu and their assistants Shvetal Vyas, Arunima Paul, Viabhal Parel, Akhil Katyal and Shivani Mutneja, participants at the Open University's London workshop on 'Contemporary

Indian Literature for the Indian Market' in June 2007, for broadening my appreciation of the current publishing and bookselling scene in the subcontinent. Lastly interviews with a number of Indian and African publishers in situ, notably with Ritu Menon, Rukun Advani, Sachin Rastogi and Ntone Edjabe, helped me assess some of the varied challenges facing the book trade in today's globalised postcolonial world. I am deeply grateful to my courteous and efficient copy-editor, Christopher Feeney. I owe a further and special debt of gratitude to four learnèd pandits: Harish Trivedi, Javed Majeed, Shafquat Towheed and Rob Francis. Where wisdom is bliss, 'tis folly to ignore.

Abbreviations of archival sources

Archival sources are cited in the text, with the following abbreviations to indicate the location of the relevant archive.

Angus	The Angus Library at Regent's Park College, Oxford
As. Soc	The Asiatic Society of Bengal, Kolkata
Balme	The Balme Library in the University at Ghana, Legon
BL	The British Library, London
BM	The British Museum
Cory	The Cory Library, Rhodes University, Grahamstown, South Africa
NAG	The National Archives of Ghana, Accra
NAI	The Indian National Archives, New Delhi
NASA	The National Archives of South Africa, Cape Town
NELM	The National English Literary Museum, Grahamstown, South Africa
Nelson	The Nelson Archive, Edinburgh University Library
NLSA	The National Library of South Africa, Cape Town
OIOC	The Oriental and India Office Collections at the British Library
OUP	The archives of Oxford University Press, Oxford
Seramp	Serampore College Library, Srirampur, India
SOAS	The manuscript collections of the School of Oriental and African Studies in the University of London

Part I

Repositionings

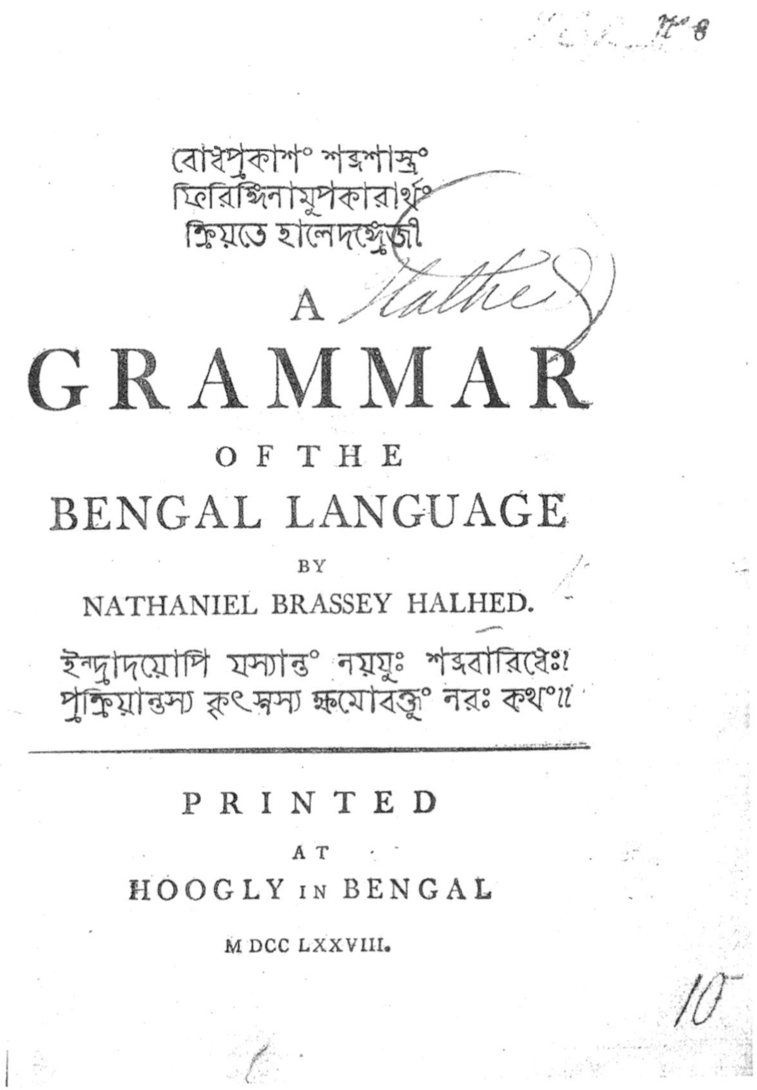

বোধপ্রকাশ শব্দশাস্ত্র
ফিরিঙ্গিনামুপকারার্থ
ক্রিয়তে হালেদসংজ্ঞা

A

GRAMMAR

OF THE

BENGAL LANGUAGE

BY

NATHANIEL BRASSEY HALHED.

ইন্দুদয়োপি যস্যান্ত নযযুঃ শব্দবারিধেঃ।
পুক্রিয়ান্তস্য কৃৎস্নস্য ক্ষমোবক্তুং নরঃ কথ°॥

PRINTED

AT

HOOGLY IN BENGAL

M DCC LXXVIII.

Figure 1.1   Title page of *A Grammar of the Bengal Language* (Hoogly, Calcutta, 1778).
Reproduced by kind permission of the British Library.

1 The problematics of print

A tale of two cities

Were you to sit amid the faded Georgian splendour of the Asiatic Society in Kolkata, or else amid the austere postmodern architecture of the Rare Books Room of the British Library in London, you might well find yourself staring at the very same page. The quarto volume that contains it is quite slender – a mere 216 pages of main text with 30 pages of prelims – but it could scarcely be of greater interest. What you would be looking at in either city is the title page of the very first book in the world to employ moveable Bangla – that is Bengali – type. *A Grammar of the Bengal Language* was compiled at Hoogly (by the banks of the Hoogly river in present-day Kolkata) in 1778 by Nathaniel Brassey Halhed, a twenty-seven-year-old 'writer' or probationer clerk in the East India Company. Halhed has signed the page near the top, so that the tail of the 'd' at the end of his surname curls across the first block of Bangla characters. That twin copies of his work can yield similar sensations in time zones set five and a half hours apart may seem slightly uncanny. In Kolkata you would need to shut your ears to the traffic in Park Street alongside the building, in London to amicable blandishments issuing from the Tannoy above your head. But lift the tome before you to eye level, and in either location you would notice, just beneath that trailing 'd', tiny indentations biting into the coarse, yellowing paper.

Considering the fact that two and a quarter centuries have passed since the book appeared, it is surprising how much has been learned about these marks. They were made by a font designed by Charles Wilkins, an accomplished linguist and writer to the Company, and cast by Panchanana Karmakara, local pandit, blacksmith and descendant of a long line of calligraphers and metallurgists. The expense of turning out both the typeface and the volume – 30,000 rupees, as Halhed's biographer tells us (Rocher, 1983: 76) – was met by Warren Hastings, Governor-General of British India, who then claimed reimbursement from the Directors.

This was evidently a collaborative publishing enterprise, and the people involved had diverse though intersecting careers. Karmakara the technician, for example, had grown up in Triveni in nearby Hooghli. Within a year of finishing work on Halhed's *Grammar* he was to be appointed as one of the Company's official print technicians. At the turn of the century he would join a famous press established by the Baptist Missionary Society in Danish-administered Serampore (Srirampur), fourteen miles upstream from Calcutta, where he would set up and oversee its type-foundry. There he evolved two different – and increasingly sophisticated – Bangla fonts for use in translations of the Bible, and a font in Devanagari – the script in which Sanskrit and Hindi are commonly written – employing 700 different 'sorts' or characters. Karmakara is also credited with the creation of fonts in Arabic, Persian, Marathi, Telegu, Burmese, Chinese and seven other tongues. He died in 1804, to be succeeded at Serampore by his son-in-law, Manohara, who would remain there for forty productive years (Ross, 1999: 46).

In the meantime Halhed had returned to England, where he became a Member of Parliament and took up residence in Charles Street, Mayfair. In 1785 Wilkins would publish an English translation of the *Bhagavad Gita*, one of the classics of Hindu spirituality. The translation would carry a Preface by Hastings dated 4 October 1784, and two years later both were translated into French. After adopting (and possibly fathering) a son by Jane Austen's aunt Philadelphia, Hastings himself would be called back to Britain, where – partly as a result of revelations by the then nascent Calcutta English-language press – he was notoriously to be impeached for corruption in 1788.

The Wilkins *Bhagavad Gita* was published in London, Halhed's *Grammar* in Calcutta but, partly because the decisions of the Company were minuted in India, we know a lot more about the production of the second. During the monsoon of 1778 it was run off on loose sheets in an edition of 1,000 copies. Five hundred sets were held for distribution in India once they had been bound, an operation which the printer advised the bookseller to delay for several months until the dry season. The Asiatic Society's copy seems to have been presented by Hastings himself. (His slightly grubby portrait in oils hangs in the library lobby just above the lockers and, as you deposit your belongings there at the beginning of a day's archival work, before him you must bow.) Twenty-five of the remaining sets were mailed to Halhed in Cape Town, where he was putting up for a few weeks on his way back to England (Rocher, 1983: 75). The remainder were shipped direct to London, followed later by two pages of errata that were to be bound in immediately after the Preface, together with an additional erratum slip Halhed himself had since added.

If the title page and printer's instructions tell you something about the book's production, Halhed's Preface discloses its purpose:

> The wisdom of the British Parliament has within these few years taken a decisive part in the internal policy and civil administration of its Asiatic territories; and more particularly in the Kingdom of Bengal, where by the most formal act of authority in the establishment of a Supreme Court of Justice, it has professedly incorporated with the British Empire. Much, however, remains for the completion of the good work; and we may reasonably presume that one of the most important desiderata is the cultivation of a right understanding between the Government and its subjects: between the Natives of Europe who are to rule, and the Inhabitants of India who are to obey. The Romans, a people of little learning and less taste, had no sooner conquered Greece than they applied themselves to the study of Greek. They adopted its laws even before they could read them, and civilized themselves in subduing their enemies. The English, who have made so capital a progress in the Polite Arts, and who are masters of Bengal, may, with more ease and greater propriety, add its language to their acquisitions: that they may explain the benevolent principles of that legislation whose decrees they enforce; that they may convince where they command; and be at once the dispensers of Laws and Science to an extensive nation.
>
> (Halhed, 1778: i–ii)

The language is confident, but it is also slightly ambiguous. The power relations invoked, for one thing, are quite explicit. The English will 'command', and the Bengalis will 'obey'. Yet it is the British who are described as 'natives', and in the process of learning a foreign language they are compared to the ancient Romans, who, whilst doing the equivalent, were once 'civilized' by the Greeks. Perhaps the most expressive phrase describes the process of assimilating Bengali, presented as an act of direct, politically motivated 'acquisition'.

Halhed's primer occupies an iconic place in the print culture of Eastern India, and in 1978 the bicentenary of its publication was celebrated publicly in Calcutta. (It was ignored in England, even in the seaside town of Lymington in the New Forest Halhed had represented as MP, having purchased the then pocket borough for £114 4s 5d.) And certainly, from a postcolonial vantage point, it may seem as if the publication of Halhed's *Grammar* was a decisive historical event. It represented, after all, the first primer printed on Asian soil for one of the most widely used languages on earth, spoken now by two hundred million people, the language of the literary polymath Rabindranath Tagore (1861–1941), and the poets Jibanananda Das (1899–1954) and Buddhadev Bhose (1908–74), the language in which the texts of the national anthems of both Bangladesh and India were both initially written, even if the latter is sung in Hindi translation. Undeniably, too, the book involved at the time a substantial advance in non-Western typography. The only previous attempt to print some sort of Bengali grammar and dictionary had been made in Lisbon thirty-five years earlier. But its compiler, an Augustinian monk called Fr Manuel de Assumpção, had been forced to transliterate everything into Roman type. This had the advantage of high-lighting lexical affinities between Indo-European elements in Bengali and de Assumpção's own Portuguese (on page 592 the Bengali for *dente* or tooth, for example, is given as *dant* or *dont*). But Bengali is a syllabic rather than an alphabetical language, and this early attempt had proved wildly inaccurate. Later, the British printer William Bolts acquired a copy (BL 16741) for 7s 6d, and on that basis attempted to learn the language and contrive his own Bangla font. This experiment had been, in Halhed's words later, an 'egregious' failure (Ross, 1999: 78). After making a nuisance of himself for six years, Bolts was deported from Bengal.

So Halhed, Wilkins and Karmakara with their purpose-made Bangla type represented a vast improvement. The question they pose for us is this: did their book, and the many others printed in Indian typefaces in the decades that followed, represent a mere technical advance, or did they also, as some have insisted, involve a fundamental shift, even a revolution, in South Asian culture? It is not difficult to adduce arguments in support of the second, more dramatic, view. Two years after the American Declaration of Independence, eleven before the French Revolution, here apparently was a revolution-in-the-making of an equally formidable kind: the exporting of the European Enlightenment, the commodification of a language, the intro-duction to the east coast of India of a transforming technology of textual reproduction, even arguably the onset of 'Modernity' itself. Print history in South Asia, broken and intermittent before, can be traced in a contin-uous line from experiments such as Halhed's, Wilkins's and Karmakara's in late eighteenth-century Bengal. The resulting transformation in modes of communication seemingly gave rise, not simply to instructional treatises such as theirs, but to the 'publication' of sacred books in myriads of tradi-tions, and the issuing of newspapers in very many languages from centres all over India. It enabled the dissemination of multiplying literary and academic genres, and of scholarly journals and monographs, across great distances. It even – so this argument might run – eventually gave rise to today's burgeoning and global artistic, political and scientific scene. Looking further ahead, one might – if so minded – attribute to the influence of these events two and a quarter centuries ago recent trends such as the emergence of the subcontinent as an international location for out-sourced printing, or the indispensable place South Asia has come to assume in the matrix of world communications.

The purpose of this and the next chapter is to investigate such claims and, with them, the problematic position occupied by the technology of print in the deep history of postcolonial cultures.

Ex Africa semper aliquid novi

One person who seems to have been convinced of the transforming potential of print for his own culture was a Setswana neighbour of the Protestant missionary Robert Moffat (1795–1883) in Kuruman, South Africa. In 1831, fifty-three years after – and 6,000 miles to the southwest of – Halhed's and Karmakara's experiments in Bengal, he was shown a page that Moffat's assistant Samuel Edwards had just run off on a wooden hand press. The press had newly been acquired in Cape Town, transported upcountry by wagon, and promptly dubbed by the locals 'Segatisho' (literally a *sharp impression*). The neighbour's reactions were observed by Moffat himself, who recorded that he

> bounded into the village, showing it to everyone that he met and asserting that Mr Edwards had made it in a moment, with a round black hammer (a printer's ball), and a shake of the arm. The description of such a juggling process soon brought a crowd to the *segatisho*, which has since proved an auxiliary to our cause.
>
> (Moffat, 1846: 563)

'Segatisho' is now in the museum at Kuruman, and is still occasionally used. Moffat and his wife had brought her up that very year along with some boxes of (Roman) type and a supply of paper and ink donated by the British and Foreign Bible Society. Soon they were putting her to good use printing parts of the Old Testament in Setswana, followed in 1848 by Moffat's own translation of Bunyan's *The Pilgrim's Progress*, the first full prose text completed at the mission. Entitled *Loeto Loa ga Mokereseti* (Christian's Journey), this is the earliest version of Bunyan's classic in any language of mainland Africa, although in 1835 a translation had been made on the island of Madagascar (see p. 109 below) and printed in Malagasy using Roman type.

There is, however, an important distinction to be drawn between the Malagasy *Pilgrim* and Moffat's, one that can perhaps best be explained by taking a look at a scene near the beginning of the book where, just before setting out on his travels, 'Christian' encounters 'Evangelist'. Bunyan's own intentions may be glimpsed in a woodcut accompanying the third English edition of 1688 in which Evangelist holds a parchment scroll and

Christian clutches a printed book, while the two men absorbedly talk and point towards the sky. Four varieties of human communication – speech, gesture, script and print – are thus brought together in one image (Figure 1.2). Now by 1835 Malagasy had been written for many centuries in Arabic script. Setswana, on the other hand, had needed to be supplied with a provisional writing system before any text could be printed. So, whereas the translators in Madagascar had at their disposal ready-made terms for both writing and reading as well as speaking and signing (even if they had freshly to transliterate them into Roman letters), Moffat was obliged to

Chriſtian, no ſooner leaves the world, but meets
Evangeliſt, who lovingly him greets;
With Tydings of another; And doth ſhow
Him how to mount to that from this below.

Figure 1.2   Speech, gesture, script, print: woodcut from the third edition of John Bunyan's *The Pilgrim's Progress* (London: For Nathaniel Ponder at the Peacock in the Poultry near Cornhill, 1688).

convey the former activities by adapting and extending existing vocabulary in a language that possessed no traditional orthography, and could as yet be written only in the somewhat approximate spelling system he and his local informants had been developing since 1826. In her seminal book *The Portable Bunyan* (2005) Isabel Hofmeyr has granted us an exposition of the significance of *Pilgrim's Progress* for cultural identity formation in Africa. It may be useful, however, to spend a moment thinking through the formative role that this classic text, together with other early missionary publications, once played in the very terms in which people came to verbalise modes of textual transmission.

In his translation of *Pilgrim* Moffat is, for instance, sometimes able to rely on vocabulary his congregation had heard from their Dutch neighbours to the south. When, right at the beginning of Bunyan's dream, Christian is revealed crying 'as he read' his Bible, his book is accordingly referred to with the hybrid term *buka*. Elsewhere the translator has sometimes had to improvise: the sentence continues *mi a buisa mo go coma, mi o rile a buisa a lela*: 'he caused it to speak, and as it spoke, he wept' (Moffat, 1848: 1). Equivalent challenges of diction faced the Bible translations published at Kuruman at this period. Setswana had soon gleaned *Bibela* from Dutch *Bijbel*, but it still required terms for the primary elements of scriptural arrangement: volume, chapter, sectional reading. So a volume became *kabo* or a portion; a chapter became *kgaolo*, a district or area; while for sections the compositors imported the typographic sign ¶. Some decisions were easy: the two books of Kings became *bukas* of *Lagosi* or Chiefs. Eden became *Edena*; Abraham *Aberahame*; Bathsheeba *Bere-sheba*. For God, however, Moffat fell back on *Modomo* (later spelt *Molimo*), who, as he bitterly complained in his journals, corresponded to a tricksome local spirit. Forty years earlier in Bengal, the Baptist missionary William Carey had wrestled with Genesis 1:21 in which God creates whales, since no whales swam in the Bay of Bengal. The Setswana Genesis of 1851 solved this problem by making the whale *leruarua*, a seamonster. A greater challenge arrived in the Gospel of St John 19:22 where Pontius Pilate, justifying the notice he has fixed to Christ's cross ironically identifying him as King of the Jews, insists Ο γέγραφα, γέγραφα ('What I have written, I have written'). As Setswana contained no words for writing, the Kuruman missionaries improvised with: *Se ki se kuarileñ, ki se kuarile* ('What I have counted out, I have counted out').

At Kuruman we are therefore faced, not simply with the introduction of one technology into this part of Africa – that is the press – but with the simultaneous inception of two revolutionary undertakings: script and print together. A few weeks were all that had intervened between Moffat's first crude experiments with Setswana orthography and his commission of a printed spelling book, published in London in 1826. This basic manual had been a spur to his own further linguistic efforts, but it was also to serve as a practical guide for the mission's compositors, once they had acquired a press. In effect, they were not printing a written language, but reproducing a language that they had written down experimentally, specifically so that they might print it.

Superficially therefore, in these historic if awkward interventions in southern Africa, we see the emergence of transformations just as radical as – perhaps more radical than – any that had taken place in Bengal, transformations that would eventually give rise to the growth of published communications throughout the hinterland of southern Africa. Multiplied many times across the continent, such changes might even be said to represent the beginnings of African publishing as we know it today. But, there again, if we were to construct an account of historical causality along these very lines, how honest would we be to the facts? Were these Halhed or Moffat 'moments' authentic revolutions, or were they accidental mutations? How much did such initiatives owe, not so much to the intervention of certain resourceful individuals, as to the pre-existent seedbed of local cultures? In his Preface Halhed prates of 'acquisition', and in his journals Moffat speaks of 'conversion', but in 1778 or 1831 what or who was acquiring or converting what or whom? Was print annexing Bengali and Setswana, or were Bengali and Setswana annexing print? These are not straightforward questions. Nor is the mindset that puts them at all simple.

The lure of a paradigm

Such queries are not, of course, new. Over the last half-century or so, the evolution of print culture (styled by Benedict Anderson 'print capitalism') out of earlier stages of human communication has been of much interest to scholars working in a number of different though inter-connected disciplines: students of the media, social anthropologists, historians of the book. Though each has brought to the subject their own angle and expertise, with hindsight it is possible to observe the persistence of certain assumptions. At the dawn of pre-history, so the received wisdom has run, all human society was governed by speech and gesture. At a given moment – differently timed in each context, but similar in its basic effects – script then emerged. With it came the possibility of correspondence between individuals across distant regions, of literature and sacred texts, even – in the view of certain more adventurous theorists – a revolution in the way in which people organised their thoughts, remembered the past and acted in concert. The Ages of Speech and Script were then superseded by the Age of Print, the consequences of which were apparently even more extreme.

Thus has the sequential trilogy of speech, script, print firmly established itself as a paradigm for human culture. A recent expression of it occurs in

David Finkelstein and Alistair McCleery's *An Introduction to Book History* of 2005, with its successive chapters headed 'From Orality to Literacy' and 'The Coming of Print'. But the paradigm itself goes back decades: at least as far as McLuhan's high-profile study *The Gutenberg Galaxy* (1962) and Ong's influential *Orality and Literacy* (1982). All societies, these commentators maintained, were once elusively oral, their sole means of communication and dissemination being speech and allied forms such as ritual and gesture. With the introduction of writing, a radical 'shift' is supposed to have occurred in the relationship between societies and texts, and across a range of cognitive fields. There followed the invention of print, attributed in this account to the invention of woodblock engraving in China in the eighth century CE, and in Europe to Gutenberg's introduction of the 'alphabetical letterpress' (Ong, 1982: 118) during the fifteenth century. Elsewhere, so it was maintained (and so Finkelstein and McCleery follow) print arrived through a process of diffusion, usually via colonial contact. McLuhan further argued that the global society of his own time was progressing beyond print culture to a fourth stage, sometimes called 'secondary orality', corresponding to the growth of electronic media worldwide.

All sorts of radical changes in consciousness have been attributed to the event that Elizabeth Eisenstein styled the 'Print Revolution', that Finkelstein and McCleery term the 'Coming of Print', and that we have already dubbed the 'Halhed' or 'Moffat moment'. According to Marshal McLuhan these included 'the stripping and the interruption of the interplay of tactile synaesthesia' characteristic of pre-print man (1962: 54), the destruction of the acoustic universe, the invention of perspective, the doctrine of scriptural infallibility, the Infinitesimal Calculus, the inception of national literatures, exams and fixed orthographies and dictionaries. Many of these claims were grossly inflated, and several hard to understand, given that McLuhan often failed to make it clear whether these supposed innovations were the result of literacy or of print or, indeed, sometimes even to distinguish between the two.

McLuhan also largely failed to distinguish between the effects of different print technologies – hand letterpress, say, and stereotyping or lithography. There was, however, a far more fundamental flaw running through his thinking, one not always recognised at the time. McLuhan wrote from an exceptionally fixed and limited cultural perspective. *The Gutenberg Galaxy* contains this magisterially chauvinist remark:

> Since the object of the present book is to discern the origins and modes of the Gutenberg configuration of events, it will be well to consider the effects of the alphabet on native populations today. For such as they *are* in relation to the phonetic alphabet, so we once were.
>
> (McLuhan, 1962: 18)

A nexus of unexamined and authoritarian assumptions underlies such apparent relativism. Who are this *they*, and who this *we*? Are none of the 'they' (whoever these are) to be conceived of as readers of McLuhan's book? Who, in any case, are these 'native populations'? Everybody is a *native* of somewhere – McLuhan himself of Edmonton, Alberta – and his use of the term is far less sophisticated than even Halhed's. In practice, of course, McLuhan means *colonised* (and therefore, to his Canadian eyes, backward) peoples. McLuhan and his followers tended furthermore to link print technology to alphabetical literacy, as if the invention of reading, writing and print had happened everywhere in a logical, pre-determined sequence. McLuhan himself took it more or less for granted that modern communications had arrived at one place and period, Renaissance Europe. From this temporal and geographical heartland it had supposedly spread out, inexorably and with the same general effects. This was the famous Gutenberg Galaxy, expanding through real time, the configurations of which McLuhan set out to illustrate through the application of some sort of literary-diagnostic version of the Doppler Lightshift. With this unwarranted and expansionist view came another: that the writing and printing systems adopted everywhere have been alphabetic (because writing, it seemed to such thinkers, is of necessity thus), and that all alphabets are phonetic.

Such were the views stemming from an approach to culture that was comparative, evolutionary and diffusionist. The first two of these two tendencies is of more assistance to us than the second and third. As Jack Goody, an anthropologist with a background in literary study, was later to remark, 'any resort to comparative work necessarily raises the evolutionary issue' (Goody, 1977: 2). There were, however, more fruitful ways of approaching this issue than hierarchy, hegemony or, indeed, any orchestrated pattern of 'development'. In place of such panaceas, Goody himself focused on what he termed 'technologies of the intellect' (ibid.: 10). By this he meant the processes through which peoples in divers times and places have learned to express themselves, the methods they have adopted to embody such self-expression and the varied consequences of these choices.

There were, it seemed to Goody, crossover points between successive technologies, most interesting of which was the inception of literacy. In his book *The Domestication of the Savage Mind* (1977) he surveyed a gamut of cultural effects attributable to the introduction of writing into previously oral cultures, concentrating on changes in the nature of texts. Literacy, he thought, involved the arrival of lists and inventories (of which many of the earliest texts surviving from, say, Sumeria or Egypt, consist) and of recipes, prescriptions or reports on experiments, as in Greece. Where reality had been immediate and concrete, abstractions now made their appearance. Written genealogies emerged which, instead of serving the needs of the moment like so many orally preserved pedigrees, purported to establish historical fact. Where texts – poems, sagas, plays – had been recited out loud, silent reading now gradually took over. And as communications systems became more complex, alphabets crystallised. A mythological way of interpreting the past gave way to annals strictly compiled and regularly revised.

Nowadays these claims again seem sweeping, but they had the undoubted effect of distinguishing the effects of writing from those of print. Thus, when Elizabeth Eisenstein turned to the inception of print culture in the West in her authoritative *The Printing Press as an Agent of Change* (1979), she was able to observe with clarity the distinctive and unprecedented transformations in intellectual dissemination arguably enabled by letterpress. For Eisenstein print was the true 'revolution', though its effects were quieter than had previously been thought. In the print age, she thought, alternate versions of texts, caused by overworked scribes, made way for definitive editions. Images, maps and diagrams newly abounded. The illuminations of medieval manuscripts ceded to the realistic possibilities of woodcut. Mnemonic aids now assisted memory, formalising though arguably weakening it: 'the nature of collective memory was transferred' (Eisenstein, 1983: 34). There occurred an explosion in knowledge and speculation, leading to a 'wide-angled' though sometimes 'unfocussed' scholarship. Accuracy became an ideal to which approximation became possible: orthographies (such as Moffat's) or errata slips (such as Halhed's) could be issued. A proliferation of fonts diversified presentation. Overall an increase in standardisation was apparent: in indices, in catalogues, in title pages (an innovation of print culture). The overwhelming effect, Eistenstein thought, was to arrest drift: in languages and in texts. As standard editions of works became feasible, so languages settled down into relatively fixed vernaculars in which national cultures could be enshrined. English literature; French literature; Spanish literature were some of the results in Europe.

Soon after these ideas were mooted, the American Jesuit Walter J. Ong attempted to bring together the work of McLuhan, Goody and Eisenstein in his work of synthesis *Orality and Literacy* (1982). Like McLuhan, Ong was interested in intersections between different cultural phases. Like McLuhan, too, he was concerned to extend the standard model beyond Europe to contexts where such intersections were currently observable; especially to Africa, where, he believed, literature had been introduced comparatively recently through outside agencies such as the missionary movement. As a literary critic, however, Ong was largely concerned with the repercussions of different communicative systems on form and style. As dialects gave way to grapholects so, he thought, 'literature' in our modern sense was born and, with it, academic study. Additive structures gave way to subordinate ones, redundancy of expression to economy. A conservative viewpoint lost ground before a radical or sceptical one, participation before objective distancing. Print, Ong thought, 'both reinforces and transforms the effects of writing on thought and expression' (1982: 117). Originality was newly at a premium. Copyright established its domain; plagiarism was identified as a misdemeanour.

The universality of such diagnoses proved impressive to many, giving rise in certain academic communities to a sort of cult. Its ambitions, however, were parochial. Though the global expansion of the galaxy of communications proved an absorbing topic – even influencing the linguistics of Jacques Derrida – few of those involved in this debate possessed any firsthand knowledge of cultures beyond the West, with the exception of Goody, whose African fieldwork inevitably stressed certain locally driven preoccupations. Nor did many of these able scholars actively consider India with its centuries-long, and highly distinctive, traditions of textual transmission. Such theories as to the history of communication, moreover, pre-dated by some years the rise of postcolonial theory in the 1990s. Little attempt has since been made to bring these fields into line with one another, or to examine what effects postcolonial perceptions might have on the commonly accepted model. A lone exception has been Benedict Anderson's seminal *Imagined Communities* (1983, 1991) with its famous view that worldwide print capitalism instilled national consciousness via a dissemination of vernaculars: in South America, in Europe and by extension in Asia and even in Africa. Such theories have proved provocative and useful. They mean little, however, until book and print history relocate themselves in an even wider geographical context, to be viewed there through critical, and postcolonial, eyes.

Homage to a five-faced Siva

One revealing aspect of Halhed's sycophantic Preface to his *Grammar* is an omission: the print founder and punch-maker Panchanana Karmakara, whom it entirely fails to mention. That he played an indispensable role in the book's production, as well as in the early history of print in Bengal, is pretty clear, however, even if Halhed himself preferred to perpetuate a heroic but extraneous myth of origin according to which Wilkins individually created Bengali typography *ex nihilo*. His praise for his countryman is profuse: 'In a country so remote from all connection with European artists', he fanfares, 'he has been obliged to charge himself with the various occupations of the Metallurgist, the Engraver, the Founder and the Printer' (Halhed, 1778: xxiv). The combination of aptitudes indicated in this encomium – acquired over a period of twelve months – would have been quite exceptional. In actual fact, as the print historian Fiona Ross has amply demonstrated (1999, 10), the task drew on the expertise and labour of at least eight different pairs of hands.

As his name indicates – since 'Karmakara' is none other than 'Smith' – Panchanana came from a hereditary caste of craftsmen. The Baptist missionary Joshua Marshman later referred to him simply as a 'blacksmith', though it seems he was also skilled in general and alloy metallurgy, and in calligraphy as well. The combination of these aptitudes suggests that he was already adept at the sort of filigree metalwork that had long been practised in India and could with advantage be turned to the fresh demands of type founding. We get a fleeting glimpse of this man on page thirty-seven of Halhed's text, where the elements of Bangla syntax are illustrated in four rhymed couplets from section seven (the *drona-parva*) of Kasirama Dasa's Bengali recension of *The Mahabharata*, one of the classic epics of India.

Figure 1.3 represents the third of these couplet as set out in the book, with Halhed's approximate Roman transliteration running beneath. An English verse translation might run: 'Everyone – youths, old men and Ponchanon – all / With red-cloaked children gathered at his call.' The name 'Ponchaanon' – a version of Panchanana – appears in the first line, and both imply 'five-faceted', referring to the five faces of the god Siva. To modern eyes the Bengali typography seems quite crude, since acceptable conventions were slowly evolving: what we are watching here, in fact, is the written transforming itself with some difficulty into the printed form. A standardised modern typesetting of the same lines would go:

সোমদত্ত বালিক আদি আর পঞ্চানন

সালু শিশু আইল পাইয়া নিমন্ত্রণ "

Bearing in mind what we know about Panchanana's background, and putting it together with our knowledge of the multiple processes involved in typecasting in 1778, it may now be helpful to bear in mind the kinds of work that went into the manufacture of the characters used in the printing of that passage, including those used for Karmakara's name. Essentially there were six stages, each of which drew on aspects of metallurgy that had been

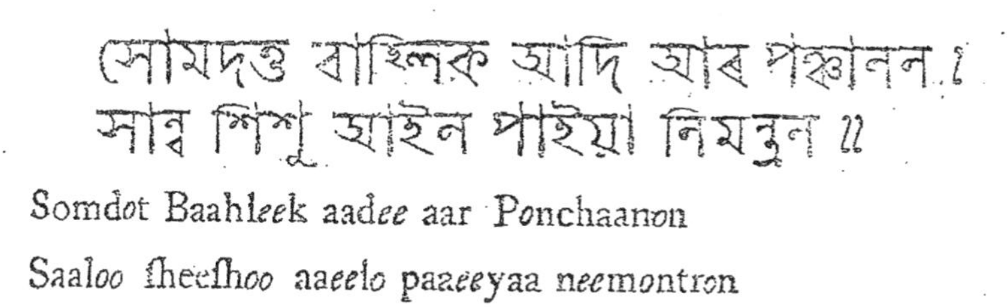

সোমদত্ত বাহ্লিক আদি আর পঞ্চানন ।
সার শিশু আইল পাইয়া নিমন্তুন ॥

Somdot Baahleek aadee aar Ponchaanon

Saaloo fheefhoo aaeelo paaeeyaa neemontron

Figure 1.3   Couplet from Kasirama Dasa's *Mahabharata* with Roman transliteration, from Halhed's *Grammar* (1778), page 37.

practised in Asia and Africa, as well as Europe, for centuries. First, there was the striking of the tools: gravers (engraving instruments to cut the metal) and files. Second, the carving of 'counter-punches', three-dimensional reverse impressions of the hollow parts of characters, the dip in an 'o', the dimples in a 'B'. Third, the creation, by Panchanana in this instance, of the all-important 'punches' – hard, three-dimensional mirror models of the required character – by painstakingly carving each on to the end of a shank of tempered steel. Fourth, the making of 'matrices' for casting, achieved by driving the punch into a softer piece of copper or brass, then filing down the edges so that it would fit comfortably into a mould. Fifth, pouring into the mould a molten mixture of lead, tin and antimony, then leaving it to set. Sixth, 'dressing' the piece of type thus formed, tidying it up by breaking off the 'jet' or excess. Once all this had been done, the character could be stored in a designated chamber in a wooden case in the print works – 'upper case' for capitals or 'lower case' for ordinary letters – so that when needed it could be selected by the compositor with his stick and placed alongside other characters, then locked into the 'forme' or printing surface ready for the press.

Nor was this all. Roman typography had developed in Europe in the late fifteenth century, and its rules were plainly set out in treatises such as Joseph Moxom's *Mechanic Exercises* in the seventeenth. The printers of Bangla texts faced a much more daunting challenge, as did printers of texts in other Indian languages, whether Indo-European in origin like Marathi, or Dravidian like Malayalam in the south. Many of these tongues possess an inherent vowel that is not separately written. In Bengali it is an 'a', though confusingly the resulting sound is close to an open 'o', and not all 'a's' are inherent. Its presence may be indicated by modification of the preceding consonant, through a diacritical mark (a subscript for example), or other mutation of the relevant letter. Mahabulul Haq's guide to Bangla spelling, published in Dakha in 1991, lists 248 such 'conjunct' characters, swelling the writing system to in excess of 300 letters. When in the mid-twentieth century the Monotype Corporation in England devised a twelve-point Bangla font (no. 470) for use in hot-metal printing, its synopsis would amount to 343 characters, though this included punctuation marks. The typeface of 1778 possessed 200 characters: 12 vowels, 34 consonants and 154 other marks, all of which had to be made up at the forge (Ross, 1999: 20). This was no simple matter when dealing with a script as angular as Bangla.

Consider, just for illustration, the technical difficulty of reproducing Panchanana's first name as it appears on that page in the *Grammar*, starting with the delicate butterfly-wing of the letter প, an unaspirated 'p'. First there was the problem of making a counter-punch to match up with its irregularly shaped spaces, then of manufacturing a punch to contain the outline, followed by the hammering of the harder though still delicate counter-punch into the punch itself to produce a matrix, into the tiny troughs of which hot metal had carefully to be poured; then the filing down of the cooled sort to maintain the precision of spider-like ascenders and descenders, and the horizontal header along the top of the character. For these tasks Karmakara would have needed every ounce of his inherited calligraphic and metallurgical skill.

Yet this was the scale of the challenge that was to face indigenous type founders the length and breadth of India as they reproduced acceptable fonts for language after language during the period up to the late nineteenth century (and in some places beyond that) when the hand press would remain the dominant technology for printing. The composing of the type into words, the printing and binding of the resulting volumes, their packaging and distribution posed further challenges, together of course with the weeks of preceding literary labour, when, as so often in this multilingual subcontinent, the book needed to be translated into parallel versions from its original text, whether that text had been in English, in an Indian language or, as in the case of the Christian Bible, in Hebrew or Greek. These were too many skills for one person to muster, and Halhed's book – using Karmakara's new Bangla font for its examples, and existing Roman type for the commentary – thus drew on the services of a number of specialists working in unison, as did all subsequent achievements in Bengali printing.

A few years later, the missionaries of Serampore were quite clear about the extent of their dependence on local know-how, linguistic, calligraphic and technical. Translation for a start was impossible without it. In 1815, by which time the works were employing 'seventeen presses with workmen of every description', together with 'a Paper Manufactory on the spot' (Baptist Mission, Serampore, 1815: 24), the mission could report in its *Seventh Memoir* 'the capacity of Native youth to acquire the Hebrew language is placed beyond all dispute by the fact that there are already found many natives of India eminently skilled in Arabic, so much more complex and copious than the Hebrew. To the Greek language the *Sungskrita* [Sanskrit] scholar already has an unerring clue. No two languages of different origin resemble one another more strongly' (ibid.: 30–1). William Carey, the founder-missionary of Serampore, and later Professor of Oriental Languages at Fort William College, had leaned on such local knowledge from the very outset. On his arrival in Calcutta in 1795, he had hired a coach, Rama Rama Vasu, to teach him Bengali. Meanwhile, with a publishing venture in view, he was negotiating for a press to be sent out from England. In the event, one could not be found, and Carey brought one for 400 rupees after reading a small advertisement in the Calcutta press. Bangla types, too, were unobtainable in England. By 1798 Carey had recognised that there was no doing without relevant local expertise. 'I have succeeded in procuring a sum of money sufficient to get the types cast', he then reported back to his sponsoring society in Leicester. 'I have found a man who can cast them, the person who casts for the Company's press' (Ross, 1999: 42). This man, of course, was Karmakara. The rest is publishing history.

Towards a new consensus

Just how collaborative early publishing in Bengal was, and just how many varieties of local skill it employed, can be gathered from this description of the works at Serampore in a letter of December 1811 from the foreman William Ward to his cousin William Fletcher in Derby. This was a period when Panchanana's son-in-law Manohara was both in charge of the type-foundry and responsible for the training of apprentice technicians. His name does not appear amongst the milling and anonymous personnel described in this passage. The only individual identified, very much stage centre, is Ward himself:

> Could you see your cousin in his printing-office, surrounded by forty or fifty servants, all employed in preparing the Holy Scriptures for the nations of India, you would, I am sure, be highly pleased. One man is preparing the Book of God for the learned Hindoos, in the Shanscrit [sic] language; another for the people of Bengal; another for those of Hindoostan; another for the inhabitants of Orissa; another for the Mahrattas; another for the Sikhs; another for the people of Assam; and for the Musselmen in all parts of the East, in the Persian and Hindosthanee languages; others for the Chinese; others for the Talingas; and others are soon to begin in the Cingalese, Tamul [sic] and Malayalim [sic] languages.
>
> As you enter the office, you will see your cousin in a small room, dressed in a white jacket, reading or writing, and at the same time looking over the whole office, which is 174 feet long. The next persons you see are learned natives translating the scriptures into different languages, or correcting the proof-sheets. You walk through the office, and see laid out in cases *types* in Arabic, Persian, Nagaree, Talinga, Sikh, Bengalee, Mahratta, Chinese, Orissa [Oriya], Burman, Carnata; Keshemena, Greek, Hebrew, and English. Hindoos, Muselmanns, and converted Natives are all busy: some composing, others distributing, others correcting. You next come to the presses, and see four persons throwing off the sheets of the Bible in different languages; and on the left are half a dozen Muselmanns employed in binding the scriptures for distribution; while others are folding the sheets and delivering them to the Store-keeper to be placed in the Store-room till they can be made up into volumes. This Store-room, which is 142 feet long, is filled

with shelves from side to side; upon which are laid, wrapped up, the sheets of the Bible before they are bound. You go forward, and in the room adjoining the office are the type-casters busy in preparing types in different Languages. In one corner, you see another grinding the printing ink; and in a spacious open place, walled round, you see Paper Mill; and a number of persons employed in making paper for printing the Scriptures in all the languages.

(*The Baptist Magazine* iv, 1812, 443–4)

It is clear from this passage that by 1811, eleven years after the establishment of the mission and its press, many segments of Serampore's diverse community were involved in the business, and in every aspect of the trade. This is the complex, multifarious and local process that the postcolonial ironist Homi K. Bhabha, citing an incident outside Delhi five years later in his essay 'Signs Taken for Wonders', calls 'the sudden fortuitous discovery of the English book' (Bhabha, 1994: 102). The precise volume to which Bhabha seems to be referring is a translation of the New Testament into Hindi made in Serampore using one of Karmakara's typefaces in 1816. With hindsight the dissemination via a Devanagari font struck by a Bengali technician, of a translation made from Greek by a committee of local pandits under expatriate supervision and run off by local compositors on paper from a neighbouring mill, does not look quite so English. Three months after Ward's letter, a disastrous fire destroyed all but five of the presses and fourteen of the precious fonts. The presses were rebuilt by local carpenters, and the typefaces listed by Ward reconstituted from the three and a half tons of molten metal collected using the surviving punches and matrices the Karmakaras and their colleagues had created over the years. Within two months, the press was in business again.

We do not know quite so much about the printing works at Kuruman, but it is evident that here too there was a team effort. Local linguists were instrumental in the process of language acquisition and translation, impressing Moffat and his friends with the pithiness and vividness of the Setswana tongue. In Moffat's unpublished notebooks (SOAS, Africa 4), there is a note on the superior brevity of Setswana to English verbs. The apostolic advice to 'Use hospitality towards one another' (1 Peter 4:9), for example, is given as *amogelana*; 'Be kindly affectionate towards one another' (Romans 12:10) is *lo homogelanc*. Moffat picked up such phrases from a succession of interpreters, using the *lingua franca* of Dutch. By the time the whole of the Bible was ready for production in one volume in 1857, local compositors were being used in the pressroom, and local catechists were employed for distribution. In only one respect was Kuruman fundamentally different from Serampore. Moffat had provided Setswana with a provisional script consisting of Roman letters with a minimum of diacritical marks, such as the ~ over the nasal 'n' in so many word-endings. So by and large he could rely on imported types, despite the availability of local expertise in metalwork. Before purchasing his boxes of type in Cape Town in 1831, he seems seriously to have considered persuading the district metallurgists to turn out suitable typefaces for him. In his journals, and also in his book *Missionary Labours* (1846: 466), there is a detailed description of a local coppersmith at work. Moffat had paid him to mend some trappings from his wagon, and plied him with questions about his work. Why was he, or somebody like him, not used? The answer can be that, unlike the German one-time goldsmith Gutenberg or Halhed's colleague Karmakara, this Setswana smith was non-literate. To involve him would have been to skip two rungs on the communications ladder, expecting a technician to turn out types in a language that he could speak, but could not as yet read.

Thus, if in South Asia the challenges facing print culture were the result of script complexity and diversification, in sub-Saharan Africa they were, to some extent at least, products of an orthography gap. Since the tenth century CE the Arabic script has been used widely along the Mediterranean littoral, across the Sahara and the Sahelian grasslands, around the East African coast and throughout Madagascar, both for the production of Arabic texts and for the replication of some indigenous or hybrid languages (Swahili, like Malagasy, before the nineteenth century was habitually written in Arabic letters). Beyond Muslim-influenced Africa, however, writing systems had been relatively scarce. Between the 1820s and the mid-twentieth century several assaults were made on these *lacunae*, both by Africans themselves and by interested outsiders. The indigenous initiatives were largely confined to West Africa, and produced a number of different writing systems, syllabic or phonetic. These were, in approximate historical order, the Vai syllabary of Liberia (1820s); the Bassa Vah system, also Liberian; the 37-letter Bété alphabet in Nigeria; the Bamum system masterminded in Cameroon by Sultan Ibrahim Njoya in the late nineteenth century; the Mende syllabary of Sierra Leone (1920s); the Kpelle syllabary of 88 graphemes invented by Chief Gbili of Sanoyea in 1935; and the N'Ko alphabet invented by Soulemanya Kante of Kankan, Guinea, in around 1946 (Dalby, 1967). All of these have given rise to written literatures, though few engaged initially with printing.

Attempts by outsiders to inscribe the spoken languages of Africa by contrast were primarily driven by a desire to produce printed books. Wary of the sort of balkanisation of writing systems to be found in South Asia, moreover, such interlopers preferred to concentrate their efforts on producing standardised alphabets with modifications on the basic Roman pattern that could be applied across the board for all African languages. The first such attempt was by the Prussian Egyptologist and linguist Karl

Richard Lepsius (1810–84), whose system of 1855 sprouted a wilderness of diacritical marks. Clumsy as it was, it proved attractive to Christian missionaries, both local and expatriate, keen to turn out devotional reading matter by the quickest practicable route. Two years later it was the Lepsius system, for example, that Ajayi Crowther, an emancipated Yoruba slave and first evangelist to the Niger, used for the first ever Igbo primer (Crowther, 1857). Lepsius continued in use until the early twentieth century, by which time his disadvantages were becoming obvious. By the First World War, Sol Plaatje (1876–1932), the veteran South African journalist, novelist and linguistic reformer, who had encountered the new science of phonetics in London, could wax scathing about the cloth-eared attempts made by Moffat and his successors to reproduce his mother-tongue Setswana through Lepsius-influenced methods (Jones, 1916). Radical reform arrived in 1927, when Diedrich Hermann Westermann (1875–1956) produced his 'Practical Orthography for African Languages', otherwise known as the New Script. Westermann, who had honed his skills as a linguist by working on the transliteration of Ewe in German-occupied Togo before the war, and who during the interwar period enjoyed widespread support from several colonial governments, outlawed many of Lepsius's symbols and simplified the whole procedure of transcription, partly to enhance inter-intelligibility, but largely to render printing more economical. His reform did not avoid controversy, mostly from enthusiasts of local authenticity worried by the ironing out of phonetic differences in so standardised a code.

I will be dealing with these matters in more detail below in Chapters 2 and 6. Suffice it to remark here that recognition of such divergent histories must perforce complicate any universalised history of the non-Western book. It also embarrasses attempts such as Bhabha's to bring book history into line with fashionable theories of colonial interaction. Just to begin with, we are faced with two somewhat different trajectories. In one of them speech gives way to a lengthy period dominated by script, leading eventually to the inception of print. In the other, oral communication gives directly onto print, with writing appearing principally as an intermediate, instrumental mode. We must, however, strongly resist any temptation to identify these two tendencies too absolutely with geography. Africa, as we have already seen, possessed some lively pre-print script traditions, though they were largely confined to specific locales: the Mediterranean coast and the Maghreb; Egypt; Ethiopia; Somalia; the Indian ocean seaboard; Zanzibar; Madagascar; the sub-Saharan Sahel. And even today there remain areas of the Indian subcontinent where long-established languages are still to be written down, as is the case with certain 'tribal' communities in Bengal, and to a greater extent in Orissa. The position a given society occupies along any purported speech–script–print spectrum is thus little reflection of its position on the map. Nor is any evolutionary paradigm of development between distinct and separable 'stages' any longer acceptable. Instead we are faced with a multivalent process that spirals off in several different directions, and in which many different combinations of orality, literacy and print culture are both possible and recorded as matters of fact.

The ancestries of print

Moreover, even where we are able to give approximate dates to times of transition between, say, a lively script culture and the inception of letterpress, the continuity involved is frequently as impressive as any apparent innovation. New technologies often rely on antecedent ones in convoluted, occasionally almost invisible ways. In any society some residual bedrock of skills exists on which any further structure of communicative efficacy will of necessity be built. Recently Finkelstein and McCleery have drawn on the researches of the German scholar Jan-Dirk Müller (1994) to take issue with Elizabeth Eisenstein's notion of a Print Revolution in fifteenth-century Europe, conceding that 'The application of moveable types by Gutenberg was, in some ways, no more than the adaptation of old materials and practices.' In particular 'the experience of the goldsmith, the writing-master, and the woodcutter all converged to create a new technology' (2005: 50–1). To be fair to Eisenstein, the term 'adaptation' is hers, but the conversion of pre-existent skills to the evolving science of print is also very pertinent to the diverse publishing histories of the non-West. Gutenberg had been a goldsmith, Panchanana Karmakara a versatile metallurgist, and no doubt the team of typecasters whom Manohara later recruited and trained at Serampore enjoyed a similar professional background. The so-called Asian print revolution deployed their skills, just as surely as it would later draw on a wide range of firmly established crafts and technologies across Asia and Africa.

Print did not therefore emerge against a background of technological nullity, but drew on an existing base of skills and mechanical arts that fed and sustained it. Metalwork, both cast and wrought, was well developed in South Asia many centuries before the first presses were set up. Just how close this existing skills base came to actual printing techniques can be inferred, for example, from the range of activities associated with the shrine of the Hindu monk Chaitanya (1486–1533), long established at Navadvip in central Bengal. Here metal stamps of wrought copper were regularly used by pilgrims to impress in vermilion ink on their skin or clothing designs associated with the saint, many of which carried verbal incantations or messages (a fine collection of such was donated to the British Museum by Robin Hawkins between 1896 and 1903). Such practices were evidently less common in regions of Africa that possessed no orthographic system to begin with. Yet metalwork was well-established in Africa, especially in the west, notably in Benin, where the *cire perdue* method of cast metalwork had been expertly practised since at least the fifteenth century. The occasional proximity of traditional stamping or painting to eventual printing, however, is strongly suggested by traditions such as the decoration of *ulu* designs on the skin, and occasionally too on inner or outer walls of houses, in the Igbo-speaking areas of what was to become Eastern Nigeria.

Nor was this technical interdependence confined to the early years of printing by letterpress in the ages of Wilkins or Moffat. As over the decades successive technologies arose, each in its turn drew on an existing base of acquired and inherited skills, giving rise in the process to a fertile marriage between home-grown and imported expertise. To take but one example to which I shall return in Chapter 5, the efflorescence of lithography – a technique which originated in Europe in the 1820s and migrated rapidly to South Asia and thence the Middle East – drew fairly immediately on centuries-old indigenous traditions of calligraphy and manuscript produc-tion The result, as we shall see, was a revolution that was to give rise to cultural configurations, and to political alignments, of urgent relevance even today.

With due deference to the complexity of the problem, and at the risk of some simplification, it might therefore be helpful at this point to illustrate some patterns of dependence between local conditions, external interven-tions and evolving modes of communication in the form of comparative charts. I have drawn up two, the first more or less satisfactory for South Asia, the second more or less satisfactory for Africa, and will be referring back to both during the course of this book (Figures 1.4 and 1.5). The find-ings cover a number of historical periods from the inception of print to digital and electronic methods. In each case I have set the results out in three columns. The first represents – in Goody's terminology – 'technolo-gies of the intellect', that is indigenous and mutating techniques of creation, reproduction or circulation, while the third lists those external factors and influences which have contributed over time to successive phases of commu-nication in the regions of the world covered. As may be expected, in each case the first column is longer than the third. In between in each chart lies a second column designating the communication shifts resulting from these twin inputs. The arrows are intended to suggest cross-paths of influence:

It may be helpful for readers to glance back at these at strategic points in ensuing chapters. Both of them, it should be noted, take the long view, and describe changes in some cases stretching over centuries, in others tele-scoped into a few decades. Sometimes, you notice, I have adopted the grad-ualistic term 'evolution', on other occasions the more abrupt and dramatic term 'revolution', a difference of usage that I hope to explain along the way.

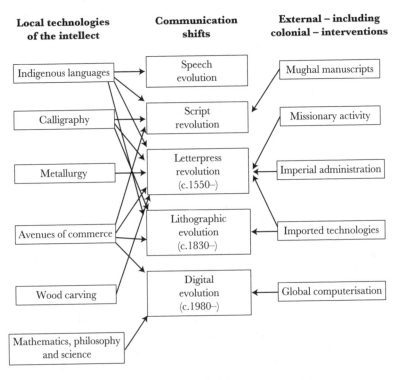

Figure 1.4 The roots of print culture (South Asia).

Neither word, however, should be understood as implying a uniform direction of progress, or even necessarily of improvement. As I shall make abundantly clear, there have always been losses as well as gains. At all stages, however, pre-conditions were present which influenced the course and direction of further development. Just to confine oneself to the substance of the present chapter, it is clear that, well before the appearance of a Halhed or a Moffat in India or Africa, fields of local resourcefulness lay ready for seeding into print technology. The adaptations involved were many, various and always vigorously localised. To forsake the regional approach suggested above, one should note, however, that there are constants that appear in the historical record time and time again. One might mention *inter alia*, and occurring across vast swaths of such pre-colonial, colonial and even postcolonial worlds:

1   The adaptation of indigenous metalworking skills to the type-foundry and, thence, to the setting of books in hand, and later, power presses.

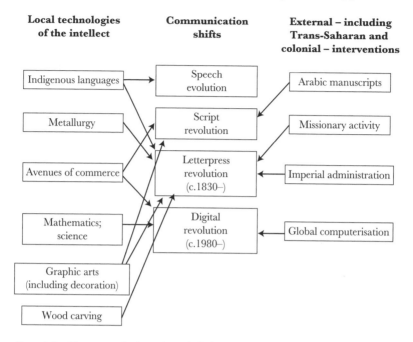

Figure 1.5 The roots of print culture (sub-Saharan Africa).

2 The adaptation of indigenous phonetic systems to mimetic elements in the hit-and-miss – and at first necessarily experimental – construction of orthographies.

3 The adaptation of special and organisational properties of manuscripts, where and when these existed, to the physical layout and 'look' of a printed page.

4 The adaptation of indigenous calligraphic techniques to writing in wax and stone, and thence to the production of – especially vernacular – books by the lithographic process (to which I shall come in Chapter 5).

5 The adaptation (especially in Africa, Java, etc.) of traditional techniques of stamping on cloth, or else of Batik, to the illustrative content of printed books.

6 The adaptation of stamping with brass seals (as with the Akan in West Africa) to the making, and use, of metal fonts.

7 The adaptation of traditional avenues of trade to the advertisement, circulation, merchandising and dissemination of printed texts.

8 The adaptation of woodcarving to the illustrative techniques of woodcuts. This proved especially important in forested parts of Africa.

9   Over large sections of the apposite regions, the adaptation of habits connected with the compilation and circulation of manuscripts to the developments of book markets as conventionally understood.

10 Last, but of profound significance to literary historians, the crystallisation from a molten and creative mass of inherited intellectual and artistic traditions – narrative, poetic, dramatic, theological, philosophical and scientific – of the notion of a fixed and definable 'text', editions of which might be physically mass produced, then sold, catalogued, shelved, and afterwards even studied.

The second, ninth and tenth of these elements represent especially significant conditions transitional towards – and leading well up to – the international book trade. All three involve the phenomenon of script entailed by, but not exclusive to, the production and consumption of manuscripts, a dispensation either ignored or sidelined by quite a lot of existing book history. For this reason I intend to examine each of these factors in turn in the next chapter.

2   Scripts and manuscripts

'Look, the sign'

In about the year 1834 Duala Bukale, an inhabitant of Jandu in northern Liberia in West Africa, experienced a life-changing dream. In it an unknown man approached him and offered him a book. Finding he could not read it, Duala asked the stranger how he could gain access to its mysteries. The dream figure then bent down and wrote with his finger on the ground, saying as he did so 'Look, the sign *I* (pronounced 'eye'). Then he wrote close to it another sign, saying, 'And that means, *na*. Now Duala, read both together!' Duala did so and discovered that he had just, for the very first time, read the word *ina*, meaning 'Come here', in his mother tongue, Vai (Koelle, 1849: 22).

It was a moment of revelation that has about it many of the trappings of the inception of a mission or cult: the dream, the book, initiation into hermetic lore. It was an encounter not unlike Christian's in Bunyan: what it produced, however, was not a conversion or creed but a particular local reading and writing revolution that would last for two centuries, and which even now has its adherents. The Vai constitute a relatively small linguistic grouping of some 75,000 speakers, the majority of whom live in Liberia, with a few thousand across the border in Sierra Leone. Though they are related to larger linguistic groupings further north, in Mali and beyond, until 1834 there was no way of writing down the language of this landlocked people. Following his dream, Bukale determined to supply one. Fifteen years later he was visited by the German-born missionary, linguist and teacher Sigismund Wilhelm Koelle, who described to the outside world the characteristics of this local writing system, whilst conveying the force of some of his own prejudices. The new Vai (or, as Koelle spelled it, Vei) script was, he disclosed, an autonomous and self-contained syllabary:

> The nature of the Vei writing plainly shows its entire independence of both the Arabic and the Latin. To prove this, I refer not so much to

the shape of the letters, though this also shows it at first sight, as rather to the fact that the Vei is a syllabic form of writing whereas the Arabic and the Latin are alphabetic. Each syllable has in the Vei writing only one simple sign for its representation. *An alphabetical mode of writing, which I believe was in all instances originally a strict phonetic one, is the most developed mode of representing thoughts to the eye ... The syllabic character, therefore, of the Vei writing speaks much in favour of its natural freedom.*

(Koelle, 1849: 19–20, emphasis added)

As set out by Koelle, and as standardised over a century later by the University of Liberia, Bukale's script contains 215 characters and is read horizontally across the page in the same direction as Arabic: that is from right to left. It is a strictly phonetic system in that it offers only one way of conveying each sound. Syllables may be combined into longer words, words into sentences and, eventually, into texts. But the physical representation of each sound is a single sign unique to itself, never – as in all Roman-derived writing systems – made up of discrete letters variously combined. Thus the relative copiousness of Bukale's script. Thus, too, its entire fidelity to the acoustics of Vai language. It was and is a way of employing signs to convey sounds, rather than achieving what Koelle with his European background seems to have felt was the purpose of most previous (and, he thought, more efficient if less spontaneous) writing systems: the rendering of thoughts directly by signs. It was a language for the inner ear as much as for the outer eye.

Hear the sign

It is a commonplace of linguistics, semiology and cultural theory from Saussure to Derrida that in all languages the sign – by which is usually meant the written or printed sign – is always and under all circumstances arbitrary. This is a fact more often stated than illustrated, and more attention has been focused on the theoretical consequences of the generalisation than the factors governing the choices. The invention – it is not too strong a word – of the Vai script in Liberia in the early years of the nineteenth century – an event no sooner initiated than described – affords us a rare opportunity of witnessing a new script in the making, and thereby perhaps of discerning what pressures may have operated locally to bring about just this scriptal formation rather than any other. This has not usually been the case with older writing systems, where the pre-determinants of the sign are often lost in antiquity and obscurity, and their influence must therefore be subject to guesswork, itself arbitrary at best.

It may be worthwhile to begin by sparing some thought for the conditions that the Vai script does not meet. It is not, for example, a hieroglyphic system, such as Ancient Egyptian, that has emerged from a picture language. Nor is it, as Koelle himself was careful to stress, in the true sense alphabetic. A syllabic system with distinct signs for each and every separately articulated sound, it makes no attempt whatsoever visually to replicate the thing referred to, as hieroglyphic systems sometimes do. Indeed, Vai possesses no signs for things as such. Nor does it have individual signs for words, unless those words happen to be one syllable long.

The elements differentiating Vai from any known alphabetic language are for our purposes even more suggestive. An alphabet consists of a relatively short series of discrete signs – the 26-symbol series beginning 'a, b, c, d' is only the best known – the individual members of which may be combined together to compose visual units representing composite sounds, and thereby things. An alphabet is a sort of linguistic Lego, the pieces of which may be fitted together to make up houses, people, chairs and also sentiments and thoughts. In Vai, there are many more kinds of pieces than in any serviceable alphabet, and they are far less flexible in their use. A sign only serves in combination with other signs to the extent that the syllable it represents acts with others to make up a lexical item ($i + na = ina$). The pieces are thus less versatile than in any alphabet. But they are also a lot closer to the sounds they represent.

What factors encouraged the inventor of the Vai syllabary to adopt this system rather than others? To some extent we will never know, but from the circumstances attending the recorded development, some considerations are very clear. Vai appeared at a time when the penetration of northern Liberia by competing imported alphabets was persistent and, from certain points of view, apparently threatening. The Arabic system had been around for many centuries, and its influence on a number of writing systems that developed, or were to develop locally, in response to its presence is comparatively easy to trace. The Roman alphabet had meanwhile been transported either by missionaries on coastal and nearby settlements, or else by the returning liberated slaves that by the 1820s onwards were to populate the English- or Krio-speaking communities of Monrovia to the south and Freetown to the north. Vai country was thus hemmed in by competing orthographies, and by the economic and social consequences of different forms of literacy.

The overwhelming need was to ensure that the Vai people, for whom Bukale intended his syllabary, should not be swamped. For this purpose they required a system that facilitated mutual communication over longish distances for all practical – including commercial – purposes, but which also set their acquired literacy apart as something quite distinctive. The principal considerations in the choices made were therefore those of, first, *communicability*, and second of *differentiation*. The writing system adopted was thus unique to the language. So close was the bond between the system adopted and the sound language it embodied that there never was, nor could be, any possibility of Bukale's brainchild being used to purvey tongues other than Vai: English, say, or Krio, or even neighbouring Mende (which a century later, as we shall see in Chapter 4, invented its own autochthonous writing system, for very similar reasons).

There was one other ingredient in this situation that is highly suggestive. The vehicles for the alphabetical invasion of the region – both Arabic and Roman – had for the most part been printed books: qur'ans, bibles and the like. There were printing presses in Freetown and Monrovia, and book imports were also common, whether from north, east or south. Yet Bukale seems to have had little desire to compete with this trade. His was a scriptal system pure and simple, and so it remained for decades to come. Bukale established a school, but not a press. This is all the more interesting, because the catalyst for his personal revelation had been a dream encounter with a (presumably printed) book that he was unable read. The script that he initiated was therefore an attempt to assert cultural autonomy and self-sufficiency. It also arguably represented a form of resistance, not just to a particular imported library of ideologically and religiously charged texts, but to print culture in itself. I shall return to this point in Chapter 5.

Cosmopolitanism, pre-coloniality and culture

Almost a millennium before Bukara, an equivalent desire to install and instil local writing systems capable of securing the communicative cohesion of language communities and marking those communities out as distinctive had been powerfully pre-echoed in the annals of South Asia. The present proliferation of scripts in the Indian subcontinent exists in marked contrast to its traditions of storytelling, poetry, religion and myth, all of which demonstrate a remarkable cohesion beneath attractive local variants. The resulting anomaly is a remarkable fact to which oriental scholars have been turning their concentrated attention over the past two decades. It is all the more striking, since for several centuries before the emergence of the Hindi, Telegu, Malayalam and a myriad of regional scripts as modes of literary diffusion, Sanskrit had remained the sole medium for the literary transmission of Vedic and pre-Vedic texts (such as the *Ramayana* and *Mahabharata*, themselves almost certainly originating in orality), and for all existing writing. The term Sanskrit 'cosmopolitanism' has been adopted to evoke this widespread scriptal dispensation: one that in some ways resembled, though it ante-dated by centuries, the ubiquitous sway exercised over respective polities by Latin in medieval Europe, by Arabic in the Islamic world and by Mandarin as written by the scribes of the Chinese empire. Benedict Anderson in his influential study *Imagined Communities* (1983: 12–19) has written with insight about the influence of such 'sacral languages' on the pre-nationalistic political and cultural formations of the relevant regions. As a sacral and universally intelligible code, Sanskrit was every bit as far-reaching, and the literature couched in it, as Sheldon Pollock (2006) has shown, was both rich and extensive.

The ubiquity of this code was something on which the intelligentsia of all regions of India *circa* pre-1200 CE could hence very much rely. The poetry of the eleventh-century Kashmiri poet Bilhana, for instance, is best known to English readers through *Black Marigolds*, Edward Powys Mathers's (1892–1939) impressionistic 1919 translation of his love cycle *The Caura-paniska* or *Fifty Stanzas*, written in jail after the poet had perpetrated a love intrigue with his sovereign's young and beautiful daughter. Mathers was relying on a Sanskrit text of Bilhana's cycle written on a palm leaf brought to light by the German orientalist Buhler in a library at Jaisalmer in 1877. It consisted of an interconnected chain of Sanskrit lyrics, each beginning with the phrase 'Even now'. In Mathers's Edward Fitzgerald-like re-working:

> Even now
> My thought is all of this gold-tinted king's daughter
> With garlands tissue and golden buds
> Smoked tangles of her hair, and sleeping or waking
> Feet trembling in love, full of pale languor,
> My thought is clinging as to a lost learning
> Slipped down from the mouths of men,
> Labouring to bring her back into my soul.
>
> (Bilhana, 1919: 9)

For what manner of audience were these passionate lyrics penned? Bilhana has understandably been claimed by critics and literary chauvinists since his death as a regional – or even national – bard of Kashmir, yet, judging from his own declared statements, this is not the view he took of his appeal. Bilhana revelled in his pan-Indian reputation. Relying on the universal intelligibility – nay hegemony – of Sanskrit amongst all who could read and, through reading, recite to others in the India of his time, he could realistically boast: 'There is no village or country, no capital city or forest region, no pleasure garden or school where learned and ignorant, young, old, male and female alike do not read my poems and shake with pleasure' (quoted in Pollock, 2002: 23).

Even in the quoted stanza there is, however, an audible wisp of longing in Bilhana's comparison of his residual desire to 'a lost learning'. Sanskrit was slowly losing its totalising grip, and the poet would have been far less likely to lodge so sweeping a claim to its universal appeal had he lived and written five centuries later. The Vernacular Revolution of the early second millennium CE saw the rise of regional writing systems the length and breadth of India. It has been called the 'vernacular millennium' by the American scholar Sheldon Pollock, who has documented the extent of the change. This process – which I have marked as a 'Script Revolution', second of the 'Communication Shifts' in Figure 1.4 above – was one in which Sanskrit, the language of the courtly elite (the word means 'sophisticated' or 'well made') proliferated and diversified, at first being transliterated into regional orthographies, then losing hold more completely as local literatures came into being couched in the colloquial tongues of each region. The process seems to have gone through a number of stages, in the first of which, starting towards the end of the late first millennium, *prakrits* ('ordinary', 'useful' or 'natural' languages) flourished as mediums for literary expression alongside Sanskrit; the second from the eleventh century onwards in which *apabhramsha* ('corrupt') varieties of Sanskrit gradually evolved into the multitude of vernaculars spoken in present-day India. 'The vernacularisation of Sanskrit', summarises Pollock, 'would begin in the last century of the first millennium in the central Deccan plateau. Here, in the course of the ninth to the eleventh centuries, Kannada and Telegu were transformed into languages for literature and political expression after four or five centuries of sub-literary existence during which Sanskrit functioned as the sole medium for the production of literary and non-documentary political texts' (2002: 28). As these new literary vernaculars grew in acceptability and expressive power, they came to be patronised by local princely courts, and to them were added hybrid dialects arising from invasion, migration and conquest. Telegu flourished under the Chola overlords of southern India and Sri Lanka. The Verna kings of Kamataka in present-day Mysore were entertained with songs in Telegu, Kannada, Avadhi, Bihari, Bengali, Oriya and Madheshiya. Later, Hindi developed at the hands of Sufi poets in areas of northern India falling, following the Mughal invasions of the fifteenth to sixteenth centuries, within the ambit of the new conquerors. To that extent at least, quite as much as Urdu – the language of the military encampments – Hindi is in its origins imperial.

The implications of these changes for book history cannot be stressed too strongly. By the early second millennium, woodblock printing or xylography had already evolved in China, and a century later it would arrive in nearby Tibet. In the twelfth century, anticipating Gutenberg by some 200 years, a form of moveable type had been devised in Korea (Diriger, 1982: 417–20). The reasons why neither development reached India at that period are still being debated by scholars: there was, after all, considerable commerce of merchandise, ideas and texts between China and India during much of this time-span. The truth is, nevertheless, that the relevant technologies did not arise in India at this stage, and the impact of print on Indian literary production can thus be traced back only as far as the sixteenth century, and then in discrete and isolated coastal locations in the south. The main thrust of print culture in the subcontinent as a whole dates, as we have already seen, from the very late eighteenth century, by which time the vernacular revolution had already set hard. It is useless to speculate, but had the apposite technologies arisen a few centuries earlier, they might well have come to enshrine the sacral ethos of an earlier age, giving rise to an indigenous and standard code, a metropolitan uniformity of print. As it transpired, English – the language of the next wave of conquerors – would come to inherit that role, whilst popular print culture was obliged to adapt itself to a multiplicity of local writing systems, idiolects and traditions. This fact would prove both a challenge and an opportunity, but the history of the printed book in South Asia cannot be understood without it.

The foregoing discussion raises a number of theoretical questions of interest to book historians and cultural and linguistic theorists alike. The most pressing concerns the relationship between the language map and unfolding methods of textual reproduction. At least one much-espoused paradigm – that of Benedict Anderson – connects the vernacular revolution in Europe from approximately the fifteenth century CE with the rise of print culture at that epoch, though it is never quite clear in that particular argument which element is supposed to have occurred first, or which to have set off the other: whether the print media arose to satisfy burgeoning vernaculars, or whether they encouraged the rise of those vernaculars in the first instance. In any case, as we have already observed, neither of these portmanteau views is of much help in South Asia, where a vast vernacular revolution pre-dated the rise of print by the better part of a millennium. Indeed, across the centuries changes in communication technology seem to have made comparatively little impact on the linguistic demography of South Asia, though, as we shall see in the next chapter, they have in the long term radically affected the shapes of individual languages. Meanwhile, however, a theoretical and diagnostic puzzle remains at global level. Has manuscript production always and everywhere served as the natural ally of what Anderson called sacral languages and, if so, does it or did it at any time inhibit the growth of regional tongues as agents for the visual transmission of texts?

The evidence is mixed, and to sift it more efficiently it will be essential in the first instance to draw certain essential distinctions, the ignoring of which has effectively blunted discussions of these questions until now. Anderson, for example, speaks eloquently of the ubiquitous spread of sacral languages such as Arabic and Latin in the ages before print. He nowhere makes clear a difference that is of fundamental relevance to the areas of the world with which we are concerned in this chapter: between shared languages on the one hand, and shared writing systems on the other. Sanskrit, for example, is an ancient and sacred language habitually written in the script known as Devanagari. For convenience the latter is sometimes referred to as 'Sanskrit script', but this term is a veritable misnomer. Sanskrit can be, and has been, embodied in any number of regional scripts; indeed the crystallisation or adoption of local writing systems for that purpose represents an important stage in the process of literary democratisation throughout India, leading to the aforementioned vernacular revolution. By the same token, Devanagari may be employed to convey several languages apart from classical Sanskrit, including Hindi, Marathi, Sindhi and Nepali. Potentially, indeed, more or less any writing system may be pressed into service to communicate just about any tongue, and, though the phonetic challenges thus set are sometimes extreme, manifold adaptations of this kind have always been made around the globe in response to a welter of internal or external socio-linguistic changes, the arrival of print being but one of them. This independence between the content and the form of all historically influenced codes introduces an added element of arbitrariness into the subject that has been frequently ignored by the disciples of Saussure, and which bedevils Anderson's well-publicised case.

Sappho in the Sahel

To refine our discussion of these elements in relation to a particular context it might be best to turn now to another scenario from West Africa, one historically intermediate between Vai and Sanskrit, and far more diffused than the first though, except to specialists, less well known than the second. The spreading, towards the beginning of the second millennium CE, of Arabic-medium and Islamic-inspired culture across a broad swath of the North African littoral and Saharan region and the Sahelian scrubland to its south – and, from a different geographical direction, across northerly stretches of the East African coast – was only partly the result of conquest. It has been characterised as a proleptic form of imperialism by certain African writers anxious to broaden their anti-colonial platform (Armah, 1973) though its principal means of propulsion was trade along well defined desert routes as much as, or as well as, duress. The cultural freight this diffusion bore with it was as visible as its other material consequences. Was it the Arabic language, or the Arabic script, that was thus spread? The answer is both, but not in the same measure, and not invariably in combination. Classical Arabic was spread by means of the Qur'an (though locally influenced dialects of Arabic were also legion). More germane from our point of view was the use of Arabic characters to convey and conserve speech and text in local tongues.

This phenomenon seems to have been widespread from quite early on. Until late in the Roman era, to take one notable example, the Berber group of languages spoken from the Canary Islands in the north to the sub-Saharan grassland in the south enjoyed their own range of scripts known to linguists as Libyco-Berber or Numidic: these were largely written in vertical columns, omitting vowels, and contained twenty-four characters with supplements. In the coastal Maghreb these indigenous writing systems were gradually swept aside by the Roman alphabet; in the desert regions to the south they were progressively marginalised by the Arabic script, retaining only a residual – yet still continuous – existence in the Tifinagh characters used to this day by the Tuareg of the Sahara region, above all by Tuareg women. When written Berber survived elsewhere, it did so by means of the Arabic script, and the same can be claimed of other languages spoken and written over this vast though sparsely populated region.

Deep in the Malian desert to the north of Timbuktu lies the hamlet and one-time oasis of Araouane, its ancient mosque now buried up to the minaret in sand. In the early medieval period it lay along the principal trade route from the saltpans of Taoudenni to the metropolis and academic communities (or madrassahs) of Timbuktu, and it was here in around 1556 that was born the scholar Ahmad Baba al-Massufi (Hunwick, 1964: 569). Drawn along the trade route, Ahmad went to Timbuktu, where he studied with several masters before migrating to Morocco, at which point he enters the European record. Ahmad was, however, almost certainly Tuareg and a Berber-speaker. In writing his mother tongue, it was Arabic that he must have used.

Five hundred miles to the south, in the Sahelian region known in the nineteenth century as Bornu, the use of Arabic script to convey texts in local languages is known to this very day as *ajami*. The library of the Caliphate of Sokoto, to mention just one notable repository, contains the most impressive collection of pre-twentieth-century manuscripts in the Sahelian region outside the famous – if insufficiently explored – archives in Timbuktu. Many are *ajami* works, and they include texts in Hausa, the sub-Saharan lingua franca spoken across a large swath of the savannah region from northern Guinea to northerly Gabon, as well as in Fulbe or Fulfulde, the language of the nomadic Fulani herdsmen living across the same area, as well as of their urbanised kinsfolk. The principal impetus behind the inscription of both these local tongues was a historic convulsion of religious certainty: not the Christian eruption of the later nineteenth century, but an Islamic jihad that preceded it by many decades, spearheaded by the inspirational, and notably scholarly, Usman dan Fodio (1754–1817), founder of the dynasty of Sokoto. Under him in 1802, spurred by the degeneracy of the times, the Fulani rose, swept across the plains and established an empire that would last until the

British incursion. It was a dominion as much of the mind as of civic laws. Literature was its lifeblood, Hausa and Fulani its shared codes. The Arabic script was its mode of written transmission.

Among the most precious items in the Sokoto collection are the poems and prose of Usman's serious-minded daughter Nana Asma'u (1793–1865). Asma'u was in her early to mid-twenties at the time of her father's campaigning; afterwards she settled in Sokoto in a large, courtyarded house close to that of her brother Ahmadu Bello, the successor to the Sultanate, where she devoted herself to literature and the education of the community's women. Among the guests who stayed there with her and her husband Gidado dan Lema – Vizier of the city and a close personal friend of Bello's – was the Scottish explorer Hugh Clapperton (1788–1827), whose accounts of his two lengthy stays in 1824 and again in 1826–7 provide us with an unforgettable impression of an hospitable, bookish and deeply learned society. Though prevented for reasons of purdah from speaking at length with Asma'u herself, Clapperton remarks repeatedly on her husband's erudition and kindness, and on the purity of his spoken Arabic, imbibed, as his host assured him, from studying the Qur'an. Invited next door to visit the Sultan, the elementary-school-educated Clapperton soon found himself way out of his depth (Bovill, 1964–6, iii: 676). He was plied with questions about the theological differences dividing the Nestorian from the Socinian Christians, but could only answer feebly that the Scots were for the most part Presbyterians. Clapperton was then shown several volumes from the Sultan's library and a pile of volumes left behind by an earlier European visitor, Captain Denham, objects of curiosity to the Fulani, not because they were books – of which the local aristocracy had plenty – but because they were printed. He was then asked when next at home to send back a substitute for the Sultan's personal copy of Euclid's *Geometry*, which had got scorched in a fire. Clapperton does not say so, but since the Sultan almost certainly could read neither Greek nor English, this was certainly a manuscript copy of one of the Arabic translations of the work through which historically Western Europe had first become aware of his existence in the twelfth century. It had been from an Arabic translation from Euclid's Greek that in around 1120 Adelard of Bath (1060–1152) had first rendered *Elementa geometriae* into Latin, eventually to be printed in Venice from an edition by Giovanni Campano in 1482. Whether aware of this complex background of cross-cultural translation or not, Clapperton seems not to have accomplished his task. He died during his second stay at Bello's house, and lies buried in the dunes beyond the city walls.

Asma'u's own works, written in vegetable dye on unbound sheets of paper, are in a variety of genres from the didactic to the elegiac. Several are laid out as acrostics, a form in which she seems to have been particularly skilled. Forty-five of her manuscripts were preserved by the family after her death, kept in a leather book-bag known as a *gafaka* (Asma'u, 1997: xvii); others have since come to light. They include texts in three languages (though several exist in more than one), since Nana's choice of medium invariably fitted the occasion. Semi-official communications she composed for the most part in Arabic; speculations on Islamic and Sufi lore in Hausa, personal poems and advice to her female acquaintance in Fulfulde. All were written down in the Arabic script in which she had been schooled as a child.

The story of the retrieval of this corpus is intriguing and can be followed through the personal papers (SOAS, GB 0102 PP MS 36) of Jean Boyd, one of the American scholars who worked on this project during the 1980s and 1990s. It was complicated by the fact that, following the incorporation of the region into Nigeria in 1901, the Roman script had made rapid strides, consigning Arabic characters to marginality. By the time Boyd and her colleague Jean Mack turned their attention to Asma'u's *oeuvre* in the mid-1970s, only a handful of local mallams were capable of construing the *ajami* texts of Asma'u's work, which had thereafter to be transliterated into Roman characters over a period of five years, before being translated into English. Across this narrow bridge-head, Asma'u's works have passed to a wider world.

The masterpiece is probably *The Journey*, an account of her father's crusade that Asma'u first wrote in Fulfulde, though only one page of this original version survives, the rest having been culled from her surviving Hausa translation. By contrast *Tindinore Labne*, her tribute to the line of women teachers stretching from the Prophet's time to her own, translated as *Sufi Women*, exists wholly in Fulfulde, as does an elegy for her husband, *Sonnore Gidado*, written in 1848/9. In it the magnanimous host evoked in Clapperton's journals is clearly recognisable, here called Jom Maslaka or the Reconciler, who 'provided accommodation for all who came. He was the same with everyone, stranger and kinsman alike' (Asma'u, 1997: 200–1). Her poem *Godaben Gaskiya*, dateable to 1842/3, tantalises us with a picture of Paradise, presided over by the Prophet's wives:

> The houses are made of gold, the clothes of silk.
> We drink from the fragrant Rivers of Salsobie with Ahmada.
> The bodies of the people are beautiful as rubies or red coral.
> The ornaments are jewels and topaz.
> They feel no sadness of heart and do not think sad thoughts.
> They are forever in Paradise with Muhammeda.
> They are all of exactly the same age as the houris of Paradise.
>
> (Asma'u, 1997: 185–6)

The theoretical point to grasp is this. We are here at a period of Sahelian history where European domination was still undreamed of, and the

Muslim hegemony all-encompassing. The medium of that dispensation was writing in Arabic letters, which was clearly commonplace. The works thus encapsulated are frequently sacred, and the position of the Qur'an, couched in classical Arabic, is pivotal to education, spiritual and moral instruction and good governance. The result, however, was not, as Anderson would lead us to expect, a monopoly of literary composition by the Arabic tongue. The Fulani ruling class, for example, seem to have conversed amongst themselves in Fulfulde and Hausa, reserving Arabic for religious observance and debate, or converse with foreigners. Likewise they wrote their works in several languages, often in parallel versions, seldom privileging one above another. The script medium was sacral and Arabic; the language medium and the content, *pace* Anderson, were emphatically vernacular.

A latish exemplar of this tradition is that of al-Hajj Umar, who flourished in nearby Gonja well into the twentieth century. Umar is thought to have migrated from Kano, another centre of Fulani and Hausa power, around 1874. He set up a school of learning, first in Gonja, then in Salaga, and travelled far afield along the established trade routes in search of manuscripts. He certainly wrote works in both Arabic and Hausa. The Scottish anthropologist Robert Sutherland Rattray, who was then conducting fieldwork into Hausa literature in northern Nigeria, met him in the 1920s. He was much taken with his learning, and reported that Umar had in his possession several odes by the pre-Islamic poet Imru 'al-Quays. He also had in his home in Gonja a manuscript treatise on Arabic prosody dating back to about 200 AH. 'Using this', Rattray reported, 'Umar had fully worked out the form and the names of the different metres for each of the 34 odes' in Imru's corpus (Goody, 1977: 31).

Nana Asma'u and al-Hajj Umar, both from the desert grasslands of a region then remote from European – though not from Islamic – intervention, are representatives of a pre-colonial literary milieu linguistically versatile, though united by faith and script. They belong to a Sahelian literary cosmopolitanism equal in reach, though perhaps not in density, to that sustained by Sanskrit. Each serves to remind us of a state of affairs that persisted right up to the onset of British colonialism at the turn of the next century and, as Rattray's testimony avers, in certain cases well beyond it. The British authorities on their eventual arrival proved reluctant to disturb this equilibrium, whose refinement and elitism appealed somewhat to their snobbism. As a consequence, following the inclinations of their first Governor-General, Frederick Lugard (whose wife in an article published in *The Times* of 8 January 1897 had coined the name 'Nigeria'), they discouraged missionary activity and its associated school network in the north of this sprawling colony for several decades. Print culture was hence slower in its penetrative effects here than in the south and east, not arriving in full measure until well into the twentieth century. Far from stimulating any resurgence in the vernaculars, it then produced in effect a restricted literary palette consisting of books in English alongside Hausa texts in Roman type. Asma'u's recovery had to wait for the scholars.

Stable instabilities

Humanity has long been established in Africa, and so has book culture. This comparatively uncontroversial statement is only likely to cause embarrassment to book historians in so far as they have fixed ideas about what constitutes a book, or indeed what constitutes Africa. To take a very early example, the corpus of literature to which in 1842 Lepsius gave the title *Das Todtenbuch der Ägypter*, and which in the English-speaking world goes by the name of *The Egyptian Book of the Dead*, dates from around the mid-fifteenth century BCE, making it a good thousand years older than the earliest surviving writing from India, and almost contemporary with Linear A, the still-undeciphered script of Minoan Crete. It is, however, likely to be looked at askance by those attempting to establish a definite lineage for the modern African book, partly because of discontinuities of time and place; mostly, I would suggest because of problems of genre. The second is the harsher stumbling block. As it happens, it also stands in the way of a number of far later examples. In a section headed 'Repositionings' it may, therefore, be as well to tackle these difficulties frankly to clear the way for the regional and historical surveys that are to follow. The problems are, I would suggest, of three kinds and can be framed as a set of inquiries, with which I would like to deal in turn. First, what exactly is a book? Second, what – and how essential – is an author? Last, and probably most fundamentally, what precisely is a text? I would like to suggest that realistic answers to these anxieties of definition, if apposite to the non-West, are very likely to be at variance with those conventionally given.

The Egyptologian *Todtenbuch*, more precisely rendered as *The Book of Coming Forth by Day*, consists of a library of spells written on papyri, individual items from which were intended for interment in the graves of the recently departed to ensure their safe arrival in the afterlife. The writing was hieroglyphic, the columns vertical, and there was never any expectation that the whole series would be kept together as an album of any kind. There existed, none the less, standard wordings that have been found in duplication at distant sites. It thus appears that such specimens were hand-picked from an available array of stock intercessions by those responsible for burial rites (including, in morbid anticipation, the dying). Following acquisition, and before bestowal, the name of the departed was written into spaces provided, preceded by that of Osiris, the god of the dead (also, according to some understandings of his role, the god of the springing corn, and hence of resurrection). Pro-forma examples have also been found with the name left blank. The probability therefore is that these documents were hawked around the houses or pegged up on market stalls for commercial display. Having acquired one of them, the purchaser would fill in the blanks with his personal details, much as we do on a present-day form, and put it by for future use. Once the deceased and the document had been interred, his submission would be read by the immortals, who would then decide to admit them into eternity or not. The point, I think, is this. While Lepsius in the pioneering days of Egyptology may have exercised a legitimate leap of the imagination by styling the stockpile of spells salvaged from various gravesites a 'book', none of those who wrote, purveyed or utilised these documents would ever have thought of them in that light. More recent scholars have to some extent fallen in with this conspiracy by styling the papyri culled from hither and thither as 'chapters', and by retaining a fairly arbitrary running order and numbering system. If this now seems appropriate, these are chapters in a volume that never did, in any conventional bibliographic sense, exist. While retaining the numbering system, Raymond Faulkner by contrast prefers the more neutral term 'spells'; he is also at pains to stress the flexibility of the purported whole. The corpus swelled and then shrank, it contained more or fewer illustrations at different locations and times; nor was the order or aggregate of items at all constant. To take but one observation of the British Museum's collection:

> Some of the earliest *Book of the Dead* papyri, such as those of Nu (BM10477), Userat (BM 10009), Kha (Turin Museum) and Yuva (Cairo Museum) contain a surprisingly small number of chapters and are further distinguished by having few vignettes. During the course of the New Kingdom, however, the repertoire of chapters grew steadily and vignettes became more prominent. Indeed during the Third Intermediary Period (about 1085–715 BC) many papyri consisted of nothing but illustrations.
>
> (Faulkner, 1989: 12)

That the result was literature there can there be little doubt. Nor, after the counter-intuitive work (1987–2006) of Martin Bernal, can any honest reservations be entertained as to it being African. Instead of 'book' or 'text', however, we need to reach for a different term.

Lest this tradition seem antediluvian, ponder an equally African example that is still extant, even if now dwindling. In the southwest segment of Nigeria, across the border in Benin and Togo, and in certain places in the African

New World diaspora, those afflicted with indecision may choose to consult a cadre of professional fortune-tellers known as Babalawos, or Fathers of Secrets. In Nigeria and Cuba, in both of which locations such counselling is known as Ifa divination, it has been described by Wande Abimbola (1976 and 1997), a one-time president of the Nigerian senate; in Benin, where it is known as Fa divination, by the French anthropologist and concentration camp victim Bernard Maupoil. In Togo, in the Volta region of Ghana, and coincidentally amongst the Igbo of eastern Nigeria, the practice is known as Afa. The rite is much the same in all of these places, however, and the ritual conducted under the eye of the god of divination, whom the Yoruba know as Orunmila. The object in every case is to arrive at one of 256 possible mathematic permutations known as *odus*, to each of which a set of texts – or *Ese* – is attached. The identifying number is obtained by a variety of means. One common method uses palm nuts, in which instance the diviner equips himself with sixteen nuts or *ekin*, and a tray (*opon ifa*) scattered with sand or dust. He places the nuts in the palm of one of his hands, and with a swift movement transfers them to his other. The expectation is that he will perform this action imperfectly, and that either one or else two seeds will be left behind. If one seed remains, he makes the mark || at the bottom right hand corner of his tray; if two, he writes |. These marks form the beginning of a binary code, on the basis of which the number will be computed conditioning the available field of textual choice. The diviner throws seven more times, until he has filled two columns and four rows. The available permutations of these columns taken together is 2 to the power 8, or 256. Once the figure has been arrived at, the diviner recites from memory and in arbitrary order at least four texts associated with it, one of which the client chooses as the oracular guide to the future. As Ruth Finnegan stresses (1970: 194) 'Since more than one piece can be quoted for whatever figure is thrown, these are recited at random one after the other, and it is for the client, not the diviner to select which applies to his particular case.' The system thus combines an ingredient of chance or destiny with a strong element of choice.

I cite this practice alongside *The Egyptian Book of the Dead* because together they suggest a certain continuity in attitudes taken towards – and in the deployment of – text that calls into question received modes of authentication. Clearly, for example, all 256 groups of Ifa *Ese* could be editorially collated to make up a proposed corpus of such *orature*. Selections have in fact already been made along these lines, but the exercise is severely limited by the fact that such 'texts' differ from place to place, and diviner to diviner. They are never, moreover, all in play at any one time, or ever offered simultaneously or sequentially to any one reader (that is, to any one supplicant). Hence any such corpus no more represents what each recipient experiences or perceives than a pack of cards represents a game of patience, bridge or whist. In much the same way, any published edition of *The Egyptian Book of the Dead* differs radically from conventional editions of the works of even as editorially disputed an author as Shakespeare. What is offered in such editions is a fairly arbitrary anthology of the available spells that happen to have survived. Besides, even within the same time-frame, those who had recourse to such verbal formulae would not have been aware of all the variants. One interesting difference between these two historically distant modes of articulation arises from the fact that in the ancient Egyptian practice it is the words that are written down, and in West Africa or Cuba a numerical code on the basis of which the words are recited and then selected (there being two stages of randomness, one subject to destiny, the other to individual choice). In both examples, however, arbitrariness on the recipient's part vitally influences the result. In effect, the reader composes the text.

The problem of attribution

This open-endedness of much oral or manuscript expression from Africa or India, and its habitual refusal to submit to ordinary editorial treatment, did not endear it to imperial commentators of the nineteenth century. In India pre-eminently there occurred, following the early generation of enthusiasts in late eighteenth-century Bengal, a rapid reversal of attitude. Halhed, Hastings and their contemporaries had lavished on the ancient classics of South Asia a certain curatorial enthusiasm, centred after 1784 on the Asiatic Society of Calcutta with its sponsored series of editions and translations. For fifty-one years a large proportion of the East India Company's budget for education was thus directed towards such scholarship, a generous annual subvention towards which was supplied by its Committee of Public Instruction. The curiosity and relative intellectual humility were not to last. Listen to James Mill, then a London-based official of the Company, fulminating in his three-volume *History of British India* of 1817 over the ancient epics of a country he had not visited, couched in Sanskrit, a language he could not read:

> Inflation; metaphors perpetual; and these the most violent and strained and often the most unnatural and strained; obscurity; tautology; repetition; verbosity; confusion; incoherence distinguish the *Mahabharat* and the *Ramayan* in a degree to which no parallel has yet been discovered.

> (Mill, 1817: ii, 364)

Mill was similarly dismissive of *Shankuntala*, the dramatic masterpiece of Kalidasa, whom the historian Stanley Wolpert (1991: 182) for one identifies as 'the greatest secular author of classical India'. These attitudes cast a long shadow. Javed Majeed amongst others has written about their impact on successive generations of British-born administrators. Suffice it to say that for several decades Mill's *History* was required reading for all who set sail for India in order to preside over its affairs. Among them was the historian Thomas Babington Macaulay, dispatched to Calcutta in 1834 as one of four members of the Company's newly created Supreme Council. On his arrival he attended the Committee of Public Instruction, then debating whether its annual grant should continue supporting the indigenous classics, or should be diverted instead to training students in the practical uses of English. Needless to say Macaulay's Sanskrit, like his Arabic and Persian, was on a level with Mill's. In the 'Minute on Indian Education' he promptly laid before his colleagues, he was adamant over his views, echoing the contempt widely felt at the time by a print for a supposedly non-print – that is a manuscript – culture:

> The question now before us is simply whether, when it is within our power to teach this language [that is English], we shall teach languages in which, by universal confession, there are no books on any subject which deserve to be compared to our own; whether, when we can teach European science, we shall teach systems which, by universal confession, whenever they differ from those of Europe, differ for the worse; and whether, when we can patronize sound philosophy and true history, we shall countenance, at the public expense, medical doctrines, which would disgrace an English farrier – astronomy, which would move laughter in the girls at an English boarding-school – history abounding in kings thirty feet high, and reigns thirty thousand years long – and geography made up of seas of treacle and seas of butter.
>
> (Trevelyan, 1889: 291)

Macaulay had been in India for some eight months when he penned these remarks, yet they swayed the committee decisively, with consequences for Indian cultural life that have been exaggerated but which were nevertheless considerable. Among them was an increasing though far from universal emphasis on English as a medium of instruction at university level, and a denigration of historical Indian mathematics and science, a prejudice that, as Amartya Sen has demonstrated (2005: 287–91), has lingered in the international mind to this day. Macaulay himself had been obliged to content himself with a pass degree at Cambridge because his own maths was so poor. He was certainly unaware of the *Sulba Sutras* of the Vedic period, containing advanced speculations on irrational numbers and the value of *pi*, or of the writings of the mathematician Baudhayana, certainly born no later than Pythagoras, who had independently discovered that the square on the hypotenuse of a right-angled triangle is equal to the sum of the squares on the other two sides. Or of Aryabhata, 476–550 CE, who had posited a heliocentric universe a thousand years before Copernicus. The extended Indian traditions in economics, linguistics and town planning also seem to have passed him by.

To place Macaulay's views in context, and to glean a more accurate impression of the nature of Indian manuscript culture in the high imperial age, it might be as well to take a glimpse at the contents of a princely library. One such was founded in the early eighteenth century, 110 years before Macaulay's arrival in India, by Jai Singh II (1688–1743), twenty-ninth Maharaja of Amber in what is now Rajastan, and a noted patron of literature, the sciences and the arts. In 1725 – the year in which Warren Hastings's predecessor Clive of India was born in distant Shropshire – Singh set about remodelling his capital. For this purpose he employed the services of the architect Vidyadhar Bhattachanja, a Bengali Brahmin deeply versed in architecture and municipal planning (Sarkar, 1984: 206), who designed the pink-hued city we know today as Jaipur, each bazaar of which, according to the visiting French diplomat Victor Jacquemont, rivalled Chandi Chowk, the main commercial street of Old Delhi. Here 'under the arcades of the palaces, temples and houses, are the shops of the artisans where are seen working almost in the open air at their trades, the tailors, shoemakers, goldsmiths, armourers, pastry-cooks, confectioners, copper smiths' (Sarkar, 1984: 33–7). He could have been describing the bustling shopfronts of present-day Jaipur.

As the heart of this grand scheme lay the nucleus of a library of manuscripts, to which Jai Singh's successors have gradually added. 'A beehive of poets, literary men, philosophers, artists and architects' is how a recent commentator (Bahura, 1971: iii) describes the court at eighteenth-century Jaipur. The scholars and craftsmen were housed in thirty-six *Karkhanas* or ateliers throughout the state, and in the royal library every aspect of their multifarious activity was represented. Held nowadays in the Maharaja of Jaipur Museum in the City Palace, its contents were listed in 1970, shortly after the thirty-eighth Maharaja expired in far-flung Cirencester. Here in abundance are versions of the Vedas of pre-Hindu India, of the post-Vedic Puranas, and multiple recensions of the *Mahabharata* and other pan-Indian classics. Contemplative works vie with philosophical treatises in the Jain, Buddhist and Hindu traditions. An illustrated Sanskrit translation in Devan-agari script of an eighteenth-century Persian treatise on geometry (ibid.: 62) sits alongside *Prastavaratnakarah*, a sixteenth-century thesaurus, also in Sanskrit. Expositions of astrology, or *Joyitisas* (ibid.: 58–62), frame a Hindi work of 1717 on the refinements of prosody. A Persian work on medicine in the Nastaliq script nestles close to a practical guide to hawking.

The catalogue in its pink dust-jacket – pink for a pink city – is itself a deeply revealing document. It is laid out in a manner approved in the 1960s by the government of independent India which, on closer inspection, turns out to be modelled on guidelines set out in 1867 by the colonial government for the registration and classification of new books. In it the collection is divided according to language, and in each language group the items are described in vertical columns, specifying the subject matter, the accession number, the title, the author if known, the compiler or editor, the size, probable date, the proportion of the original manuscript that survives, with a report on its physical condition.

The columns are full of precise details, with two significant exceptions. First, a precise date of 'publication' is seldom specified beyond an indication of the century of provenance. Second, and from our point of view more tellingly, the name of the author is often left blank. Of the third Sanskrit item, for example, a great deal is known. It is a good nineteenth-century copy of the *Gotra-pravaradhyayah* of the afore-mentioned mathematician Baudhayana (here spelt Bodhāyana), complete and in the Devanagari script (ibid.: 2–3). This, however, is the only one of the eleven items on the same page that is attributable to a named author. For all the other items the author column is empty, a tendency that is recurrent in the catalogue as a whole. In fact, the only language group for which the author is specified in every instance is Latin. This is hardly surprising since the principal items it contains (ibid.: 76) are the first and third volumes of *Historia Coelestis Britannica* (The Story of the Skies over Britain) by the first British Astronomer Royal, John Flamsteed (1646–1719). Acquired in the early eighteenth century, they are evidence of Jai Singh's international reach, and of his wide-ranging curiosity about both cosmology and human nature. Flamsteed, as Stephen Hawking in his *A Brief History of Time* (1988: 199–200) recounts, had recently quarrelled with Isaac Newton, withholding calculations on which Newton wished to draw for his own work. Newton had them seized and published in a pirated edition by Edmond Halley, better known for his comet. Flamsteed then seized every copy he could find and burned them in front of the Royal Observatory at Greenwich, where he was the director, at which Newton deleted every reference to him in the next edition of *Principia Mathematica*. The scandal may well have reached Jaipur and the ears of its Maharaja, a keen judge of both people and stars. When two French Jesuits visited Jaipur in January 1734 (Sarkar, 1984: 213), they appear to have brought with them the official edition of Flamsteed's work, published posthumously in London in 1715. The Jesuits, we are told, broke their journey overland to make use of the astronomical observatories the Maharaja had set up at Benares, Mathura and Delhi.

Other volumes in the library attest to Jai's omnivorous appetite for astronomy and maths. Like the Sultan of Sokoto, for example, he was anxious to read Euclid's *Elements*, and for this purpose had acquired that Greek work in the Arabic translation later known to the Sultan of Sokoto. Unlike the Sahelian sultan, however, this Indian prince was unable to read Arabic, so he persuaded his astronomy tutor Jagannath Pandit to translate the book into Sanskrit for him (Bahura, 1971: ii). He was also keen to take into account the geocentric cosmology set out in Ptolemy's *Syntaxis*, with which the more accurate heliocentricism of the much earlier Vedic astronomer Aryabhata was famously at odds. So again Jai acquired the standard Arabic translation of the Greek original known as the *Almagest* (from which Ptolemy's work had first been translated into Latin, much as Euclid had in the late Middle Ages, thus entering the mind of Dante and Europe). Again he got Jagannath to make him a manageable Sanskrit translation (Sarkar, 1984: 213) entitled the *Siddhanta Samrat* (or sometimes the *Siddhanta Kaustuva*).

Texts and repertoires

Attention to this one royal library is thus more than enough to dispel the ignorant attitudes of the literary supremacists of the mid-nineteenth century. It also serves to raise two important questions of definition for book history. Authorship, for example, is of primary strategic importance to the Western tradition: bibliography employs it as an alphabetical aid and much of the hype of book promotion is currently based around it. In India, however, and as we shall see in Africa as well, we are in an environment where historical expression, whether conveyed orally or by manuscript, was until the later decades of the nineteenth century very often collaborative and cumulative. In Jaipur, for example, whilst scientific and philosophical works are mainly ascribed to person, time and place, theological and mythological ones are not. This leads to asymmetry of a kind between the language groups. Of the Sanksrit works in the library about a third are attributable to one author, of the Hindi about half, of the Arabic and Persian around three-quarters. The reason is not hard to seek: the catalogue itself boasts a title page: many of the Hindi or Sanskrit items listed do not. Instead, in most cases there is a scribal colophon identifying the subjects treated, but rarely an exact date, place of publication or even the name of the writer or scribe. Such details, after all, are products of a particular kind of publishing culture, one partially embraced in the Arabic- and Parsee-speaking lands, where manuscripts of the codex form known in Western Europe were more deeply entrenched.

Such disparities possess an edge more radical than Roland Barthes's famous assertion in mid-twentieth–century France that the author henceforth was dead. Authors are products of print culture, and, in conditions of vigorous manuscript production and exchange, they may not readily identify themselves in order to be killed. We can take the measure of this fact by comparing the Jaipur catalogue with another recent literary inventory, Ananda and Sukanta's *Shakespeare on the Calcutta Stage: A Checklist* (2001). This vouchsafes the details of around 200 productions in that drama-obsessed city, in English or Bangla. The first is an all-male benefit *Othello* advertised in *The Bengal Gazette* in December 1780 (Lal and Chaudhuri, 2001: 15). It was staged at the Calcutta Theatre (1775–1808, sponsored by William Garrick and later restyled the New Playhouse) at the crossing of Lyons Grange and Clive Street. The theatre's manager, Mr Soubise, starred in the title role, the editor of *The Monitor* appeared as Iago, and Mr H., 'a gentleman of doubtful gender' as *desdemona* (*sic*). The last production listed (Lal and Chaudhuri, 2001: 136–7) is a two-handed one-night performance of the same play staged in Arabic by the touring El Teatro company from Tunis in March 1999. In every case the venue is known, as in most cases are the names of the cast. The utterly consistent fact, however, is that the writer in every instance can confidently be given as William Shakespeare, whose biographical identity, and the extent of whose collaborations, may be in doubt, but who exists none the less as a fixed authorial reference point in a way in which Vyasa, the putative author of the Puranas, does not.

One aspect of the Maharaja of Jaipur's library is obvious to anyone, even at the most superficial glance. The ancient literary epics of India are very fully represented. There are, for example, five Sanskrit redactions of the *Mahabharata* and four of the *Ramayana* in the catalogue. The *Bhagavad Gita*, the episode in dialogue form from the former in which Krishna reconciles Arjuna to battle, is separately present in nine different versions. Careful examination, moreover, will reveal that the 'text' is not identical in these cases. I thus come to the last of the general questions that I wish to raise in connection with South Asian manuscripts – and, indeed, with manuscript and oral culture in general. What, after all, *is* a text?

The parameters of such a discussion can tentatively be established by returning once more to Shakespeare. Despite widespread talk in the heritage industry and among conservatively minded teachers of a 'Shakespeare canon', it is quite clear that the complete works of this ubiquitously performed dramatist can never be set in stone. The impossibility of any such enterprise has been highlighted since the publication in 2007 of the Royal Shakespeare Company edition of his works, which returns to the text of the First Folio printed by Shakespeare's actor colleagues after his death. This differs from, but does not supersede, the words as presented in, for example, the Arden or New Cambridge series which have drawn selectively both on this Folio and on the individual Quarto format editions of each play issued in Shakespeare's lifetime. The differences are legion, if for the most part minor, even if Hamlet's last soliloquy disappears. Despite these shades of preference, and maybe of opinion, it is relatively clear of what *Othello*, for example, consists, and radical departures from it appear as blatant, and are occasionally as deplored, in Africa or Asia, as they are in Stratford. When El Teatro of Tunis performed *Othello* in Calcutta in March 1999, the *Telegraph*'s drama critic was irate. What dismayed him in this North African interpretation was not that it was delivered in Arabic, but that it represented 'a most unlikely deconstructed rendering ... ruthlessly edited, sliced up and reassembled in a purposely random nonsequential manner starting from the end, while slides projected the equivalent English passages and a TV played the Orson Welles film' (Lal and Chaudhuri, 2001: 137) and a tape recorder reproduced diatribes by Bill Clinton against Saddam Hussein.

Fewer dissenting voices were raised in the 1980s, when the British director Peter Brook re-interpreted the *Mahabharata* for the Paris and Glasgow stages; nor are they raised the length and breadth of India when countless local variants of the same epic are delivered in different tongues. This is not because the Indian intelligentsia *is* any less vigilant over this revered Indic epic than over the British bard. The *Mahabharata* is just a very different sort of work from any by Shakespeare, the history of its reception is far more complicated, its canonicity an altogether more brachiated question.

Arguably, indeed, *Mahabharata* is less a text than a swarm of stories featuring common characters and themes from which a choice is made in any given recitation, reading, manuscript redaction or printed edition. As Sumanyu Satpathy (2005) has remarked, the *Mahabharata* is 'not one but many texts'. Several times in the twentieth century scholars attempted to organise this fecund mass into an authorised and definitive edition. The results illustrated nothing as much as the difficulties involved. The most exhaustive – even heroic – attempt was made early in the century by V. S. Sukhankhar, mathematician and Cambridge wrangler. On his return to India in 1917, Sukhankhar applied his scientific intelligence to the preparation of a comprehensive critical edition of this epic cycle extending to 74,000 verses and 1.8 million words. A team of scholars at the Bhandakar Oriental Institute in Pune worked for forty-seven years on the project. The outcome, issued between 1919 and 1966, was an edition of 13,000 pages contained in nineteen rexine-bound volumes. The index added a further six.

The fascicles were received with some scepticism by the Indian world at large, since, despite the length of the critical edition with its copious accompanying textual apparatus, readers in each region instantly identified gaps. These were not the same in each case, since by common consent the *Mahabharata* had over the centuries branched out into a forest of local variants. This proliferation had been the perhaps inevitable consequence of the vernacular revolution described earlier in this chapter. As local scripts, and the literary codes they embodied, had separated out during the early years of the second millennium CE, so the story-line of this most prized and promiscuous of poems had burgeoned into a congeries of local forms, each of which had added distinctive digressions and episodes. This had heightened a general sense of the work as a pan-Indian masterpiece; by the same token it had made standardisation well-nigh impossible. As Pollock (2003: 109) explains, 'the spread of *Mahabharata* manuscripts largely followed the boundaries represented so frequently in the text itself. These are visible in principal "recensions" deriving from different script traditions: Nepali, Bangla, Grantha (Tamilnadu), Malayalam (Kerala), Nagari (comprising north-central India down to Maharashtra and Gujarat), and Shanada (Kashmir and much of West Punjab).'

Hundreds of local variants or interpolations bear witness to this process. To illustrate it, we might take one strand from the Bangla text of the epic known as the *gaudiyasampradaya* or, colloquially, the Bangla vulgate. Most versions of the work dwell on the role of Krishna in his role as counsellor, notably to Arjuna during the episode known as the *Bhagavad Gita*. In Bengali mythology, however, this facet of his personality is dwarfed by what Richard Blurton (2006: 47) has called his 'blissful sporting with Radha in the eternal land of Vrindavana'. The episode concerned ultimately derives from a thirteenth-century CE poem from Orissa known as the *Gitagovinda*, the 'Love Song of the Dark Lord'. Written by the poet Jayadeva near Puri, this was translated into English by the Welsh orientalist (and co-founder of the Asiatic Society) Sir William Jones in 1793 (1807, iv). It was independently translated and published in the Oriya tongue by the Mission Press at Cuttack in 1840. In Bengal, meanwhile, it resulted in a flourishing cult of Krishna as a gentle, bucolic, love-struck and flute-playing cowherd. The local version of the *Mahabharata* dwells on this youthful aspect of Krishna whilst those established elsewhere subordinate it to his reputation as a lawgiver and sage, just as they ignore an episode in Bangla versions of India's other great epic the *Ramayana* where Rama, who is about to invade the kingdom of Lanka to fetch back his wife Sita, sacrifices to the goddess Durgah. She demands from him 108 lotuses; when he falls short by one, he offers one of his own eyes.

These examples should convince anyone that a standardised and definitive form of either work on the Shakespearean model is a lost cause; indeed, Johannes van Buitenen, a more recent editor of the *Mahabharata*, candidly admits as much (1975: 20–2). This in no way reflects a failure of scholarship, but a radical inappropriateness in this context of the very notion of 'the text' as something that can be standardised, even in the most liberally disposed variorum edition. Text is arguably no longer the right term. My practical suggestion, whether we are dealing with Yoruba orisa, with *The Egyptian Book of the Dead* or with the *Ramayana*, is that from now on we refer to such expressive manifestations, to use a term employed by Faulkner (1989) and

Barber (1991) amongst others, not as texts – which as I shall demonstrate in Chapter 6, are themselves products of print culture – but specifically as 'repertoires'.

Those conscious of any one ingredient in a given repertoire are not necessarily, as with a text, aware of all – or any – others. Those in ancient Egypt who acquired spells for their own posthumous use were certainly not aware of any greater collation to be known to future Egyptologists as *The Egyptian Book of the Dead*. Those in Nigeria or Egypt who grapple with a set of *odu* pronounced by the Father of Secrets are probably not aware of the other 255 that might have been offered had the arithmetic of the seeds yielded a different sum. And those who sit entranced in Bengal to this day listening to the *patua* or itinerant storyteller recounting an episode from the *Ramayana* with the assistance of a painted scroll may well be unaware of the whole corpus of tales that supports his recital.

In any case, many of the above examples cross the borderlands between the recited, the written and the printed. In the light of this fact, divisions between the oral, the spoken and the published – either as sequential or as simultaneous modes of textual transmission – can also no longer be maintained. It is to the constant interfusion of these modes in the regions in question that I would like to turn in the next part of this book.

Part II

Places

3 Transmitting the word in South Asia

A new woman

Indulekha, heroine of Oyyarattu Chandumenon's 1890 work of that title – the first novel ever to be published in Malayalam – must rank among the most formidable characters in nineteenth-century world literature. Part New Woman, part bibliophile, part amateur musician and hostess, she spends her hours in her matrilineal family's home in Travancore on the southwest coast of India playing the piano, receiving guests and lolling on the sofa whilst perusing the works of Kalidasa in large-type Sanskrit, either by sunlight or else by the fitful beams of a spluttering kerosene lamp. Naturally the guests include suitors, one of whom, a libidinous buffoon called Nambuthiripad, is presented by the writer as a ludicrous study in comic satyriasis. Indulekha rejects him, to the dismay of her family, since he is egregiously rich. It is less her independence in this matter of marriage that concerns her relatives, however, than the apparent cause of it, for Indulekha is addicted to print. Two of her uncles are debating this interesting anomaly in the downstairs living-room, where one of them has just indicated the bookcase:

GOVINDAPANIKHA: What is the necessity of them reading all this? Can't they read the *Ramayanam* or the *Bhagavadan*? [Manuscript 'vulgate' versions of the *Ramayana* and *Bhagavad Gita* in Malayalam.]
PANCHMENON: That is what I too say. There are so many books in our literature at Poovally. No one touches them. All the volumes which are *aalekham* [written on palm leaf] have disintegrated beyond repair. I had told Modhavan long ago to dust them and keep them clean – he has not done so yet.
GOVINDAPANIKHA: Can't Indulekha clean them?
MANCHUMENON: She is contemptuous of *aalekhan* volumes. Do you think that people will touch anything other than printed books? It is the height of *kaliyuga*.

(Chandumenon, 2005: 48)

Chronology is clearly of the essence here. Manchumenon's outrage over his niece's behaviour is governed by a sadly limited vision of female education – Indulekha's job is to dust manuscript books, not to read printed ones. It is also dictated by Hindu historiography. *Kaliyuga*, or the 'Black Age' is the most debased of the four ages of increasing degeneracy described in the Sanskrit classic, the *Surya Siddhanta*. It began in 3102 BCE, and during it all sorts of undesirable events are to be expected including, apparently, the advent of printing and the publication of Chandumenon's book, the Preface to which was finished at Parappangali on 9 December 1889. Chandumenon, a local magistrate, had started the text on 11 June and finished it on 17 August. The novel was issued in January of the following year by the Spectator Press in Calicut, whose superintendant, a Mr Kochukunyan, helped with the proofs. Reviewed favourably in *The Madras Mail*, the three hundred octavo copies sold out by March ('Quarterly Returns for Madras 1889–90', BL SV 412/33). A 'revised and improved' second edition of 1,000 copies appeared in June, the price having dropped from 2 rupees to 1 rupee and 8 annas. Within a year an English translation was issued in Madras.

Chandumenon was part of a busy local literary culture in Travancore and Cochin (within the present-day state of Kerala), but it is also interesting just how much he reflects trends elsewhere in the world. His concerns with the New Woman question reflect themes in Hardy and Shaw, as well as Benjamin Disraeli's novel *Henrietta Temple* (1837), which he was reading at the time, though they also address ongoing tensions in his own matrilineal Nair society. He was a talented satirist, but the passage quoted seems double-edged. As far as their reading preferences are concerned, is it the avuncular busybodies who are out of line, or the plucky niece? I am tempted to think the first – indeed a feminist reading of the text would probably insist on this point. For, though *Indulekha* debates the battle of the sexes, cheek-by-jowl with this discussion runs another concerning textual transmission. The name of the eponymous heroine means both a crescent moon and a first draft. Her bookishness is clearly admired by the author, who none the less gives her uncles a strong case as well. Why exactly is Indulekha so devoted to the printed word, and why are the precious palm-leaf manuscripts being so neglected? Manifestly, in Indulekha's eyes, to be modern is to espouse the liberating ideals of the printed book, and, then as now, 'education' – in Macaulay's sense of the word – is bound in with this particular cultural priority. In her uncles' eyes, however, print is a distortion. Proper books for them, even as late as 1889, are manuscripts.

The age of iron

Were these elderly gentlemen of late nineteenth-century Kerala reaction-
aries and extremists, or were they realists? Before dismissing their attitudes
out of hand, it may be helpful to take a look at the history of textual transmission in South India from their point of view. One hundred years after
Halhed, was print the normative condition for text? An equally valid alternative is possible: that in India the subliminal norm was then – and was for
some time to remain – script, a condition towards which – even in the high
Victorian age of machine reproduction – print constantly tended to aspire.
To enter the South Asian environment, or to be born into it, involved main-
taining a critical distance from print's imperialistic claims to superior efficacy, claims underlying book history to this day.

For commentators of the ilk of McLuhan and Ong, in every place and
clime print has been an advantageous technology, sweeping all before
it, broadening mental and cultural horizons as it goes. But consider such
counter-arguments as might have been mustered by Indulekha's family.
Print can be viewed as a technique that diminishes writing, depriving it of
the personality of the individual hand, disturbing distinctive and personal
relations implicit in manuscript production between writer and text, text
and page, page and volume, volume and reader. In the process not just one
rhythm, but a whole gamut of reciprocal rhythms dissolves. The speech-act
(to use Peter Stillingworth's term) is of necessity personal. The script-act
may be almost equally so, though confined to paper, pen and ink. When
text is printed, its visual form is at the disposition of publisher, designer
and compositor, aided, abetted (and sometimes resisted) by the author at
one stage alone: proof correction. To understand the implications of this
arrangement, witness the panic of a writer when he or she first receives a
complimentary specimen copy of their latest book. In the first few minutes
of frenzy, the pages are eagerly scanned for printer's errors, the cover for
flaws, the index for omissions. The author has lost control to what Pierre
Bourdieu once called 'the field of cultural production'.

Or, as Indulekha's reactionary uncles are more likely to have argued,
consider the potentially adverse effects of print culture on language. Malayalam is a Dravidian tongue written in a curved script remotely deriving
from Brahmi. At the time of this conference of uncles it had been printed
for under seventy years. The first font was designed in 1821 in Kottayam
in Travancore by Benjamin Bailey of the Church Missionary Society, a
thirty-year-old Anglican priest, amateur poet and one-time associate of
John Keats (who had once stayed with him in Oxford, afterwards writing
him some of the most memorable letters in English literature). Shortly after
arriving in Travancore in 1819, Bailey carpentered his own termite-prone

wooden press and set about translating the New and then Old Testaments into Malayalam. To print them he contrived a delicately rounded typeface consisting of 56 basic characters with 600 compound letters or conjuncts. In the 1860s the Basel missionary and grammarian Hermann Gundert added several more characters, making up the full complement of 900 'sorts' used by the Spectator Press in their two editions of *Indulekha*. To set a whole novel in so multifarious a type was clearly a demanding task, though possible without distorting the script. Late nineteenth- to early twentieth-century Malayalam typography is distinguished by its sinuous beauty.

Disaster struck in the late 1960s when typewriters became common in local offices. To fit the language on to a conventional keyboard, the Bailey/Gundert font had to be reduced to a tenth of its full extent. In 1969 the Kerala Language Institute, which was promoting Malayalam as the official state language, presided over the necessary truncation, insisting as it did so that the revised character set should be used only in typewriting and printing and should not be used for teaching children. Despite this stipulation, by 1973 it was being used in school textbooks, and a generation grew up reading it. This drastically pruned writing system is still in widespread use. Employing computer technology, an orthographic revivalist movement, 'Rachana', has been able since the late 1980s to restore something of what was lost. Currently most newspapers in the state – where literacy levels have now reached over 90 per cent – use for their banner headlines a digitalised font developed in 1993. Its name is 'Indulekha'.

For the letterforms of Malayalam, print has thus been a mixed blessing. Its impact on vocabulary and syntax has been just as ambivalent, and in this Chandumenon himself was instrumental. As well as his typeface and translations, Bailey compiled in 1844 a dictionary 'of high and colloquial Malayalam', printed by the CMS Press and dedicated to the Rajah of Travancore, who contributed 1,000 rupees towards its cost. While extending Bailey's typeface, Gundert also produced in 1872 a fuller dictionary and grammar that drew its vocabulary from every sector of society, boasting in its Preface that 'the materials for this work have been collected during more than twenty-five years' study of the language. The words have been taken from all available sources, from the lips of speakers of all ranks, castes and occupations, from the letters and records of many different districts, and from the writers in prose and poetry of every age.' Quoting these words (Chandumenon, 2005: 234–5), Anitha Devasia, whose English translation of *Indulekha* appeared from OUP India in 2005, argues that Chandumenon inherited this verbal richness only to constrict it. His novel is set securely amongst the upper-caste and aristocratic Nair, whose speech patterns pervade his writing. In his Preface Chandumenon insists that he has kept Sanskritic words to a minimum, yet his apparent partiality is for high Malayalam rather than low, and such has been the novel's influence that this preference has pervaded the written language ever since. 'To this day', comments Devasia, 'there is a certain tension between the more inclusive form of the language symbolized by Gundert's initiative and Chandumenon's more elite usage' (ibid.: 235). Both of which, it should be added have – like the modern Malayalam script – been moulded by local print history.

Thus if Jack Goody was right in claiming that any comparative study of intellectual technology of necessity involves some notion of cultural evolution, evolution does not seem, in this instance at least, necessarily to have entailed enhancement. In any case, the various modes of human communication frequently exist side by side. Script does not always given way inexorably to print. And neither has ever completely supplanted the substratum of speech that, along with song, is forever present in culture. Successive technologies may therefore best be regarded as alternative transliterations of a ubiquitous vocal medium into competing systems of signs. As Stuart Blackburn has persuasively argued when discussing Tamil folk culture, print may in fact give speech a second lease of life. 'Time and time again', Blackburn has insisted (2003: 3), 'whenever a specific case has been investigated, we find that print, writing and oral traditions tend to co-exist, although sometimes for different purposes, usually in different spheres and often with different consequences.' One might add that under such circumstances the residual presence of performance and writing frequently exercise an abiding influence on literary taste and the consumption of printed material.

The purpose of the present chapter is to examine such co-existences, survivals and transmutations within a broad South Asian context. In conformity with my argument I shall be stressing continuity rather than fracture, and will therefore begin by concentrating on repertoires that have appeared in different presentational modes, either successively or, more interestingly, in the same period or place. Throughout, none the less, I shall be posing the same basic questions: 'Is it ever possible truly to talk of script supplanting speech, or print script? How do these dimensions of communication cross-fertilise, and with what essential effects?'

'Speech is immortal.' Oral forms: a study in survival

Orality is a permanent aspect of the South Asian scene. In the state of Kerala, not far from Chandumenon's Poovally, a male chorus of Namboothiri Brahmins may occasionally be heard intoning a text in disciplined unison. Rhythmically, and with much systematic repetition of final syllables, they chant each verse on a half-sung reciting note, deviating to form slight melodic inflections or decorations, returning at the beginning of the next line. They are performing the *Rig Veda*, one of the oldest texts known to humankind, more ancient than the Hindu religion itself, so ancient that King Bhoya, the eleventh-century monarch of present-day Madhya Pradesh, excluded it from the canon of recognised *kâvya* or 'literature' on the grounds that it possessed no known agency, human or divine. The Veda was – and even now occasionally is – acquired by a process of *smirti* or rote learning, its public performance expressing what Sheldon Pollock (2003: 49) has described as 'an archaic conviction about the efficacy of its purely phonetic dimension, embodied in the traditional training of syllable-by-syllable reproduction without attention to signification'. The Namboothiri recitation, though increasingly rare, employs Sanskrit with a raised accent that is believed to be one of the last remnants of proto-Indo-European. Listening to it, even on a track recorded in 1983 by Pribislav Pitoëff and collected in the album *Voices of the World* issued by the Centre de la Recherche Scientifique and the Musée de l'Homme (1996), one is in contact with a tradition that pre-dates both script and print, yet has influenced both.

A few miles to the east, where Malayali and Tamil country merge, a group of Nadars congregate as night falls across a temple at Nancil Nadu to enact in song and dance an episode from eighteenth-century dynastic history. The Nadars are a low-caste group who traditionally make their livelihood cropping Palmyra trees for toddy. Unlike Chandumenon's Malayalam-speaking Nairs, they are Tamil-speaking and patrilinear, and they may not pass within eighteen paces of a Brahmin (Blackburn ,1988: 5). Their instruments are a long (10–14-foot) bow with a Palmyra-wood frame along which nine variously pitched cowbells are strung; a clay pot struck by paddles; several wooden blocks; and an hourglass drum. In the hours before midnight these accompany the lead singer as she tells of an outrage committed in 1731 by one of the more illustrious Malayalam rajas that have for centuries dominated the area. If in the eyes of Indulekha's uncles Kali Yuga is characterised by print, in the bow-song of the Tampimai brothers, transcribed by Blackburn in 1988, it involves strife between castes, languages and systems of inheritance. The king, Marthanta Varma, offers the marriage cloth to his female cousin, an act that, in conformity with Malayalam matriliny threatens to disinherit her brothers. They insist he recognise their rights. When he refuses, they meet him in battle:

> The sea which circles the earth
>   Rose up in angry waves,
> And rolled towards the raja,
>   Who screamed, 'It's the kali juga!'
>   (Blackburn, 1988: 115)

He quashes their revolt but, through the kind offices of Siva, the Tampimai, champions by implication of the disadvantaged, are vindicated and then deified. The performance closes with a dance of possession celebrating the resurgence of such human gods.

In Rajastan, 2,000 miles to the northwest, a party of singers gather at dusk before the central shrine in the Durgah at Ajmer. They squat on their haunches in a double semi-circle, facing the shrine as their leader plays a keynote on a portable harmonium and then leads them in the evening *qawwali*, singing each line in a passionate tenor before his co-musicians repeat it, clapping and swaying at the hip. When I attended this Sufi shrine in December 2005, most of the songs were in *ghazal* form: protestations of love for Allah, couched in quasi-erotic terms. The form is dictated by its rhymes: a couplet or *malla* whose end-word or *radif* is then repeated at the end of every other line, supplemented by a supplementary rhyme or *qafia* on its penultimate syllable (Kanda, 1995: 1–2). This subtle genre, at least 700 years old and at once literary and musical, is of Mughal origin and originally couched in Farsi, though most *ghazals* now are in Urdu or Punjabi. Among its literary practitioners in Urdu was Bahadu Shah Zafar (1775–1862), last of the Mughal emperors, who, exiled to Rangoon in 1858 after the tragic Sepoy Rising, spent the rest of his days extemporising on his fate in impeccable and moving *ghazal* laments. In Ajmer – among the most revered Sufi shrines in all India, erected to the memory of the saint Khawaja Moinuddin Chisti (1141–1230 CE) – the form is a ceremonial one, and the note of personal complaint, as Qureshi (1995) points out, strictly subordinated to the love of Allah. The poems exist in both manuscript and book form, though the musicians compose a guild, and texts may pass by ear from one male generation to the next. The group I heard performing varied in age from seventeen to seventy.

Across the Gangenetic plain in Kokata, Purusottama Lal, who is seventy-seven, settles down for an hour of recitation. The day is Sunday, the place the city's library hall, and Professor Lal will now deliver the next few *slokas* of his on-going 'transcreation' from Sanskrit into English of the *Mahabharata*. He has been at his task since 1999, and recites the results week by week. His version takes in all known variants in all their known recensions. It is now 100,000 *slokas* long, the task is far from done, yet Lal is convinced of its relevance. First, because the epic is about modern India: 'Its characters still walk the Indian streets, its animals populate our forests, its legends and myths haunt and inspire our imagination, its events are the disturbing warp and woof of our age' (*The Hindu*, 2 January 2005). Second, because face-to-face recitation is the undying medium through which this great work has been, is being and probably always will be delivered. Even as the Professor declaims before his audience in Kolkata, he is confident in the knowledge that this

2,000-year-old epic, in very many regional transformations, enjoys an existence through various kinds of live presentation, at home and throughout Southern Asia: through shadow puppetry in Andhra Pradesh, with a Telegu text and inter-dispersed by comic episodes with clowns; through the marionettes of Rajastan such as I witnessed perform an episode outside Jaipur; accompanied by gamelan orchestras in Java; or recreated by a visiting Italian puppeteer in Hyderabad. Across north India it lives as *Alha*, with a text and *dramatis personae* updated to the Kali Yuga age (Shoner, 1989). Once a generation or at times of public crisis in Garwhal, in the mountainous Uttaranchal – India's newest state – it is performed by village amateurs at the nine-day-long *Pandav lila*, or the Dance of the Pandavas. Before the performance the local children enact its principal conflict in a tug-of-war, Pandavas against Kauravas. And in nearby Chandpur bards stride backwards and forwards across the town square reciting the epic from memory. 'Sometimes', observes William Sax (2002: 54), 'the performing bard is pointedly and formally challenged by another to recall an abstruse detail from the *Mahabharata* story. If he is able to do so, he continues his recitation; if not, the challenger takes over.' As one of these bards concludes:

> The bird flies, but the summit remains.
> Man dies, but the Pandavas' story remains.
> Speech is Immortal, the seasons are immortal,
> Nothing else in this world lasts.
>
> (Sax, 2002: 38)

I have deliberately selected these four snapshots of alive-and-well oral recitation, so different in scope and genre, and stemming from four corners and various religious and linguistic cultures and social levels within India, because each illustrates – but also embarrasses – the relationship between the spoken, written and printed word. All of these oral texts possess written and printed embodiments that complicate any attempt to allot them to any given semiotic sphere. The scripted history of the *Rig Veda*, for example, is even older than the Sanskrit script in which it has traditionally been written. At first, by common agreement, its preservation was exclusively oral, a method preferred even after redactions made in the Middle Ages in the Gupta and Siddham scripts. 'Thus in the seventh century CE the pre-eminent scholar of Vedic hermeneutics reasserted, in writing, of course, that learning the Veda from a concrete text-artefact – "by means contrary to reason, such as from a written text" – could never achieve the efficacy of the Veda learned in the authorised way, "by repeating precisely what has been pronounced in the mouth of the teacher"' (Pollock, 2007: 79). The earliest surviving manuscript dates from the eleventh century CE. When in 1847 the German

Indologist Friedrich Max Müller set to work on his grand printed edition, he worked from manuscripts in the Bibliothèque Royale, and others borrowed from the French orientalist Eugène Burnouf and copied on tracing paper. To print the book Müller moved to a city he Sanskritised as 'Ukshatarana' (Ford of the Ox), whose university press possessed a set of Devanagari type designed by the Sanskritist Horace Hayman Wilson, formerly of the Asiatic Society, now Librarian to the East India Company, which was financing the publication. The proofreading was done by a British compositor who knew not a word of Sanskrit. When Müller asked him how he managed, he replied 'Well, sir, my arm gets into a regular swing from one compartment of types to another, and there are certain movements which never occur. So, if I suddenly have to take up types which entail a new movement I feel it, and I put in a query' (Chaudhuri, 1996: 135). Several copies went to the company; others were presented to various, mostly princely, libraries in India. The second edition of 1890 caused an office furore. It was to be underwritten by the Maharaja of Vijayanagara, who, having guaranteed a deposit of £2,600, then forgot all about it. Henry Frowde, litigious publisher to the university, pursued him with lawyers, to the disgust of Müller, who wrote in mitigation, 'He [the Maharaja] did not realise what a Deposit meant ... But the legal mind is above such things' (Müller to Frowde, 21 January 1889, OUP archives).

Few imaginative forms illustrate more fully the complex and shifting relationship between the oral and the literary than the bow-songs of Tamil Nadu. The description given above of one live performance is drawn from the field research of Blackburn related in 1988 in his vivid book *Singing of Birth and Death*, where, as he himself stresses, reading is as an integral aspect of the whole event. The bow-song tradition in general perplexes Ruth Finnegan's often-cited distinction (1977) between short lyrics prepared in advance and longer sagas improvised on the spot. In fact, it steers a lot closer to the Homeric practice of collation from a series of stock phrases or segments as analysed eighty years ago by Milman Parry in papers collected in his post-humous *The Making of Homeric Verse* (1971). In the bow-songs, however, the agent is often a written text in the shape of a palm-leaf manuscript handed down from bard to bard. Such texts may be used in preparing performances but, as Blackburn goes on to explain, they may be carried on stage:

> In certain temples, these performances are actually verbatim recitations from an official palm leaf manuscript. The manuscript is held by one man, read line-by-line to the lead singer, who immediately turns each line into song. Such recitations are not conducted in every, or even most temples, but they so remind us of a basic truth in the study of oral tradition: fixed, written texts are not necessarily inconsistent with

oral performance. In the bow-song performance they literally go
hand-in-hand.

(Blackburn, 1988: xxi)

But printing technology has long been active in the neighbourhood,
the first press having been set up there in 1820, the same year as Bailey's
experiments in Cottayam. Printed copies of these bow-songs now exist as
pamphlets run off at 500 copies a time, and purchasable for a few rupees
from a wayside stall. Interestingly, although these printed versions follow the
manuscript texts word for word, they are never used in the temples, because
they are considered to be ritualistically impotent. Only script conveys the
magic of the gods.

The history of the transmission of the *ghazal* is equally complicated, and
markedly transregional. Unlike the much-older Vedas, or the younger bow-
songs, its origins lie well outside India but, as with them, its transmission
seems at first to have been oral. Integral to the training of its adepts, both
in Persia and later in northern India, was the memorisation of thousands of
texts. The first known manuscripts are in Persian and date from the fourteenth century. With the Mughal invasions of the fifteenth, the *ghazal* enters
Indian book history. In the eighteenth and nineteenth centuries it became
the mainstay of the *tazkirahs* or script anthologies, whose provenance and
diffusion have been charted by Frances W. Pritchett, anthologies that
circulated in multiple manuscript copies throughout the relevant communities on both sides of – and across – borders (Pritchett, 2003: 864–70).
The museum at Jaipur today contains two Persian *diwan* (or collections) of
the work of Hafez dating from the eighteenth century. In the meantime,
the form entered international print history through the intervention of
certain Western orientalists, whose motivations do not always coincide with
the suspicious theorising of Edward W. Said. The first *ghazal* translations
into a European language were from the fourteenth-century Persian poet –
and contemporary of Tamberlaine – Hafez. As Kitty Scoular Datta (2008)
reminds us, they were in Latin, though the same year, 1771, saw the inclu-
sion of several Hafez *ghazals* into mannered English in Sir William Jones's *A
Grammar of the Persian Language*, a book whose title anticipates Halhed's. From
the 1840s onwards, with the burgeoning of print technology right across
north India, printed *tazkirahs*, in Urdu and Persian or a combination of the
two, appeared employing the new technique of lithography. They have
continued to be produced by this method ever since, signalling the perpe-
tuity of the *ghazal* as a printed form. In the meantime the birth of recording
technology has ensured the survival – indeed the rebirth – of *ghazal* as a
vocal and musical genre in the shape of the pop *ghazals* that are to this day
so marked a feature of popular culture in both India and Pakistan. *Ghazal*,

then, represents a vocal-cum-written-cum-published-cum-recorded tradition. It is ceremonious and demotic, amorous and sacred, indigenous and foreign, old and new, refusing to subscribe to arbitrary divisions, whether of transmission or of taste.

The transmission of the *Mahabharata* has been complicated by its epic length, but once again it affords an example of a text that has resolutely refused to lie still, stealing as it constantly has between versions, redactions and reproductive modes. Its attribution to the poet Vyasa is almost certainly apocryphal, although unlike the *Ramayana*, that other saga of classical India, its preservation from early days was as much literary as it was oral, the first known Sanskrit manuscript dating from the second century CE. From the very beginning it has shown a tendency to proliferate into regional variants. Since the fifteenth century this most venerable of pan-Indian epics has, for example, enjoyed a fairly independent history in Orissa in the form of the *Mahabharata of Sarala Das*, written in Oriya with localised references and a localised pantheon. It has also split up into sub-texts, the *Bhagavad Gita* – a dialogue between Arjuna and Krishna – being only the most prominent. When, in 1785, Charles Wilkins translated the latter into English he was simply perpetuating its existence as an independent, mostly devotional text, a history stretching from the tiny *Gita* now in the Jaipur museum, to the pocket-sized editions carried around by several of the characters in the novels of R. K. Narayan. In the early nineteenth century print simply reinforced this diversity. The year 1883 alone, for example, saw several printed versions in Sanskrit from centres all over India, as well as a Telegu version published at Trivetor High Road Madras, and a *Mahabharat-t-Manzum* versified in Urdu from the Persian translation by Faizi and issued by Bhawan Naval Kishore, the leading Lucknow publishing house of the period. Attempts to hammer all of this prolixity and inventiveness into a standardised classic have proved fairly futile, despite the forty-seven years spent over the task by a team of scholars led by the one-time Cambridge-trained mathematician Vishnu Sukhankhar, who devoted a lifetime to collating myriads of local manuscripts into a supposedly definitive nineteen-volume text. Efforts are made no easier by the inveterate tendency of the *Mahabharata* to burst out once more into unbridled live performance. Professor Lal's weekly renditions in Kolkata are only one manifestation of a tendency exemplified elsewhere by a recording of the *Bhagavad Gita* on DVD, or Peter Brook's dramatisation of the 1980s, performed in English in Paris and Glasgow, and later on film.

The perpetuation of oral texts through alternative technologies is thus a major fact of South Asian cultural existence. In this process of transmission and variegation, the decisive factor seldom seems to have been print, but the transliteration of original texts into writing in the form of sometimes one, sometimes several regional languages and scripts. The intervention of the printing press by and large had the effect of enshrining a range of expression articulated and preserved over many centuries by the script cultures of the region. It is to the material dimension of script in the history of South Asian book culture that we must therefore turn next.

Script galaxies and the universe of script

South Asian script culture is an infinitely complex phenomenon. Over thirty million manuscripts are estimated to exist in India alone, though when the Commission for the Restoration of Manuscripts, launched in February 2003, has finished its work, that figure may well rise steeply. Properly speaking, too, we should refer to 'script cultures' or perhaps, adapting McLuhan's fanciful terminology, to 'galaxies of script'. One is, after all, dealing with reper- toires in very many tongues: a lot more than the fourteen major languages recognised in the 1947 Indian constitution, but somewhat less than the 544 dialects recognised in 1903–22 by the demographer George Grierson. One is also confronting a range of technologies deploying different *physical* mate- rials to various ends within diverse cultural and religious traditions that have spread out and overlapped. Over-generalisation is difficult to avoid, but it may help to break the subject down into distinct dimensions. I shall deal in turn with writing substrates and implements, binding techniques, ways of reading and – perhaps most relevantly for our general discussion – patterns of distribution and circulation. I shall end with some remarks about the strategic significance of script as a communicative form in the South Asian milieu.

The oldest known substrate or surface is stone, and the oldest examples of Indic writing of which we are aware thus survive in the form of inscriptions. On a hill overlooking the Cuttack–Puri road, some eight miles to the south- east of Bhubaneswar – capital of the modern state of Orissa – stands a low knoll with bare outcrops of rock, on the tallest of which an elephant is carved in relief. Nowadays the lower slopes are protected by wire, behind which you can just make out a number of shallow inscriptions. Written in around 262 BCE, in a Magadhi dialect and in the Brahmi script, they commemorate a victory by the Maurya Emperor Aśoka – 'Beloved of the Gods' or 'Piyadasi' – over the local rulers, the Kalingas. It is stated that 100,000 men have died in this battle, and 150,000 been taken prisoner. Such was Aśoka's revul- sion at the slaughter that he converted to Buddhism: hence the elephant, acknowledged by Pali lore as symbolic of that spirituality. The inscrip- tion announces his change of heart and addresses the local Mahamatras, appealing for them to refrain from further bloodshed. The appeal is unique among the rock edicts issued by Aśoka; the rest of the text echoes fourteen he had carved elsewhere in India. The sentiments – admired in modern times by liberal intellectuals as diverse as H. G. Wells and Amartya Sen – are also echoed in texts Aśoka caused to be set up – or should one say published? – on free-standing granite columns across northern India and Afghanistan. One such can be seen on the ridge above Old Delhi, about half a kilometre from the Mutiny Monument. Originally raised in Mehrut (modern Mirat) in Uttar Pradesh, it was brought overland, breaking in five pieces *en route*. In the nineteenth century the section containing the text was sent to the Asiatic Society in Calcutta, where it joined a small rock edict discovered at the town of Bairat in Rajastan. Its eight-line text was deciphered in 1837 by James Prinsep (1799–1840), assayer of the Calcutta Mint and secretary to the society. With all of the emperor's idealism and humanity, it condemns the practice of animal sacrifice described in the Vedas: 'This I desire, that of all ye priests and princesses, religious men and religious women, yea every one of ye, every hearing thing, bear it in your hearts! This is my pleasure; I have caused it to be written; yea, I have devised it.'

Prinsep's connection with the mint was a help to him, as epigraphy in India benefited from numismatics, and the study of inscriptions in turn has fed into our understanding of early scripts. Metal – principally copper – is therefore the second substrate for writing and drawing that we know of. Techniques involved in coin-making were complex, and bear indirectly on skills adapted much later to the science of printing. Basing his conclusions on coins of the Gupta period, Prinsep himself identified punch-marking, die-striking and casting as apposite methods. All of these are found again when copper plates were used to enshrine deeds of covenant or land grants, examples of which have been found over much of India. An early survival from the Gupta period, now in the Asiatic Society, is an inscription of the seventh or eighth century CE by King Sridhirana Rata of Samatata, recovered from Khailan in present-day Bangladesh, granting twenty-five *patakas* of land to a local Buddhist monastery. Another land grant of much the same period, originating in Nimgachi forest in the Padma district of Bengal, is kept alongside it. Incised on both sides of a small copper plate, it bears in place of a seal the likeness of the ten-armed god Sadasiva fixed to an elliptical projection in the middle of its upper edge.

Copper was not the only mineral to be used. Especially in southern India, where the humidity renders softer materials perishable, bronze, silver, clay, ivory and even gold are in evidence. The treaty of 1691 between the Samorin of Calicut and the Dutch East India Company is written on one rolled-up sheet of gold (Blackburn, 2003: 21). In northern India, the climate is kinder, and birch-bark, wood, parchment, hand-made and glazed paper (substances imported from China when printing itself was not) are all found. Machine-made paper was introduced in the late eighteenth century, at about the same time as typesetting. Such is the material used by rural *patuas* or peripatetic folktale tellers in rural Bengal for the painted *pats* or scrolls with which they illustrated their recitations of the classics. Examples showing the stages of the *Ramayana* epic in successive registers or tableaux survive from the 1820s. Perhaps the most impressive example is the 13-metre-long Gazi scroll painted in the Sunderbans of the Ganges delta around 1800, and relating the life history of the Sufi saint Gazi in fifty-four horizontal tableaux (BM 1955 10-8 095). It represents the fine point of a vigorous and resilient tradition, as latterday *pats* for tourists may be picked up in the bazaars of Kolkata to this very day. Further to the northeast, in adjacent Assam, strips of woven silk were sewn together to make up textile sheets that served much the same function. A seventeenth-century example telling the exploits of Krishna through repeated graphic figures between rows of Bangla script has been in the British Museum collections since 1905 (BM As 1905 1-18.4).

The ubiquitous substrate for Indian manuscripts, however, is palm leaf. Early manuscripts, especially in South India, are made from the broad fronds of the Talipot palm, which grows wild as far south as Sri Lanka. But in the sixteenth century the female Palmyra plant was introduced from East Africa. Its leaves are smaller but tougher, especially when treated chemically with oil extracted from lemon grass. The resulting sheets are characteristically light yellow in colour and wider than they are tall. Across India, the common practice was to superimpose the pages of a given text, then bind the stack with a single chord running though an aperture in the middle. To read such a manuscript, or *grantha*, you turn the pages, not horizontally in either direction, but away from you perpendicular-wise. Wooden boards, sometimes carrying painted illustrations of the contents, often served as book covers. Other arrangements have also been known: in the great Hindu shrine of Jagannath at Puri, the temple records are preserved in pages sewn together end-to-end, then rolled into drums (Banerjee, 1980: 109).

Whatever way you regard them, however, and however they are bound, *granthas* are books, just as surely as were the scrolls of ancient Rome or the codices, or book-shaped manuscripts, of medieval Europe. Outsiders though may have to revise their ideas of reading – formerly performed whilst squatting backwards on the heels – and even more drastically of writing. Once again, many styles are apparent: in Tamil Nadu the practice was to hold a metal stylus with the right hand while propelling it from behind with the left; in Orissa to hold the stylus vertically whilst drawing the leaf beneath it, going across the grain to avoid splitting the fibres. The peculiarly loop-like letters of several Eastern Indian scripts – Oriya and Malayalam, for example – probably result from a desire to avoid the leaf damage likely from incising straight lines. Later, a mixture of ash, charcoal and oil was rubbed into the incisions to make the words stand out. These are skills rarely on show nowadays, except for inquisitive outsiders.

The technicalities of manuscript production are less significant for Indian book culture as a whole, however, than the very fact of their existence across the subcontinent for many centuries before the existence of print. The survival of the Aśokan edicts in rock and pillar form demonstrates just how deeply rooted writing cultures have been in India for over two millennia. The flowering of literatures within this distended period, first in the trans-regional and cosmopolitan high tongue of Sanskrit and later in regional *prakrits* in myriads of local scripts, represents a revolution in South Asian culture far deeper and wider than that modernist glitch that in Chapter 1 – and in satirical mood – I dubbed the 'Halhed moment'. Hence if in the European environment we are capable of speaking with Elizabeth Eisenstein of a 'print revolution' in the fifteenth century CE, in India we are far more justified in referring to a deeper and earlier script revolution over a far longer time-span. Listen to Sheldon Pollock on the cumulative impact of this sustained and diverse event, and the challenge it poses to the hegemonic claims made for the print 'revolution' by certain book historians:

> An alternative case could certainly be argued, that the truly historic event for literary cultures in India, and what defined them in the peculiar contours they often still bear, was the invention, diffusion, and eventual conquest of manuscript culture, in its specific symbiotic relationship with the antecedent oral culture. The epistemic revolution of literacy, the production of manuscript books (over thirty million manuscripts are still extant), their dissemination in often massively reproduced and relatively stable form, and perhaps most important, their oral performance before large audiences over long periods of time, have had an effect on shaping imagination, sociality, and power arguably deeper and more extensive than any attributable to print, middle-class book consumption (stunningly low in India), and the culture of private reading reinforced by print (though hardly generated by it).
>
> (Pollock, 2007: 77–8)

What Pollock calls here 'the epistemic revolution of script' is known to have occurred in a number of stages. Brahmi, the script in which the Aśokan edicts were framed, was an administrative code ensuring the communication of, and complicity with, the liberal commands of the emperor, and the polity of his chancery or court. The high language of Sanskrit is a later development, and its purposes and ambiance were literary. Through it the classics of Vedic India, devised in an oral environment, were newly transmitted, and more recent texts such as the *Mahabharata* inscribed and spread. Sanskrit was a minority code and its ubiquitous existence at certain social levels ensured that the potential galaxies of script were held within a script universe accessible everywhere to a transregional literate elite. The third stage of this story concerns what Pollock has called a 'vernacular revolution', associated with the diffusion of political power following 1000 CE between regional spheres of influence and regional courts. The emergence of locally diverging writing systems now enshrined the diversity of *prakrits* and *desa-bhasa*, or tongues of the place. This multifoliated process is itself thought to have occurred in two phases that have been termed *literisation* and *literarisation*, separated in most localities by a period of some three centuries. In the first phase the traditional and cosmopolitan texts of the elite were transmitted through the new code, a diversification of communication involving the evolution and authentication of local scripts (Devanagari, Malayalam, etc., in any of which Sanskrit could be written) and of local dialects. In the second phase local languages and writing systems evolved their own autonomous literary traditions, giving rise to what we can confidently address as Kannada literature, Marathi literature, Bengali literature and so forth.

Print adaptation and print reinforcement

The principal effect of print culture in South Asia, certainly in its earlier manifestations, was to reinforce these developments. Though Halhed, Wilkins and Karmakara, with whom we began this study, are of great importance to print culture locally in Bengal, theirs was very far from being the first book printed in South Asia. That honour goes to an edition of St Francis Xavier's *Doctrina Christiana* produced in 1557 by Portuguese Jesuits in Goa (Kesavan, 1985: 17). Twenty-one years later, a Tamil translation of the same text by Padre Henrique Henriques (1520–1600) and Padre Manoel de San Pedro was published on the Malabar Coast under the title *thambiran vaNakkam*. Henriques seems to have been Portuguese by birth, and Manoel his Tamil assistant. Working with a combination of letterpress and what looks suspiciously like woodblock, they printed off sixteen octavo pages from a single sheet, an exemplar of which is held nowadays in Harvard.

The fact that, within two decades of arriving in India, these Roman Catholic missionaries were adapting the received technology of the hand press to the letterforms of one of the more widespread Southern Indian vernaculars brings these early developments in sharp and meaningful focus. To answer a question raised in two parallel contexts in Chapter 1, what seems to be occurring is that print is not so much annexing Tamil as Tamil is acquiring print. Where the Catholics had trodden, the Bible-loving Protestants soon followed. By the early eighteenth century Tamil types were being cut by German printers working in Holland. In October 1713 they were used in a diatribe against Hinduism published by Dutch missionaries in Tranquebar. When it came to printing the first Tamil translation of the

New Testament, they proved too clumsy, and were replaced by a font cut in the mission's own foundry, reputedly using lead extracted from cases of Cheshire cheese sent out by the Society for the Propagation of Christian Knowledge. The following year a further edition of the gospels and the Acts of the Apostles was run off in the same location, using a fresh set of largish (13.5 point) German-made types. A copy of this text can be inspected in the library of Serampore College on the spot of Carey's eventual mission, the Tamil letters looking very much like those on contemporary palm-leaf manuscripts. The British were not far behind and, with their customary insouciance, they did not build their first printing press, but stole it. In 1761 a three-year-old printing press was requisitioned after a raid on the French colony of Pondicherry by the British general Sir Eyre Coote. He brought it back to Madras (Chennai), where for decades it was used by SPCK missionaries in the suburb of Vepery.

Yet these miscellaneous initiatives, useful as they were, hardly add up to a continuous national print history. Before 1778 print culture in South Asia was very much a start-and-stop affair: the product of discrete communities working in separate locations using improvised methods. The authentic contribution of the closing years of Halhed's eighteenth century was one of consolidation and diffusion. Starting in certain strategically placed centres – Goa, Madras, Calcutta – the techniques of print production gradually spread out until by the 1840s they covered most of the subcontinent. As they did so they adapted themselves to various regional writing systems, striking new fonts when and where it became necessary. Manohara Karmakara's type-foundry at Serampore undoubtedly played a major part in this achievement. After making a new Bengali typeface for the Bangla Bible of 1800, it went on within a very few years to produce a Devanagari font for the Sanskrit and Hindi testaments, an Urdu font for the so-called Hindustani testament, and equivalent typefaces for Persian, Arabic, Punjabi, Maharathi, Oriya, Burman, Tibetan and even Chinese. Within two decades Benjamin Bailey and his assistants further south were turning out reading material in Malayalam. The proliferation of fonts continued until by the mid-nineteenth century the literisation and domestication of print technology to the existing language systems of the subcontinent was almost – though not quite – complete.

In each and every region, a similar scenario is enacted. A team of local pandits transmits a language with its lexis, syntax and associated calligraphy to an intermediary. The intermediary – missionary, administrator, or educator – then employs a technician who adapts metallurgical and other traditional skills to the task of turning out a font. With the assistance of numerous local consultants – many of whom will not feature in the official accounts – the desired texts are then collected or translated. By means of long-established patterns of trade, the resulting books then circulate. Before we revert to styling this scenario a revolution, it is as well to consider what sort of changes it did, and did not, characteristically effect. As one might expect it introduced wholesale the paraphernalia of Western para-textual arrangement. Where palm-leaf manuscripts had colophons, books printed in Calcutta or Madras possessed title and contents pages, tables and indices. Certainly, too, print increased the speed and scope of propagation; *grantha* took months to reproduce in multiple copies, and reached perhaps scores of readers. A book might be printed in a few weeks, and then reach hundreds; judging by extant records, until late in the nineteenth century print-runs of over 500 were quite rare, though of course the deep-seated habit of reading aloud to others often ensured that many of these texts were consumed aurally by a large number of people. Certainly, too, as we shall see, the existence of print encouraged the development, among particular and expanding coteries, of some imported genres: novels such as *Indulekha*, for example, or short stories.

It is equally incontrovertible that print did not instantly transform popular literary taste, and that it had surprisingly little effect on the chosen languages of diffusion. The fonts devised for missionaries for proselytising purposes were rapidly turned to other ends, which in practice frequently meant the perpetuation of the Indian classics, often translated into a local vernacular. Despite the endeavours of some, the Roman script resolutely refused to catch on for languages other than the administratively fostered tongues of English (in British India and some allied princely states), Portuguese (in Goa) and French (in Pondicherry). Books printed in these languages at first initially took the form of either government edicts, or school and univer-sity textbooks. It is remarkable how little such publications influenced the overall cultural demeanour of a proliferating publishing scene. With limited exceptions, a printed national literature in English took a full century to develop. Imperial myth has it that, following Lord Macaulay's Minute of 1835, English stole a march on its indigenous rivals by securing a place for itself as the principal language of secondary school education within areas governed by the East India Company, and later the Crown. The precise effects of this measure on the educational system, and the reading habits of the educated, have been questioned by historians such as Javed Majeed. Its ramifications for publishing history are a matter of exact record.

Until the 1860s, to the regret of some observers, few records of print production were kept. A decade after the Sepoy Rising of 1857–8, however, the surveillance instincts of the British got too much for them. Act XXV of the Year 1867 accordingly decreed that, in each of the seven Presiden-cies of British India, publishers should submit details of each publication issued in any language or format, with full details of its author, genre, place of publication, the print technology used (letterpress or litho), size (quarto, octavo, duodecimo), number of pages, price and print-run. These details were then collated and published in a quarterly catalogue, with comments on the usefulness and, sometimes, on the political tendency of each item entered in a separate column. The Catalogue for the Presidency of Madras for the first quarter of 1890, for example, (BL SV 412/33) informs us that in January of that year *Indulekha*, a work of fiction written in Malayalam by O. Chandu Menon was printed by P. C. Achutan Brothers at the Spectator

Table 3.1   Book production in Bengal in 1874, subdivided by language group.

Subject	Books Printed in English And Other European Languages	Books Printed in Bengali	Books in Classical Indian Languages	Books in More Than One Language
Biography	1	14	0	0
Drama	15	90	7	12
Fiction	1	66	5	1
History	9	12	0	14
Language	7	43	31	24
Law	17	14	1	1
Medicine	2	19	19	6
Miscellaneous	71	167	0	42
Poetry	10	201	18	24
Politics	0	0	0	0
Philosophy	0	16	10	47
Religion	18	177	21	0
Science (Material and Mechanical)	9	39	0	1
Science (Natural and Others)	10	177	21	0
Travels and Voyages	2	3	0	0
TOTAL	171	894	114	174
Original Works	131	504	90	152
Translations	2	181	24	30
Republications	33	209	0	2
TOTAL	171	894	114	174
Educational Works	46	112	8	36
Non-educational Works	125	784	106	138
TOTAL	171	894	114	174

Source: 'Annual Report on Book Production in India for 1874' (BL IOR MF 1/198).

Press in Calicut. Three hundred copies of an octavo volume of 498 pages were issued at a price of two rupees, copyright having been registered under the name of the author. The inspector comments that this is 'A novel in Malayalam written by a District Munsif in Malabar, useful as a delineation of Malayali society. The plot concerns a Nair girl in love with a graduate of the university and wishing a marriage against the proposal of her relatives.'

Nor is this all. The quarterly returns for the year were subsequently collated in Calcutta (after 1911 in Delhi), and issued in an annual report, the statistics in which afford a bird's-eye view of book production across British-administered India throughout the year in question. They run from 1867 until well into the twentieth century and, while allowance must be made for non-compliance with the Act, they still constitute a quarry that book historians have scarcely begun to exploit. For present purposes, the strongest revelations concern the balance maintained between different genres and languages of transmission. Table 3.1 gives the statistics for books published during 1874, forty years after Macaulay's championing of the medium of English, in Bengal – that most anglophile and anglophone of provinces – broken down according to subject and language group.

One or two elements here seem slightly suspect: for example the non-existence of political works in all columns, suggestive of self-censorship or else non-registration. Such absences may also indicate that politically orientated books may well have been entered under another category to avoid prying eyes. Other features are peculiar to the presidency, such as the preponderance of educational over non-educational publications, or the prominence of drama in Bengali, a vehicle for public controversy popular then and since among the liberal bourgeoisie or *bhadralok* class of Calcutta, and one of several categories into which the non-appearing polemical works may well have been squeezed. What is flagrant is the quantity of items in Bengali compared to those in English. In some categories this discrepancy is by a factor of twenty or more. Even for educational publications there are twice as many Bengali works, probably reflecting the rise of local centres of vernacular textbook production such as Dakha. The only subject where English comes out top is law, and nearly half the anglophone titles appear in a miscellaneous row that includes official circulars by the government. These boost the English sum a little, but even so the Bengali total dwarfs it by six to one. English is even exceeded by the 'classical' tongues of Persian and Sanskrit.

The figures are far from untypical of India as a whole. That same year the Director of Public Instruction in the Punjab noted that 4.12 per cent of the book production had been in English, 77.74 per cent in the vernacular, 14.28 per cent in oriental languages and 3.84 per cent in more than one language. In this busy and polyglot presidency vernacular production

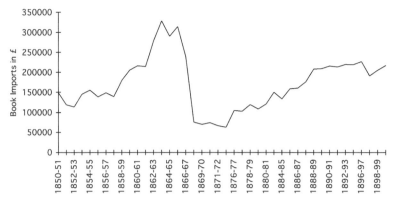

Figure 3.1   Book imports into India, 1850–1901 (from Joshi, 2002a: 40). Reproduced by kind permission of Priya Joshi and Columbia University Press.

was split between Urdu (including a translation of St Augustine's *Confessions*), Hindi, Punjabi and Pashtu. The same impression pertains, however. Sixty years after Halhed, the net effect of print culture in India has been to reinforce the vernacular revolution of several hundred years before, with Macaulay's influence or without it.

Another aspect of the table that will strike many modern observers: there is one work of fiction in English to sixty-six in Bengali. Three caveats should be noted: in 1873 the novel in Bengali was beginning its rapid rise to prominence; second, the Bengali total includes translations from English; third, English novels had been imported from Britain for some time, and such sales were – for the time being at least – able to satisfy the needs of the English-reading classes, both expatriate and local. The statistics above enable us to survey the mid- to late-Victorian book scene through the eyes of local producers. To gain a fuller view of the trade as seen by booksellers, librarians and readers we therefore need to supplement them with Graham Johanson's and Priya Joshi's research into book imports and the impact, over the last quarter of the nineteenth century, of 'colonial editions'. In her book *In Another Country* Joshi, for example, makes great play with the annual proceeds from book imports across the second half of the century. She sets them out as a graph, the Himalayan folds of which have much to tell us about the vagaries of the book trade at the time (Figure 3.1).

As Joshi acutely observes, between 1850 and 1865, book imports into India are seen to treble in value, and 95 per cent of the titles are from Britain. The contours of her diagram, however, describe a commercial topography more complex and interesting than this. At first imports rise slowly, at a few per cent per year. There is then a spurt in 1857–8, following the Sepoy Rising in North India, and a further sharp rise in the early 1860s. The summit of the import book trade occurs in 1863, with a subordinate peak four years later, the very year when the introduction of presidential catalogues and centrally produced records enables us to track local production for the first time. Almost immediately there is a sharp fall, so that by the beginning of the following decade the figures stand lower than at mid-century. The remaining survey discloses a gradual rise at quite a slow gradient, so that by 1889 the value of imports has reached the same level as 1850. By the end of the century, after many a ripple and crag, the figures are some £25,000 higher than they were at the start.

Why all the bumps and slopes? Beneath this terrain surge two opposed tectonic plates: the inexorable rise of indigenous Indian publishing, and the expansionist energy of British firms in search of fresh markets. The shift in educational policy signalled in 1835 by Macaulay's notorious Minute had produced a decisive increase in the demand for books, especially in English, largely satisfied at the time – in the absence of a fully-fledged local publishing industry – by the importation of British titles though normal trading channels. One, quite well charted, repercussion of the rising in 1857 was a further large hike in educational investment, partly intended by the authorities as a counter-insurgency measure. By this time, however, local firms – whether expatriate-owned like Calcutta's Thacker and Spink or under local management like Lucknow's Bhawan Naval Kishore – were far better positioned to take advantage of increased demand. The result was a successful challenge to imported titles mounted by material locally authored, edited and manufactured: a development evident from quarterly and annual returns. The reaction of publishers in Edinburgh and London was to fight back through a set of marketing policies targeting particular segments of the colonial readership, notably students and readers of fiction in English. It is against this background that the rise of British-based 'colonial editions' and educational series from the 1870s onwards is best interpreted. By means of such careful and angled strategies, the sales of British books in India eventually regained much lost ground – though somewhat against the commercial grain.

Editions of metropolitan fiction specifically for the imperial market, for instance, go back to October 1843 with an abortive scheme by John Murray for a list for British and overseas readers entitled Murray's Colonial and Home Library. It reached forty-nine titles but closed after six years since, as the name of his series indeed implies, Murray had not sufficiently separated out colonial requirements. But in 1870 the Forster Education Act made instruction in the three Rs available for the first time to everybody in imperial metropolises. The resulting literacy rates forced British publishers to think hard about various categories of reader. A burgeoning of budget-priced series ensued, most consisting of reprints of English classics or other works out of copyright. Fairly typical was Cassell's National Library, launched in 1886 with Macaulay's *Life of Warren Hastings*, and aimed at elementary school products in clerical employment like my maternal grandfather. It was issued in weekly volumes, at 3*d* in boards or 6*d* in cloth, the price being defrayed by the advertisements carried by each duodecimo volume for Morson's Preparations for Pepsine Indigestion or Singer's Cycles 'for Health, Utility and Pleasure'. The manageable price differentiated it from Cassell's middlebrow Standard Library at twice the cost – still far less than a contemporary Cassell title on the theme of the Great Game: *The Coming Struggle for India* by Professor Arminius Vambéry, complete with coloured map showing 'Russian Advances towards India', all for a hefty 5*s*. The cut-price library boomed.

Publishers soon took advantage of this winning formula to plan their very own outflanking assault upon India. First in 1878 came the firm of Bentley, whose Empire Library was to go through two series, launched respectively in 1878 and 1885. The success of the second suggested rich pickings were to be had in the colonies, provided the field was properly scouted. Accordingly in 1884 Maurice, scion of the flourishing family firm of Macmillan, undertook a tour of India, Australia and New Zealand, combining it with his honeymoon (Morgan, 1944: 187). He became an imperial enthusiast, and two years later launched Macmillan's Colonial Library, overwhelmingly as an outlet for contemporary middlebrow fiction, much of which was still in copyright at home, and the royalties from which thus served to boost the incomes of his much-valued living British authors. The cutting of the Suez Canal had by now reduced the voyage to Calcutta or Bombay to a mere three weeks and the cost of freight as well. Thus each quarto title could be sold to local booksellers for a price of 3*s* plus discount, the company ensuring this concession did not compromise the British market by marking copies 'Not for Resale'. The library was to include 1,738 titles by 1960, rebranding itself from 'Colonial' to the more jingoistic 'Empire' in 1913, then to politically more acceptable 'Overseas' in 1937, reflecting the changing political susceptibilities of the times. Its scope was empire-wide, but a more territorially specialist ambiance is evident from 1894, when Bells took over the stock of the defunct company of E. A. Petherick. Petherick had been buying in sheets from other companies and repackaging them for the general colonial market. Bells restyled the exercise their Indian and Colonial Library, under which rubric they were to bring out 1,386 titles between 1894 and 1918. The Scottish firm of Blackie were pioneers in two respects: first producing an earmarked Indian series, then opening a branch in Bombay to service it.

Soon Macmillan, like Nelson, Longman and other firms, were applying the formula to educational provision by commissioning textbooks and readers for school and college classrooms throughout India. It was a far more competitive field, and one in which a whole gamut of local publishers with advantages of location, access, know-how and low overheads had long been active. This was nowhere truer than in the Punjab, fast becoming one of the most vigorous publishing centres in all India. By 1892, Rudyard Kipling's father, John Lockwood Kipling, a noted educator and head of the art college in Lahore, is writing to Macmillan's directors in London letting them know that, in the face of such sustained and well-informed local competition, the firm's new set of readers does not stand a chance with the education committee: the 'chief of the Delhi Mission College objected to it on the grounds that the moral lessons were not moral enough and that the gradations did not fit in with the school courses. A more reasonable objection – I forget whose – was that the Explanations and Comments of the early numbers are in English' (BL Add. MS. 54940).

Book marts and reader constituencies

By the 1890s, then, book-crazed Indulekha and her contemporaries were faced with multiple choices at their local bookshop or pavement booth: between competing genres; between different languages and scripts; and between local or imported titles. Already the vertically crammed shelves of the thirty-odd booksellers crowded cheek-by-jowl in the growing book mart along Calcutta's College Street offered these three parameters of variety: displaying English- or Bengali-medium textbooks published in Dakha beneath novels from Edinburgh, beneath Urdu tracts from Lucknow, beneath locally produced journals and even erotica. Such in the closing decades of the century was the Canning Library at the corner of College and Harrison Roads, presided over by one Babu Yogesh Chandra Bannerjee. Here Bipichandra Pal, later a prime mover in the Indian National Congress, recalled playing truant from Presidency College across the road whilst 'freely rummaging for hours and hours together' among stock 'both in Bengali and English' (Pal, 1973: 181). Prominent, then as now, were cribs for the degree papers at Calcutta University down the street, or entrance exams into the coveted ranks of the 'pukka' ICS, the Indian Civil Service, produced on rough paper for a few annas by jobbing neighbourhood printers. One of the candidates for the Indian Civil might have been Kim, the Irish-born, Lahore-bred and Lucknow-educated protagonist of Rudyard Kipling's novel, issued by Macmillan as number 414 of their Colonial Library in 1901. Kipling never mentions the cribs.

The book scene in South Asia at the turn of the twentieth century was therefore an exceedingly diverse one. Much has changed in the interval, with the growth of nationalist movements everywhere, with the coming of independence to India, Pakistan, Bangladesh and Sri Lanka, with more Asian authors writing across more genres with – in some cases – far more international exposure, and with additional and more efficient print technologies speeding the flow. These changes, though, have represented for the most part – albeit large – transformations of scale. Arguably, as we shall see in Chapter 8, the actual balance of publications on offer in the internal South Asian book market – between language groups, between exports and domestic production and between the kinds of publication on offer – is not so radically different today from that which pertained in 1900. Increasingly, though, Asian publishing has itself become part of a globalised communications network. Before examining this and other complications of modernity, we must turn our attention to parallel developments in Africa.

4   Transmitting the word in Africa

A child of his time

Chinua Achebe's character Obi Okonkwo is a son of print. The anti-hero of Achebe's second novel *No Longer at Ease* (1960), sequel to the more celebrated *Things Fall Apart* (1958), he is a university-educated higher civil servant arraigned for corruption while attempting to make ends meet in fast-moving Lagos, capital of post-independence Nigeria. Obi is found guilty but, before his fall, he makes a return trip eastwards in his new Morris Oxford to his home village of Umuofia in Igboland. There he wanders into the study of his father, Nwoye, a missionary product and a preacher, himself the son of the non-literate but proverbially wise Okonkwo, tragic protagonist of Achebe's famous first novel.

In *Things Fall Apart*, Nwoye is portrayed as a great disappointment to his profoundly traditionalist father, but in *No Longer at Ease* we discover what kind of a person he has turned into in the interval, especially in his reading habits. At his baptism he has chosen the Christian name Isaac (which, interestingly, turns Okonkwo, Obi's grandfather, into Abraham). As a representative of Umuofia's first generation of schoolboy literates he has, moreover, come to believe implicitly in 'the written word, or better still, the printed word' (Achebe, 1960: 126). So firm is his faith in fact that in the presence of his non-literate Igbo relatives Nwoye/Isaac is nowadays fond of quoting Pontius Pilate's disclaimer from St John's Gospel in the local Onitsha dialect: '*Ife nke ndegolu, edegom*' (translated by Achebe as 'What is written is written'). Now, scouting his bookshelves, his son finds them packed with mouldering books and papers, 'from Blackie's *Arithmetic* which he used in 1908 to Obi's Durrell, from obsolete cockroach-eaten translations of the Bible in the Onitsha dialect to yellowed Scripture Union cards of 1920 and earlier'. Isaac Okonkwo, we learn, 'never destroyed a piece of paper. He had two boxes full of them. The rest were preserved on top of his enormous cupboard, on tables, on boxes and on one corner of the floor' (Achebe, 1960: 127).

Achebe's inventory of this personal library is bibliographically very precise. Blackie's *Arithmetic* 'for secondary schools and pupil-teachers', for example, was published in Edinburgh in 1883, and was widely used in schools in Nigeria from the 1890s onwards. Scripture Union 'cards', containing daily Bible readings and questions, were first issued to schoolchildren in 1879. They were replaced by so-called 'Notes' in pamphlet form in 1923: no wonder Isaac's are yellow. The most informative items, however, are the cockroach-eaten tomes. The New Testament in the version Achebe cites was issued in the Onitsha dialect by the British and Foreign Bible Society in 1893. The gospels of Matthew and Mark were translated by Henry Johnson, 'Archdeacon of the Upper Niger Territory', Luke and John (whom Isaac quotes) by Henry Hughes Robinson, 'Archdeacon of the Niger'.

By the late 1950s these versions had long since been rendered 'obsolete' since in 1913 the Society had reissued the entire Bible in 'Union Igbo', a 'central' compromise between four rival dialects recently adopted for convenience by the Church Missionary Society. The Anglican Church (of which both Achebe and the fictitious Isaac are members) had stuck to this Union translation long after the government in the 1960s had gone over to a later compromise orthography known as 'Standard Igbo' (which in 1999 Achebe would publicly attack). Thus old Isaac, with his Onitsha dialect testaments, is a good two trends behind the times. The illuminating point in Achebe's account is this: Onitsha Igbo is – and certainly was in Isaac's youth – a living tongue. Union Igbo, on the other hand, was spoken by nobody in particular, and was introduced principally to universalise the printed language over a larger geographical area. Amid the mildewed clutter of his room therefore, this ageing bibliophile has carefully preserved bound evidence both of his faith in print and of his nostalgia for regional speech. His mind is layered, each stratum representing an affinity with a particular, phased mode of verbal communication.

In this chapter I shall be looking at such layering across Africa, and investigating its repercussions on verbal transmission across a range of media, printed and otherwise.

A question of speech

Any honest account of communication in Africa must begin with a frank recognition of the extreme linguistic and expressive balkanisation of the continent. When it comes to modes of converse and forms of the imagination, Africa is quite exceptionally prolific. The dimension of language yields a basic sense of this range. When I was preparing my book *West African Poetry* (1986) I became interested in the number of languages spoken in the comparatively confined area of the world I was then covering. I sought the advice of a computer at the School of Oriental and African Studies in London, which responded that the answer depended on what was meant by a language. The Africanist and linguist David Dalby, who provisionally mapped the languages of Africa in the 1970s, had employed two different criteria (Dalby, 1977): either counting every language group that recognises itself as a distinct unit, or extending each grouping as far as it reached before its speech became unintelligible to its neighbours. The first tally is obviously larger than the second. In the case of West Africa the respective totals turn out to be approximately 1,250 and 700 (Fraser, 1986: 7). For the continent as a whole one would have to quadruple these figures. Each item in the aggregates, moreover, possesses it own 'oral literature' – to use Ruth Finnegan's (1970) now somewhat discredited term – or its own *orature*, to use a term that has been in vogue since the 1980s. The range of expressive forms is as a result very large indeed, and shows little of the corporate cohesion that we have already noted in South Asia. Again, to sustain the terminology we defended at the end of Chapter 2, each and every such orature displays a kinetic legacy of *repertoires*, rather than of texts as such. The flexibility, as well as the scope, of these repertoires is remarkable, and passes well beyond the regional variorum effect noted in the perpetuation of the classics of India. Much of it indeed, is extemporary, and takes the form of spontaneous variation on sets of remembered, and communally recognisable, metaphors or tropes.

The extent and versatility of such traditions may be hinted at by sampling examples of local fieldwork, one of the liveliest of which is Karin Barber's astute and highly committed account (1991) of the phenomenon of *oriki* in one comparatively small Yoruba town, Okuku in Nigeria's Oyo state, where the relevant performances are for the most part the prerogative of the women. 'Praise names' is how *oriki* were earlier described by Finnegan (1970: 112) or 'permanent titles held by individuals, given to them by friends or, most often, by the drummers', but this grandiose and formulaic description hardly covers the practice in Okuku, where spontaneity and improvisation have always been the order of the day. Barber evokes the scene as an artist takes her pitch before the object of her attentions and proceeds to riff on, around and between a complex network of references, allusions and verbal echoes, each one of which she can confidently expect her client and all the onlookers to summon up from brimming recall. Each individual example of *oriki* is thus a patchwork of cryptic quotations, or rather half-quotations, the residue of which, and connections between which, the audience must fill in for themselves:

> Rather than seeing an *oriki* text as a 'whole', divisible into a number of discrete 'parts', it might be more productive to see the performance

as a process of juxtaposing elements from a repertoire of utterances which *float*: that is, elements which make sense when taken on their own but which can be brought into conjunction with other elements in variable combinations and variable contexts, acquiring new meanings in the process.

(Barber, 1991: 264)

Oriki may provide an extreme instance of this sort of authorial freedom, but much the same may be said of the Yoruba *ijala* or hunters' songs earlier analysed by Adeboye Babalola (1966), or indeed of the songs newly recorded by his much younger namesake, the jazz percussionist Lekan Babalola. That panegyric in Southern Africa too possesses something of the same one-off, eclectic quality can easily be established from listening to the froth and spume of *izibongo* – chiefly salutes – collected by Mazisi or Daniel Kunene in the 1970s. That improvisation on this level continues as a continent-wide tendency can further be substantiated from the highly improvisational and politicised lyrics in Swahili collected along the East African coast by Kelly Askew (2002).

As a consequence, the idea that Africa remains *par excellence* the continent of orality enjoys both a long provenance and widespread currency. I have proposed it myself (Fraser, 1986), and it lies behind a number of critical readings of published texts in all of the genres whose presence is attested north and south of the Sahara: poetry/song, drama and prose, to list them in the order of their frequency. Yet the primacy of the oral word in African literature is an idea that has recently been subjected to thoughtful revision, by Stephanie Newell (2006) and Ruth Finnegan (2007) amongst others. The essential problems are these. The oral forms that have existed, and continue to exist, in Africa are simply too various in kind and function for us to be able to isolate a single, meaningful strand that can be designated *orature*. Besides, the present evidence for pre-print oral forms often exists in the form of recordings (most of which were made subsequent to the introduction of print, and many of which themselves have come to be printed) and of transcriptions, the most widely diffused of which have necessarily taken the form of printed matter. (Even the internet in this respect has functioned as an electronic print medium.) The eclecticism of African oral performance, moreover, often takes in much that is derived from scripted or printed sources, thus complicating the picture even further. Popular theatrical forms, the Yoruba opera or Ghanaian concert party of West Africa to take but two examples, have for long drawn on pre-existing published material. Here is Efua Sutherland, the *doyenne* of Ghanaian theatre in the 1960s, quoting Bob Johnson, 'ace comedian' of the colonial Gold Coast, in her book on that musical artiste, whose career began at the Optimism Club in Takoradi in the mid-1930s, benefiting from the outset from a well-known commercial compilation of music and texts published in London in 1934:

> 'Our teachers used to say "Empire day is coming. Let's learn songs." And we used to learn songs from a book called *Lawrence Wright's Album.*' One of these songs stuck with him and became an important influence on the beginnings of his theatre. It was called Mini the Moocher, and part of it goes:

> But Mini the Moocher
> She was a low-down Hoocher Coocher.
> She was the roughest, toughest frail
> > But Mini had a heart
> > As big as a whale.

> (Sutherland, n.d.: 6)

Wright's 'monster' album contained piano solos by Duke Ellington among others and a selection of Al Jolson songs, on many of which Gold Coast Johnson leaned. But his mimicry was broadly assimilative. In 1936, in anticipation of the crowning of Edward VIII in far-away Westminster Abbey, his company performed *The Coronation*, a full-dress imperial mock-up 'complete with an Archbishop, an Admiral, an Altar Boy, and of course, the King'. Naturally the props included a Prayer Book with which 'before the crowning ceremony the Archbishop conducted a full Communion Service for the King' (ibid.: 20).

It is, of course, weakly feasible to draw a line between the so-called 'traditional environment' in which most borrowings are aural, and a 'city environment' in which some of them have come from books, the radio or television. However, the time is long past, if it ever existed, when such a dichotomy is robustly realistic. Whenever and wherever we study oral forms in Africa we are in truth observing phenomena in living shapes influenced, to a greater or lesser extent, and in subtle or not-so-subtle ways, by print culture. From the early twentieth century onwards it is especially difficult to separate out alternative strands of transmission, since print and non-print media have long existed side by side, interpenetrating one another in vigorous and rewarding ways. Repertoires remain repertoires; they none the less draw on texts, sometimes in fragmentary form. As we have already observed above with Igbo, and in Chapter 1 with Setswana, it is as a result extremely doubtful whether any such a thing as a purely oral register can now be isolated for study. Languages change as they are written down, and so in turn do artistic forms. The effect of pre-existing orature on early African literature has been extensively addressed, pre-eminently by Fritschi (1983), Obiechina (1975) and Okpewho (1990). In what follows I shall instead be examining a number of early literary examples from Southern and West Africa in the hope of demonstrating something more complicated and interesting: a mutual inter-dependence between oral and printed norms in which it is often difficult to perceive where one ends and the other begins, or where authenticity – that vexed ideal of the critics – ultimately lies.

The Mfecane of print

The resulting nexus can take many forms, one of which is the conversion of a flourishing repertoire into a printed text under particular, localised condi-tions. It is a process best observed in a milieu where the records of the early presses are fairly full, as they are in the Eastern Cape of South Africa. The fuller the records, however, the more complex the relevant transformations of medium sometimes turn out to have been.

I mentioned in Chapter 1 the critical attitude of the novelist, journalist and pioneering nationalist Sol Plaatje to the cloth-eared attempts of mission-aries of an earlier generation to convert his mother tongue, Setswana, into a print language. Plaatje's own contributions to communication as news-paper editor, as propagandist, translator or as linguist are well attested. It is thus with some interest that we turn to the print history of his only work of published fiction, *Mhudi*, sometimes cited as the first novel – as opposed to set of memoirs – in any language written by a black African and published by an Africa-based press. (Its only rival, *Ethiopia Unbound* by Joseph Casely-Hayford of the Gold Coast, had been issued in 1911 in London.) *Mhudi* was first issued in 1930 by the Lovedale Press, set up in 1823 at Gwali in the Tyume Valley by John Ross of the Glasgow Missionary Society, who had used a small Ruthven hand press and types and paper, acquired, like Moffat's, in Cape Town. Destroyed in a frontier war of 1834–5, it was replaced by a second machine in 1839, on which, with the assistance of Dukwana the son of Ntsikana, several issues of a bilingual Xhosa–English newspaper, *The Morning Star*, had been run off before this piece of equipment was destroyed in its turn in the so-called War of the Axe, the type being melted down to provide bullets for the British militia. It was on a third machine at Lovedale that Tiyo Soga's important Xhosa translation of *Pilgrim's Progress* was printed by a team of local apprentices and journeymen in 1861.

By Plaatje's time the press had been reorganised, and surveillance tight-ened over its affairs by a committee of missionaries and local consultants. From 1927 its director was Robert Shepherd, an individual with firm views both on local culture – a question on which he had been influenced by Booker T. Washington-inspired communities in the United States – and on the Xhosa language, over publications in which he exercised an iron

control without being able either to read or to write it with much competence. Linguistic standardisation in the early 1930s was as much a fad in
Southern Africa as in Isaac Okonkwo's Nigeria. Following Westermann
and his International Institute of African Languages, Shepherd chaired a
committee overseeing the overhauling of Xhosa in line with a new standardised orthography, involving the introduction of three new letters and of
double vowels and diacritical marks. 'The awesome effect ...', concludes
the historian Jeffrey Peires in his summary of these changes, 'was to turn
every literate African into a functioning illiterate' (1975: 161). Plaatje, who
watched in alarm as his mother-tongue Setswana was similarly affected,
wrote despairingly to the editor of *The South African Outlook* in August 1931
– the year following the publication of *Mhudi* – 'the muddle brooks of only
one solution, i.e. not to write in Sechuana at all'. *Mhudi*, needless to say, was
written in English.

Soon the Lovedale Press was insisting that all vernacular manuscripts
submitted to it should subscribe to these new, Westermann-influenced,
guidelines. Tiyo Soga's son, John Henderson – who, ironically, had served
on Shepherd's committee – was among the first to experience the inconvenience of these provisions. He submitted his history of the Ngugi and Lala
peoples to Lovedale in 1926, only to be told that the entire manuscript had
to be revised in line with the new script. Henderson agreed, but he proved
unequal to the effort; as a result his valuable book has never been published
(Pieres, 1975: 163–4). Successive runs of correspondence in the Cory Library
at Rhodes University (Cory Ms 16 423) demonstrate how waves of would-be
authors used to send in their work to Shepherd, who would then submit it
to the linguistic scrutiny of his fellow committee-member D. D. T. Javabu
at Fort Hare College. If it did not meet the new standards of lexical and
orthographic purity, the proposed work was either rejected or returned for
wholesale recasting. Unsurprisingly, many authors, faced with this extra and
unwelcome hurdle, preferred not to publish at all.

It was in this atmosphere of editorial constraint that Plaatje sent his English-
language novel *Mhudi* to Lovedale, after several unsuccessful attempts to
interest commercial publishers. The typescript can be viewed at the Cory
Library (Cory Ms 16 323) and confirms suspicions first raised in 1978 by
Stephen Gray and Tim Couzens while editing the book for the African
Writers series. In his Preface to the first edition Plaatje thanks Shepherd
for helping him with the proofs, but comparison of the printed text of 1930
against the typescript illustrates something far more extensive: a mixture
of interference, collusion and resistance as Plaatje struggles to reconcile his
deep sense of local, orally-transmitted, history and life with, on the one hand
literary models inherited from the West and, on the other, the expectations
of a local print culture governed by narrow missionary dictates.

From biographical and other clues it seems likely the work was first written around 1917 when Plaatje was much involved in the campaign to oppose the segregationalist land policies of the recently established Union of South Africa. As a consequence Plaatje was much concerned to project a local literary personality. He was also, however, conscious that the African folk tradition had already been absorbed, and to some extent appropriated, by British writers in the romance mode, especially by Rider Haggard, whose swashbuckling tales of South African life were cutting a swath in the imperial metropolis and, to some extent, in Africa, too. With this end in view, Plaatje had couched his story in the form of an oral narrative expounded by one 'Half-a-Crown' – who is possibly the son of Mhudi, the capable protagonist herself, and her husband, Ra-Taga. Both are militantly engaged in the struggle for survival mounted by their own people, the Rolong clan of the Tswana, against encroachments by Ndebele armies, who themselves have been uprooted by the Mfecane, the recent burgeoning of Zulu power to the southeast. All of this was well in line with orally transmitted history; as Laura Chrisman has proved, it was also quite close to material covered by Haggard in his romances of Zulu life, principally *Nada the Lily* (1892), whose example Plaatje was resolved both to echo and to answer. In intention, then, *Mhudi* seems to have been conceived as an early example of 'writing back'.

But on the typescript there also appear a series of manual deletions in Plaatje's own hand, eliminating the narrator Half-a-Crown altogether and converting the text into a narrative told by an impersonal third-person narrator. The Christians of Lovedale, it seems, were just as much concerned with literary as with linguistic standardisation. The likelihood is that they required a novelistic chronicle with less subjective, rawly political power than Plaatje's original version had supplied. In his eagerness to see his work between hard covers, this is what Plaatje at length agreed to. It was this self-censored text that was set up in hand press in 1931. Copies were run off, and the beds of type laid aside on racks for future use.

But this is not the end of the matter, and the subsequent history of the book illustrates that conjunction between history, ideology, editorial input and evolving technology on which Third World writing has so often depended. The sales were a modest success, and in 1957 a paperback edition was called for. The 26-year-old 'formes' or beds of type were promptly brought out of store. In the intervening period some of the type had worked itself loose in the wooden 'furniture' or frames. The typescript had also gone missing. The compositors restored the missing words by guesswork, giving rise to an occasional – and ideologically influenced – idiosyncrasy in the paperback text.

For twenty years this remained the standard trade version of *Mhudi*. In May 1976, however, the Soweto Rising occurred in protest against the imposition of Afrikaans as a teaching medium in black schools. Whereupon the jittery authorities in Lovedale moved their archives, and the mislaid typescript of *Mhudi* came to light. The scholar Tim Couzens had been working for some time on an edition for the American market. He scrutinised the rediscovered typescript, and was alerted to the discrepancies with Lovedale's official text. That year Heinemann Educational Books in London were preparing an edition of the novel for their African Writers series. Rather than reproduce Lovedale's existing version, they decided to have the whole book reset in Gandhidham in India, using the up-and-coming process of filmsetting. This enabled Couzens and his co-editor Stephen Gray to restore the wording of Plaatje's typescript, with the exception of a handful of explanatory glosses. Back came the oral narrator, along with several ethnographic nuances the missionary text had distorted in an attempt to bring the story into line with received preconceptions of 'native' life. What print culture had once eliminated, print culture could now restore.

It would, nevertheless, be naïve in the extreme to claim that the resulting, and now widely accepted, version of *Mhudi* is any less ideologically driven – any less the product of a prevailing *Zeitgeist* – than the bowdlerisations it replaced. Gray and Couzens's account of their interventions is orchestrated by a liberal-anarchic serendipitous destiny miraculously timed to coincide with the iconic disturbances of 1976. In that year, they were to claim in 1978, 'it *so happened* that the typescript of *Mhudi* was discovered'; 'Simultaneously, *as it happens*, Heinemann ... decided to reset their edition' (Couzens and Gray, 1978: 201, my italics). This train of events, and the way that they were perceived, have paved the way for post-Soweto readings of the novel, notably Laura Chrisman's (2000) and Elleke Boehmer's (2002), in both of which Plaatje features as a proleptic Panafricanist, feminist and enthusiast for the Rainbow Nation. Chrisman, indeed, writes as if the rediscovered typescript and the photo-typeset edition of 1978 were *the very same thing*. They were not, since the second represented an act of deliberate restoration along lines heavily influenced by the collectivist politics of the time.

Mhudi as we have it is thus as layered as any other piece of African literature, representing the imposition of a latter-day liberal authenticating impulse on a body of words earlier warped by draconian, print-driven imperatives over an authorial typescript, itself a blend of a deliberate 'writing back' to colonial models and a conscientious drawing on – and in a double sense a translation of – age-old oral repertoires. One is reminded of some of the editorial shenanigans described in our last, Asian chapter. Ultimately *Mhudi* represents a complex communicative process masquerading as a cultural fact. In other words, it represents what we have come to understand by a 'text'.

Blinkards and drinkards

The publication of *Mhudi*, along with the Moffat 'moment', represents another of those points of apparent inception in global communication that turn out on closer inspection to be a mirage. In Africa as a whole several factors conspired to transform a traditional scene energised by active repertoires into a library of fixed and edited texts. Literature in Africa – whether spoken or written – has, as we saw in Chapter 2, been a feature of the scene for centuries. Despite this, and in marked contrast with South Asia, literacy as such was for much of this period a fairly patchy affair. To take West Africa as an example, already in 1842 the Yoruba-born Ajayi (Samuel) Crowther, later Bishop to the Niger and currently *en route* for that very river, was loading on board his sea-going craft a printing press at Cape Coast Castle in what is now Central Ghana. Printing, it seems, was a well-established business in the Castle, which, remarks William St Clair (2006: 65), 'was better supplied with books than many a gentleman's country house in England and Scotland', and where there was a flourishing literary society, known as 'the Torridzonians'. Only four years earlier, on 15 October 1838, the romantic poet Letitia Landon, wife of the Castle's governor, George Maclean, had expired there after ingesting prussic acid: she lies buried in the forecourt. Crowther and his colleague James Schön were soon benefiting from the services of a locally trained journeyman printer. As they wrote in their log-book:

> The Governor has a small printing press in the castle, and a printer employed continually. One of the printer's former apprentices is now employed in the expedition, without whose aid no use could be made of the printing press on board. The Governor kindly allowed me to print an Address to the Chiefs and People, which I translated into the Hausa language.
>
> (Schön and Crowther, 1842: 21)

It is an intriguing question whether this Hausa address was couched in *ajami* Arabic script, which the local chiefs could have read easily. Be that as it may, Crowther and Schön had soon introduced print culture to the coastal towns of Bonny and Port Harcourt in what is now eastern Nigeria. Little wonder that, in the early twentieth century, Port Harcourt would become such a breeding ground of books. By contrast print, even writing, did not arrive in the interior of Igboland – just a few hundred miles inland – until very late in the nineteenth century, the period evoked by Achebe in *Things Fall Apart*. Again, large parts of inner Sierra Leone were non-literate until the eve of the Second World War, though an active press culture – even routes of transcolonial book distribution – had been centred in the coastal capital of Freetown at least since 1827, the year in which Fourah Bay College – the first institute of higher education between Timbuktu and the Cape – was set up. Crowther had been its very first student.

The complexity of the resulting cultural map means that practically all the grand foundation myths espoused by agencies, literary historians and other interested parties – the 'first series', the 'first press', the 'first novel' – are misplaced. 'African literature' has been going for a great deal longer than most experts have believed, and it has taken a multitude of shapes. There are, however, common factors. In all cases a vigorous vernacular orature enshrined in a local language with its regional dialects has encountered rupture or an opportunity – depending on your point of view. The causality of such events was never consistent. Sometimes innovations in communication simply spilled over from a contiguous community; sometimes they were deliberately introduced as a matter of policy by governments, or by philanthropic individuals working under the auspices of a missionary society or an educational trust. The penetration thus achieved was often gradual, depending on such factors as the amenability of spoken languages to transliteration, existing social structures and the mobility of individuals (trade patterns were evidently instrumental). The 'literature bureaux' established in Africa East and West in the late colonial period turn out to have been one of the major catalysts, both of literacy and of literature, unsurprisingly regarded as linked processes. All the signs are, however, that acute moments of cultural trauma like that evoked by Achebe at the end of his famous first novel were actually quite rare.

What is absolutely clear, *pace* the self-congratulatory claims of certain international publishers, is that African literature and its dissemination began, and was initially fostered, on the spot. It was never 'introduced', or principally nurtured, from outside, though in the later twentieth century overseas agencies undeniably broadened its appeal, transported it across borders and enhanced awareness of it in Europe, America and elsewhere. Well before that had happened, however, a decisive impulse towards literary production had come from two internal sources: rising affluence caused by increasing involvement in an urban cash nexus and the perceived need to arm populations with relevant intellectual skills as part of a gradual preparation for self-government. I shall deal with these in turn.

The effects of rising affluence can be observed most clearly in West Africa. The great economic success story of the first half of the twentieth century was the Gold Coast (now Ghana), where cocoa planting combined with forestry and gold and manganese mining produced a commercial surplus rapidly invested in physical and cultural infrastructures. The economic indicators are decisive and can fairly easily be correlated with

Table 4.1   Average annual trade in the Gold Coast, 1899–1926.

Years	Imports	Exports	Total
1899/1905	£1,505,428	£787,143	£2,292,571
1906/1912	£2,346,286	£1,683,857	£4,030,143
1913/1919	£4,127,857	£4,353,286	£8,481,143
1920/1926	£8,545,286	£8,694,857	£17,240,143

Source: Report of the Governor, Brigadier-General Sir Frederick Gordon Guggisberg to the Honourable Members of the Legislative Council, Gold Coast Colony, Legislative Council Debates Session 1927–8, 3rd March, 1927 (Accra: Government Printer, 1928), 29.

the growth in book culture. A glance at patterns of import and export for the period will set the background (Table 4.1), all the more impressive since the census of 1911 had calculated the population of this perky colony at only 1,503,386.

The figures are even more impressive when broken down by tonnage. Manganese exports, for example went up ninefold within a decade: from 4,016 tons in 1916 to 344,933 tons in 1926. Cocoa was the commercial mainstay. Exports in this one commodity leapt from 10,000 tons in 1907 to 92,000 tons in 1917; in 1926 they stood at 231,000 tons (*Report of the Governor … 1927–8*: 30). By the 1940s the Gold Coast, then producing two-fifths of the world's crop, was in a position to loan the British government a substantial sum towards fighting the Second World War.

The effects of this rising wealth were plain for all to see: a deepwater harbour at Sekondi-Takoradi; a railway network connecting the timber-rich forest with the coast; prestigious secondary schools at Achimota College in Accra and Mfantsipim in Cape Coast. Educational investment shot up. In 1919 the schools budget was £54,442, by 1925 it was £116,140, and by 1932 £266,000 (*Government of the Gold Coast*, 1919–57: 1932, 48). The effects on general print culture proved decisive. Wherever you look, local publishing, distribution, newspapers or bookshops, the Gold Coast of the early twentieth century provided a lively and expanding scene. Already by 1911 it had produced its first novel, *Ethiopia Unbound* by Joseph Casely-Hayford, reviewed in the November 1912 issue of the local *African Times and Oriental Review* (pp. 7–8) as 'this somewhat speechifying book'. By 1915 the social repercussion of these developments was vigorous enough to lay itself open to parody in *The Blinkards*, a bilingual Shavian comedy by the Fante lawyer and man-of-letters Kobina Sekyi (1892–1956). Here in Act Two is the 'young blood' Mr Okadu attending a garden party in Victoria Park, close by Cape Coast Castle:

A product of the Low School, embroidered by the High,
Upbrought and trained in similar products here am I.
I speak English to soften my harsher native tongue:
It matters not if often I speak Fanti wrong.
I'm learning to be British, and treat with due contempt
The worship of the fetish, from which I am exempt.
(Sekyi, 1974: 46–7)

That the root cause of all of this affectation is bibliophilia is established in the very first scene, delivered in Fante, in which the evolué hostess Mrs Brofusem berates her maid for disturbing some dried petals carefully inserted between the pages of one of her favourite books: 'Minke inkyire w'de, Aburekyir nuhu wodzi ahaban hyihye *mbuukuw* m'ma woakyinkyin na wowie kyinkyin a, wodzi *mbuukuw* n'atutu mbre wogyi hon mfefuw enyiwa bi a?' ['Haven't I told you that, in England, leaves are placed in the *books* to dry, the *books* when the leaves are dry being placed in drawing rooms?'] (Sekyi, 1974: 18–19, my italics). The satirical point here, needless to say, is not that the maid needs instructing in the refinements of European book culture, but that Mr Brofusem treats her library as a status object rather than as the rich cultural resource it deserves to be.

The incremental diffusion of print is further suggested by the rise of book-shops in the following decade. In 1923, for example, the Methodist Book Depot, one of the colony's leading outlets, possessed just one shop. Five more were quickly added: at Kumasi (1925); Sekondi (1926); Accra (1931); Swedru (1933) and the gold-mining town of Tarkwa (1937). Their turnover rose from £2,200 in 1924 to £21,816 in 1935 (Bartels, 1965: 197), a nine-fold increase that reflects the rising income from, say, manganese. A more obvious symptom was a burgeoning of newspapers, both local and national, serving as a mouthpiece for an alert and politically conscious intelligentsia. Already by 1912 the *Western Echo* was carrying a column called 'The Owl' in which Casely-Hayford scrutinised every move of the colonial bureaucracy. Sekyi himself was a frequent contributor to – and reviewer for – the *Gold Coast Times,* a later publication that gives the flavour of journalism in the late 1920s and early 1930s. Published in Beulah Lane, Cape Coast, it was distrib-uted through twenty-one outlets in the south of the colony, and catered for the business community and the professional class. Here, between court proceedings and notifications of the sailings, inbound and outbound, of the Elder Dempster Shipping Line – lifeblood of the colonial economy – were book advertisements, reviews, poems. 'The Event of the Year' for 1926, for example, was the appearance of *The History of the Akan Peoples of the Gold Coast* by W. T. Balmer, the promotional puff for which indicates very clearly the sort of readership the *Times* was aiming to reach:

DID *YOU* KNOW?

The origin of your race?

The derivation of the word 'Guinea'?

Why the Fante confederation was formed?

What effects the Danish occupation had on the life and customs of the Akan peoples?

If Mohammadanism [*sic*] had a good or bad effect on the Gold Coast peoples?

(*The Gold Coast Times*, vol. iv, no. 153, 2 January 1926)

These were just the sorts of question that concerned the local literary and debating societies, the proceedings and programmes of which were also covered by such newspapers. On 15 February 1929, for example, the Cape Coast Literary and Social Club was considering the merits and demerits of the matrilinear system of inheritance, and the following month they received a lecture on 'The Road to Freedom', both faithfully noted by *The Times*. Two sorts of meeting stand out: one was 'Table Talk', a debate or open forum on issues of the day, another 'mock divisional courts' in which these future lawyers and politicians practised their calling in advance. That they situated themselves in a broader colonial context is suggested by the frequency of features in these broadsheets covering developments elsewhere in the empire or the wider world: an interview with the black American poet Countee Cullen, an article by Rabindranath Tagore in *The Times* for 21 June 1930 on 'The Indian Situation'.

In her book *How to Win the Game of Life*, Stephanie Newell has charted the characteristics of this vigorous salon culture: the well-stocked library of Dr Aggrey, assistant headmaster of Achimota, the literary and debating societies, the magazines, the book imports, the beginnings of a 'popular' literature. The scale seems small by international standards, yet the activity covered much of the country, and was not confined to expression in English. By the 1930s the Achimota College Press in Accra was turning out books in English, Twi, Ga, Fante and Ewe; the Government Press in the capital Accra offered the same linguistic range, as did various branches of the Methodist Mission Press. The Presbyterian Press meanwhile was producing texts in Ga and Twi, and their Keta branch catered for Ewe. Though a regional library network was not to grow up until after 1945, and bookshops were largely confined to the cities, the number of voluntary associations involved in the dissemination of this literature is impressive, especially as many of the organisations, like the Ewe Literature Improvement Association in Keta in the east or the Nzema Literary Association in Sekondi towards the west, flourished in places quite distant from the metropolitan hub.

What in the meantime was happening to the oral repertoires? They flourished side by side with early print culture, even as the literati of the towns seemed sometimes to turn a deaf ear to them. The coming together of the two streams is perhaps easiest to illustrate in Nigeria, where in 1948 Chief Daniel Fagunwa (1903–63), Yoruba master at a Lagos secondary school, submitted a story entitled *Ogboju Ode ninu igbo Irunmale* to a competition run by the Ministry of Education. Published with another of Fagunwa's tales, *Igbo Olodumare* (Forest of God), in a reader by Thomas Nelson and Sons the following year, it would later be translated into English by Wole Soyinka under the title *The Forest of a Thousand Demons*. Fagunwa's five novels set a trend for published fiction in Yoruba; they also served as a catalyst for Amos Tutuola (1920–97), an elementary-school-educated motor mechanic, who, influenced by both Fagunwa and Bunyan, was to produce a stream of picaresque tales couched in West African English, beginning in 1952 with *The Palm Wine Drinkard*, often mislabelled the first African novel. It was not that, but the result of a confluence between, on the one hand, living oral repertoires and, on the other, international models and idioms, which anticipated much that was to come.

Sign and sound in Sierra Leone

The other internal source for book culture in black Africa was related to the first. The economic forces unleashed across the continent were clearly not going to give rise to vibrant and autonomous political systems unless the mass of the people were involved, able to read and thus to discriminate and vote, and armed with a body of relevant literature to feed their curiosity. Thus it came about in the mid-twentieth century that an array of literacy campaigns went to work in consort with publishing outlets and planned deliberately to stimulate contemporary writing in languages both indigenous and Europhone. The result was sometimes to give rise to a new body of writing and sometimes to stifle a nascent one, as we can clearly see in the case of rural Sierra Leone.

Languages, needless to say, are a product of history, and Sierra Leone has a particularly complex one. The country owes its corporate identity, and the capital Freetown its name, to the fact that the coastal strip was settled in the early nineteenth century by emancipated slaves 'repatriated' from America. The scheme was partly overseen by Olaudah Equiano (*c.*1745–97), born in the east of what is now Nigeria, himself an emancipated slave and anti-slavery campaigner; in his *Interesting Narrative* (1789), published in London in the year of the French Revolution, he narrates his exploits and gives some impression of the new polyglot communities set up along this stretch of the coast. The slaves originated from all parts of West Africa: the requirements of mutual communication thus necessitated the inception of Krio as an English-based lingua franca, no sooner spoken than printed and along with it a busy local press and, from 1827, a university college.

Outside the capital the language map was diverse. Of the major linguistic groups in the north of the country, Limba and Temne had both acquired Roman-derived scripts in the nineteenth century, and with them the beginnings of a printed literature. In both cases, however, the process involved privileging certain dialects over others, resulting in tensions that have been felt up to the present day. Further south, towards the border with Liberia (itself the site of an emancipation settlement), the picture was embarrassed by ethnic differences and by patterns of work and migration. Several dialects remained unwritten and unprinted for decades. An important exception was Vai, spoken predominantly in Liberia but also by several thousand people in southern Sierra Leone. As we have already seen in Chapter 2, Vai (originally spelled Vy) evolved – quite separately from any developments elsewhere, and without external intervention of any kind – its own syllabic writing system in the 1830s.

The adjacent Mende-speaking areas provide us with an interesting countervailing example. Numbering less than a million (now 1.6 million), the population were rice-, yam- and cassava-farmers whose ancestors migrated from the Sudan by 1500 CE and spoke a language generically related to Bambara, one of the principal tongues of Mali. Several alternative scripts had been proposed for their language, including one Arabic-based system. In 1921, furthermore, Kisimi Kasara (c.1890–1962), seemingly motivated by the same vision of a dialectical relationship between writing and power as had earlier inspired the impresario of the Vai script Duale Bukare, devised for Mende a syllabary of 195 symbols. Possibly this was influenced by a secret – and now lost – script then cultivated in Mauritania for relaying messages in Arabic: its letter forms were however, quite distinct from both Arabic and Vai, though like the former it was scanned from right to left, and like the latter it was purely phonetic, with an individual character for each sound in the language. Kamara called his writing system *ki-ka-ku* after the first three characters conveying syllables beginning with a hard 'c'; throughout the 1920s and 1930s he busily disseminated it at a school he maintained in Potoru. Figure 4.1 shows it in the form published by David Dalby in 1967.

If this system was intended as a challenge to government-sponsored modes of writing and communication, the authorities soon fought back. By 1943 the mission-administered International Committee for Christian Literature, based in London but with affiliates on the spot, was reporting that literacy among the Mende-speaking people – by which they meant literacy in any phonetically modified system – was running at around 4 per cent; the Mende, for example, would not possess a complete Bible translation in Roman script (or indeed in any script) until 1959. In official quarters there was some anxiety that the resulting situation left these regions exposed and

	i	a	u	e	ɛ	ɔ	o
p							
w							
mb							
b							
kp							
gb							
f							
v							
t							
l							
nd							
d							
s							
j							
nj							
y							
ŋg							
g							
k							
h							
-							

Nasal syllables

	ĩ	ã	ũ	ẽ	ɛ̃	ɔ̃
h						
m						
n						
ny						
ŋ						
-						

other combinations

wɛi	gɛi	ɛi	ŋgua	gua	kua	ñua
mua	ŋua	fã	lɛɛ	hel	hou	mũc

Figure 4.1   Kisimi Kasara's Mende script. Consonants in rows; vowels and dipthongs in columns. Reproduced by kind permission of Jason Glavy.

Source: Dalby (1967). Print font and graphics by Jason Glavy, 2006.

vulnerable in the planned drive towards independence and citizenship. It was in these circumstances that in August 1943 an 'experiment' was devised to introduce Roman-based literacy at an accelerated and concentrated rate: to raise it in fact from 4 per cent towards 25 per cent within six months (SOAS, CBMS/ICCLA Box 23, 526: 'Report on the Experimental Literacy Campaign at Bunumbu, Sierra Leone, 1943'). The location of this exercise was the town of Bunumbu; the ingredients of the programme a small team of local teachers, a lorry with some basic field equipment for demonstrations, a cinema van for advertising purposes and, vitally, a printing press at the local mission headquarters capable of turning out readers, textbooks and exercise books several hundred at a time. For if rising rates of literacy were conceived of as being the ultimate end of the Bunumbu experiment, the production of a literature was thought of as a means integral to the process. As the organisers explained:

> It is useless to teach people to read unless they can be provided with a certain amount of literature. There should be literature suitable for each stage as they make progress in reading ability, for unless interest is maintained, and they are able to obtain reading material as they go along, they would soon relapse into illiteracy.
>
> (Young, 1946: 1)

The Mende literacy campaign of the 1940s thus became a Mende publishing campaign, the fortunes of which enable us to examine the birth of a local printed literature (with its roots in a well-established local *orature*) in close miniature. The pedagogical methods involved also have much to tell us about what can happen when a tongue spoken for hundreds of years (and, in the case of Mende with its Sudanese antecedents, for well over a millennium) comes face to face with an educational establishment and a print culture resolved on quick results. The teaching approach adopted, the so-called Key-Word Method, had been honed in India in the 1930s. Its object was to render peoples literate in their mother-language as quickly as possible, and it consisted of breaking up sentences into units – syllables first, and then whole words – which were transliterated into a very slightly modified Roman script, assimilated, then scanned by groups of learners visually from blackboard, flashcard or page, without recourse to the aural memory. The inventor of the method, the one-time missionary Frank Laubach, later to expand his ideas into a programme for global intellectual, political and moral re-armament in idealistic tracts such as *Teaching the World to Read* (1948), was convinced that orality lay at the root of traditional linguistic and textual transmission. Orality, however, was an aural mode and, he believed, deleterious to the assimilation of visually based reading methods. For a proper literary mode to take off, such habits would need to be broken. As the project leader of the 1943 campaign himself dogmatically asserted:

> Reading is not memory-work but eye-work. The learner must concentrate not on sound memory, but on visual memory. It is most important to remember that most Africans will quickly learn a lesson by heart, so that they can repeat it verbatim, but this is not reading.
>
> (Young, 1946: 30)

With hindsight we can now see that what these official activists and reformers were trying in effect was to distil – by shortcutting – a Saussurian semantic logic. In Saussurian linguistics (as inherited for example by such theorists of literary transmission as the Algerian-born Jacques Derrida) signified meaning communicates itself via signs. 'There is', quoth Derrida (1976: 14), 'no linguistic sign prior to writing'. In Africa – so these pioneers believed – no signs of this sort had existed, and all communication had been wedded to sound. Locally engendered syllabaries, such as the Vai and Mende systems, had specifically catered for this predisposition. They provided, as no later system quite would, for what T. S. Eliot called the auditory imagination and Ong was to term the interiority of sound. The plan now was to foreshorten such an equation by substituting eye-recognition for ear-recognition, proceeding directly from signified to sign, with the minimum interruption from the ear.

As the organisers duly reported back to base, the policy worked, though in a way heavily influenced by local conditions. The most efficient teachers turned out to be the children, who, on their release from school in the afternoon, were co-opted to instruct the adults in the evening, by the light of a flickering hurricane lamp. The unsatisfactory luminosity, however, affected the results, so that recitation frequently took over from perusal, and a reliance on aural memory returned unawares. The organisers had instructed the printers in the village to run off flashcards, and syllables were also painted on wooden blocks which could be lined up to form words. By this means 210 out of a total adult population of 390 were taught basic Roman literacy within six months. The press had also printed a primer in advance; it proved a success, and demand rapidly exceeded supply. Soon reprints were asked for, and the range of titles was expanded. It was important for all concerned that local authors should be involved at every level. What had started as a utilitarian literacy campaign thus rapidly turned into a project to initiate and sustain a new and relevant literature. Feelers were put out to established literates who might be interested in producing booklets on such subjects as 'Mende Proverbs', 'Mende Law', 'Our Home and Villages' or 'Swamp Rice Cultivation'. Within a couple of months the hard-worked press at Bunumbu was able to report that it had completed fifteen booklets in Mende on a variety of themes, had thirteen manuscripts ready for printing and a further eight in preparation. The only limiting factor was a temporary shortage of paper. Of the twenty-one books in the process of publication, five were on matters of health, two were collections of Mende stories, eight concerned public instruction on practical matters; only six had any overt Christian content. By April 1945 printing operations had moved to the larger town of Bo, turning out material for the whole of the Protectorate – that is the hinterland of Sierra Leone beyond the colony enclave of Freetown – mostly booklets on health and citizenship, the mainstays of a future democracy. 'There is', reported the director, R. R. Young, 'no reason why the majority of the people in this country should not be literate by 1955, and the Mende people could be literate by 1950' (Young, 1945: 1). Within a year, the press at Bo had been rechristened the Protectorate Literacy – later to become the Sierra Leone Literature Bureau – and was turning out self-help booklets in ever-increasing numbers.

Within a generation Kasara's syllabary had more or less died out. Why did it founder? That it enjoyed no colonial, or later government, backing or funds must have been a contributing factor. A strong ancillary cause, however, seems to be that its functional uses were confined to the private medium of correspondence and the utilitarian purpose of record-keeping. It was never viewed (as Vai seems to a certain extent to have been viewed) as a medium of mass communication, and few attempts were made to replicate texts written by means of it in multiple copies. The syllabary did not give rise to a marketed literature, nor did Kasara have access to a printing press. Without this sustaining lifeblood, and against a tide of concerted print-linked competition, *ki-ka-ku* soon wilted. The 'literacy campaigners' of the following decades were wrong about many matters. They misconstrued the languages that they taught, and they cruelly lopped them off from their roots in orality and tradition. But they discerned the vital bond between a reading culture and an energetically produced print literature, and for this reason alone the visually orientated pedagogical initiatives of the missions thrived, strangling in the process the aurally more astute approach characterised by local syllabaries.

'The Clean Book': repertoire as text

The evolution of a local literary scene from pedagogical activity to local literary production illustrated by the Bunumbu project goes some way to correct prevailing conceptions of the inception of African literature and its relationship to local print culture. Similar scenarios were to be duplicated many times over across sub-Saharan Africa. National literary bureaux, for example, became a proactive and influential feature of the post-war and post-independence scene. They caught on especially in East and Central Africa, where they played a major role in the nurturing of new literatures, both in the vernacular and in English, not simply serving new writing, but actively soliciting and shaping it.

Some indication of their role is afforded by, say, the East African Literature Bureau's publication in 1957 of *Helps and Explanations for African Authors: Some Forms of Writing*. This was a guide for aspiring writers that nudged them decisively in the direction of treating their prospective readers as citizens of a future democracy needing assistance with the niceties of voting, self-education and the like. It also, however, provided hints for imaginative writing, both in English and in African languages. Would-be authors were asked a series of questions: these and the suggested answers yield insights into perceptions that were to produce nascent schools of writing across several genres. 'What are you going to write about?' was the first query. (Answer: 'If you are going to write fiction you need to have imagination, and to be observant, so that your stories become interesting and your characters like human beings': Richards, 1957: 2.) 'For whom are you going to write?' was the next. (Answer: 'This is a matter in which African authors can take an important part in the development of literature, because they have the intimate knowledge of the life and thought of their own people which is needed. There is an African style of telling a story, or of conveying information, by using parables, giving instances, and quoting riddles or proverbs: try to use a style like this, which will be readily understood because it customary', Richards, 1957: 3–4.) 'Africa', the compilers of this suggestive guide went on, gesturing towards existing repertoires (Richards, 1957: 7), 'has an embryo literature in its own oral traditions. The earliest literature in England was the writing down of such traditional tales; in writing them down the African author may be helping to lay the foundations of African literature more surely than by any other form of writing, since they are, and will still be, of the people. In Africa the need for books on it is still very urgent, because so much of the lore of past ages is being forgotten.'

Already the bureau was able to point to a number African texts that had already set an example (Richards, 1957: 5), including Camara Laye's *L'Enfant noir*, a novel in French from Guinea that was yet to be translated into English, *Mine Boy* and also *Wild Conquest*, both by the South African Peter Abrahams, and *People of the City* by Cyprian Ekwensi from the Igbo-speaking eastern region of Nigeria. The first of these had been published in Paris, the rest in London and Edinburgh. Though such books may have raised expectations and ultimately persuaded East African authors to seek international exposure through publication abroad, all the signs are that the initial impetus towards creativity stemmed from local bodies such as the bureau itself. The first novel written by Kenya's Ngugi wa Thiong'o, for example, found international exposure when issued by Heinemann Educational Books under the title *The River Between* in 1962. Under its first and provisional title *The Black Messiah*, it had earlier been submitted for a competition organised by the bureau, winning the first prize of £50 (Sander and Lindfors, 2006: 2). With hindsight it is possible to see just how faithfully it, and so much of Ngugi's early fiction, followed the guidelines laid out in *Helps and Explanations*: it sketched local life, it drew on communal folklore, it portrayed the trials and tribulations of a generation struggling to come to terms with education, human rights and citizenship. In all of these respects it was characteristic of the first generation of African literary writing as a whole, much of which steered closely to the suggestions of the pan-continental bureaux with their focused, and politically liberal, notions of cultural development.

Among the notable products of the ethos cultivated by the bureaux was one of modern Africa's poetic classics and fount of the so-called East African Song School: *The Song of Lawino* by Okot p'Bitek. Okot (1931–82) was from the Acholi people of the Gulu region along the Uganda–Sudan border. Poet, novelist, anthologist, educator and a one-time professional footballer, his first published book had been the novel *Lak Tar Miyo Kinyero Wi Lobo* issued by the bureau in Acholi in 1953, four years before *Helps and Explanations* but much along the lines of the programme set out there. Twenty years later – and a full two decades before Zadie Smith's bestseller of the same title – it was reissued in English as *White Teeth*. Okot's best-known work also had roots in the mid-1950s. *Wer pa Lawino* was a lament in Acholi placed in the mouth of the discarded village wife of Ocol, a plutocratic politician-on-the-make. In 1955 its author was making his living as a teacher of general subjects at the Sir Samuel Baker School, founded two years earlier to cater for Gula's few secondary school students. One of them was Taban lo Liyong, subsequently to emerge as a writer both of poetry and of prose. He was later to describe Okot, then his biology teacher, reading the poem aloud in class. Clearly in every sense the poem was a gesture towards oral repertoires and intended for recitation. Already, however, and even in its 'oral' form, it demonstrated the effects of imported print literature, rhyming for the most part in a variant of *terza rima* derived from Longfellow's *The Song of Hiawatha*. Though written for the most part in standard Acholi, it was moreover linguistically and stylistically exceedingly hybrid, reflecting the mixed nature of Gulu's border culture and drawing on various dialects of Luo from adjoining Kenya. Parts of the text were in Lango, others in Alur, Jonam or Jo-Palwo (p'Bitek, 2001: xiv–xv). It also echoed the Acholi hymnbook and local translations of the Christian scriptures. It was in-jokey, bustling, at moments quite anarchic.

Ten years later, having failed to secure publication, Okot was working on a free-verse English translation of the poem, though perhaps the more apposite term would be 'transcreation' or 'version': the text known around the world as *The Song of Lawino*. By Okot's own admission he had in the process 'clipped a bit of the eagle's wings and rendered the sharp edges of the warrior's sword rusty and blunt' and had moreover 'murdered rhythm and rhyme' (p'Bitek, 1966: iv). The truth is that *The Song of Lawino* was a very different work, in feel and sound, from its African-language original. The rhymes had disappeared as had the *terza rima* stanza form, and its linguistic scope had dwindled. It was, as a result, markedly less cosmopolitan. *Wer pa Lawino* had been couched in a dozen or more registers mimicking, for example, demobbed servicemen's clumsy attempts to talk in Swahili; the *Song* was cast in a fairly uniform, if lively, English idiom. The Acholi poem had been jokey and had passed from idiolect to idiolect; the *Song* was blandly witty, commending it to an Anglophone, school-bred audience, and a sympathetic but occasionally patronising international readership. The result was a simulacrum necessarily in contradiction with itself. Lawino herself is non-literate: to represent her damning the urban classes in English was effective, but somehow limiting. This is nowhere clearer than when she denounces her partner for his partiality for reading, the Acholi Bible in particular:

> My husband
> Looks down on me;
> He says
> I am a mere pagan,
> I do not know
> The way of God.
> He says
> I am ignorant
> Of the good word
> In the Clean Book
> And I do not have
> A Christian name.
>   (p'Bitek, 1966: 111)

The joke here is levelled at Protestant missionaries to Acholiland in the 1930s. At a loss to describe the Holy Spirit, they had rendered Him as *Cwiny Malen*, 'the Clean Ghost'; the Holy Bible, in which He appears at Pentecost, became *Kitabo Malen* or 'the Clean Book'. To render this absurdity in English was not to destroy it, but the jibe now requires a gloss, where the original had gone straight home to the local audience for whom it was intended.

Okot found a publisher for his English-language text in the East African

Publishing House that had emerged from the bosom of the bureau. In 1966 it was issued as a 12 × 18.5 centimetre paperback as part of their Modern African Library series, and printed locally by the East African Institute Press in Sudhanha Lane in Nairobi, with humorous woodcuts by the South African artist Frank Horley. Okot followed the international success of his poem by turning out several English-language sequels. *Song of Ocol* represented the husband's rejoinder; *Song of Prisoner* was spoken by a political detainee, *Song of Malaya* by a Nairobi prostitute. Three years later the press at last issued the Acholi-language original, including its fourteenth chapter, omitted in the English version (Taban, 1993: 87–92). In due course there were to be imitations by others. On the poet's early death from a liver infection his daughter published her own *Song of Farewell*.

The internationalisation of Okot took its course, and Heinemann Educational Books in London bought up the rights to all of his *Songs*, which they issued in their high-profile African Writers series. As far as the world was concerned, the Englishing of the poems had now eclipsed the Acholi originals, which few people could remember. The exception was Okot's one-time student Taban, who in 2001 reminded his readers that the *Song* was in actual fact a shadow of an African-language masterpiece by publishing in Kampala his own alternative translation. *The Defence of Lawino* was not a substitute for the *Song*, but an attempt in the translator's words 'as faithfully as possible to reproduce Lawino's thoughts in as rhythmic an English as suits her mode of discourse' (p'Bitek, 2001: xvi). A product of the twentieth-century *fin-de-siècle*, the *Defence* was arguably a feminist vehicle, whereas neither the original *Wer pa Lawino*, nor the enthusiastically womanising Okot's own translation, had been quite that. In comparison with Okot's own English version it was more rhetorical, and gave even less leeway to the husband. It was, moreover, a refreshing sign, at the turn of the twenty-first century, that it was once again an African-based publisher that had issued it.

Part III

Powers

5 Resistance and adaptation

Rewriting the script

So far in this book we have been concerned with resetting some essential bearings, and charting the chosen terrain. For the remainder I will be speaking about the dynamics of book history in the regions under discussion, dynamics that are best interpreted as a set of clashes between competing forces, some of them plainly revolutionary, others constructively conservative. Book history, I believe, cannot and should not be construed as a process of inevitable, irreversible evolution, or even as the product of intelligently ordered design. It is a battlefield in which technologies slog it out and voices strain to be heard, and where economics and commerce vie or conspire with the needs of self-expression. The chosen model is thus an open-ended one in which there are continuities as much as there are ruptures. What happens is a balance of attrition. It is with this contest between stasis and change that I shall begin.

Some patterns of resistance

I briefly considered in Chapter 1 the anthropologist Jack Goody's term 'technologies of the intellect' as a way of describing various ways in which people in different environments choose to transmit verbal texts. Goody himself seems to have favoured a revised evolutionary approach: profoundly suspicious of models assuming cultural supremacy or a one-way procession towards a teleological goal, he retained none the less some sense of successive cognitive regimes leading one to another, the vital cross-over point in his scheme of things being the attainment of literacy. I want to replace this angle with a more flexible one in which orality, writing and print are viewed as genuine alternatives which none the less often co-exist: print on top of writing above a substratum of orality, but also in other combinations as well, such as orality on top of writing above a substratum of print. I will get to some of these less conventional combinations shortly, but want to begin by separating these elements out and examining the ways they occasionally clash. Conflict between them has indeed been a recurrent feature of the scene, observed most clearly when one regime threatens to supplant and wipe out another, with all of its strengths and weaknesses. We will only be able to make sense of this phenomenon if we recognise that orality, for example, possesses distinctive strengths that other systems can unthinkingly suppress.

When looking at phases of transition between alternative technologies, it is therefore important to avoid the mistake of regarding the process of change as either inevitable or smooth. As a matter of historical fact, new methods are often resisted, and not only for reasons of sentiment. An interesting case in point is the resistance of liturgically sophisticated communities in India to writing as a means of propagating the Vedic scriptures several centuries after they had become aware of its availability. Writing, we now know, was an established feature of the Indian scene from the third century BCE. Despite this, the great epic the *Ramayana*, for example, continued to be communicated orally for many centuries before it was written down, a fact suggested by its opening prelude, in which the poet Valmiki is described reciting the whole poem to two young acolytes with the intention that they should commit it to memory entire. A nostalgic, but none the less authentic, memory as to the epic's oral origins thus persisted in the teeth of other traditions suggested by an eighteenth-century manuscript from Udaipur (BL Add MS. 15295) in which the work's manner of eventual diffusion is depicted as manuscript transfer from hand to hand. In actual fact, as Pollock insists (2007: 79), there had occurred during the earlier period a number of 'conscious refusals of technology marking the history of literary and manuscript culture ... due to characteristic satisfaction with suitable sophisticated oral practices'. As we saw in Chapter 3, several relevant orally orientated practices survive in different rural and urban contexts to the present day.

Just as important was the wholesale and centuries-long resistance of Indian cultures to the technology of print, long after it had become established elsewhere in South and Southeast Asia. Again, the reason seems to have been a refined sense of what manuscript could achieve and print could not. Woodblock printing had been practised in Tibet since the eleventh century CE, as well as in China, with which there existed throughout this interregnum a busy textual trade (Sen, 2005: 161–90). Yet, with the possible exception of some closed Buddhist communities in Bengal, print was long shunned in the subcontinent. Its progress after the Jesuit experiments in Goa, Kerala and Sri Lanka was, moreover, slow. As a result, what we have already called the Halhed 'moment' looked then like a leap in the dark, despite such earlier experiments.

We need, however, to separate out resistance to writing from resistance to print, since they are far from the same phenomenon, or even similarly motivated. Beginning with the first – refusal of script by a culture habituated to word of mouth – it might be helpful to unravel for a moment Pollock's phrase concerning 'suitable oral practices'. What, we might well ask, in an intellectually refined society, constitutes suitability in the recital of the spoken and remembered word? I would propose three elements: a trinity of retention, reciprocity and intervention. An actress remembers her lines; she delivers them to an audience; and she reacts to their presence: usually by facial expression, sometimes by verbal deflection as well. A stand-up comic definitely does all three, and fairly constantly. The modern theatre is an oral form with a printed substrate, as we have already seen in the case of the bow-songs of Tamil Nadu. Stand-up comedy is more purely oral, though since many comics write out their jokes, it may be said to possess a written substrate, just as drama did over much of India prior to 1800, or Shake-spearean drama in England before the appearance of the early quartos. The oral model is a classical one. All religious celebrations too are acts of elaborate *orature*. They are this more than they are anything else, even if they may follow the rubric of a written or printed liturgy. All of this the world well knows; yet some book historians persist in referring to the 'print age', the 'age of orality' and so forth.

Resistance to writing is comparable to the regret we feel when silently reading a play. We have gained certain benefits – silence, concentration – but we have lost a live interaction: laughs, gasps, the odd comment off. Of course we can have both, but the resistance to writing is caused by a quite comprehensible concern that one may supersede the other. This is what, in p'Bitek's poem, the non-literate Lawino has to say about her bibliophile and graduate husband, Ocol:

> My husband
> Has read at Makerere University
> He has read deeply and widely,
> But if you ask him a question
> He says
> You are insulting him;
> He opens up with a quarrel
> He begins to look down on you
> Saying
> You ask questions
> That are a waste of time.
>   (p'Bitek, 1966: 140)

Reciprocity and intervention were clearly not encouraged by the new literates of late colonial Uganda. Contrast such boorish behaviour with the mutual give-and-take and the open textual structures evoked by Karin Barber (1991) when one of her female *oriki* singers delivers a panegyric to a gratified male recipient, or the equivalent reciprocity and textual openness that Pongweni (1997) observed in the 1970s during the performance of Chimurenga songs in War of Liberation Zimbabwe. In both instances, as Pangweni observes when alluding to Barber's work, the form achieved is the result of active collaboration between performer and audience:

> As Barber (1984) observes in relation to Yoruba *oriki*, folk poetry does not have the 'wholeness' that written poetry does with its parts strategically 'placed so as to give the poem its boundaries', so that it does not merely end but 'achieves closure with a feeling of inevitability and finality' because of all that had preceded the closure. 'Oriki' are in this sense akin to the 'Ndarinyo' on which Chimurenga songs are based: if at any performance of the song the audience can contribute their own lines, it follows that a change of audience will most likely lead to a change of combination and, therefore a change in 'text'. A change in the purpose of the performance will also trigger some changes not merely in the 'text', but also in the order in which the parts are marshalled.
>
> (Pangweni, 1997: 66)

Okpewho (1990) notes the same sort of flexibility in successive performances of the *Ozidi* saga amongst Ijo communities from midwest Nigeria as filmed and transcribed by the playwright John Pepper Clark (1977). The fluidity of performance, the elements of reciprocity and spontaneous invention, are obvious on film. Clark's previously published verse translation of the cycle (1966) inevitably forgoes it.

Loss and resistance are thus inevitable aspects of the transaction between performance and writing. They are correlative aspects, too, of the transition between writing and print. Print settles a text in a definitive or quasi-definitive form, all the more so when the print medium has been imported. The result is frequently a campaign of passive resistance, all the more deepseated when the appearance of writing and print coincide. In certain parts of Africa indeed, though far from universally over this vast continent, a coincidence has sometimes occurred between the appearance of print and the arrival of writing systems that were either imported, or else improvised on the spot in response to encroaching print norms. This is one explanation of the spontaneous invention, in Sierra Leone, Liberia and Cameroon, during the nineteenth and early twentieth centuries of indigenous scripts resistant to the invading Roman alphabet. A more emphatic, if less constructive, reaction has been the occasional Luddite destruction of presses: the Lovedale Press in South Africa, for example, fell victim to border skirmishing on a number of occasions (Shepherd, 1941: 400). Destroyed during the sixth Xhosa war of 1834–6, it was replaced in 1839, only to have its type melted down to make bullets during the War of the Axe (1846–7).

Yet the pre-existence of script, as in India, does not necessarily make print any the more welcome. The key variables here seem to be the kind of script previously espoused and the nature of the print font on offer. If print culture arrives in the guise of an alien writing system, both may be rejected at once. Such is the case in societies in which the inception of print has coincided with the arrival of one writing system seemingly bent on superseding another with a long tradition of written literature behind it. The resulting tensions have sometimes led to political consequences way beyond the strictly cultural sphere.

A well-documented case-history in point is that of the island of Madagascar in the early nineteenth century. Here there had flourished a long oral tradition, notably of recitations of the epic poem *Ibona*. Side by side with this were twelve centuries of experience in writing the Malayo-Polynesian Malagasy language in Arabic script, supporting in turn four centuries of written literature. In the 1820s all of this came up hard against a print dispensation bent on rendering all textual communication via the Roman alphabet. (This situation was to be echoed in Somalia, Zanzibar and other places on the East African coast. Madagascar, however is relatively isolated, and the realities were correspondingly more intense.) In 1820 the London Missionary Society sent out two volunteers, David Jones and David Griffiths who immediately set to work rendering the Malagasy language in a modified Roman orthography (omitting the letters C, Q and Z), into which one by one they translated the books of the Christian canon, assuming that they had fallen among 'a people without a written language' (Freeman and Johns, 1840: 74). Four years later, the society dispatched a printer and a press with 150 reams of paper. The printing works was evidently modelled on that of the contemporaneous Indian Baptist Mission at Serampore (Moss, 1875: 1–15), and consisted both of a letterpress for books and a still quite experimental lithographic press for maps and music, manned by a combination of local apprentices and 'mechanics' brought across from Mauritius. By 1830, under intense surveillance from the island's newly acceded and highly sceptical queen, these Christian Soldiers had run off a *Testimenta 'ny Jesosy Kraisty* (New Testament), followed by a Malagasy–English dictionary, portions of the Old Testament and, eventually, *The Pilgrim's Progress*. All were in Roman script, even though by recourse to the wider mission field the team might easily have acquired a perfectly serviceable Arabic typeface. Unsurprisingly they met with official resentment directed both against their religious teaching and the technology that apparently accompanied it. Was this feeling fired by resentment at an imported religion, an imported technology or an alien writing system? The letters of the Madagascar-based LMS missionary the Rev. James Cameron to his mother and sister survive in the School of Oriental and African Studies in London (SOAS GB 0102 Ms 380685); like so many of his persuasion and generation he seems to have been convinced that the resistance he felt around him was motivated by pagan obduracy, a view endorsed by the successive annual reports of the mission's directors in London (SOAS CWML H698). The evidence, though, suggests a clash of cultures and communicative systems.

Through a dramatic account of 1840 by Freeman and Johns we can follow the sequence of events that led to the suppression of the press, the temporary suppression of Christianity and Cameron's exile to South Africa. Tensions came to a head in 1833 since 'in the latter end of the year the slaves were strictly forbidden to read or write' (Freeman and Johns, 1840: 90) lest they question their condition. The following March 'orders were issued that all persons who had read any books from the Europeans, whether directly or indirectly, should deliver them up, and not conceal a single leaf, on pain of death' (ibid., 142–3). Griffiths was soon in trouble with his students for attempting to teach them a text as secular as Watt's *Logic*. Soon 'everything printed was prohibited' and 'the natives who had been taught the art of printing were no longer permitted to assist in any such design' (ibid., 151). In July 1836 the missionaries and their printers fled, burying seventy of their precious copies of the scriptures in the earth, and sequestering the last few in various hiding holes around the island. One of the 'buried bibles' to survive the 'killing time' that followed is in the possession of the British and Foreign Bible Society. It had been preserved for a quarter of a century in a cave high up in the mountains used as a smallpox hospital, and protected from assorted dangers by being rebound with vegetable fibre and covered in animal skin (Darlow and Moule, 1903–11, ii: 1032).

The subsequent history of the island manifests that meeting between cultural convenience and the vicissitudes of colonial power on which so much of the world community for so long depended. Cameron did not return to Madagascar until 1862, and the stalled print industry did not fully take off again until the French imposed a protectorate over the island with British agreement in 1885. This time publishing thrived without interruption, as did the Romanising of Malagasy, in writing as well as print. When the world belatedly turned its attention to Madagascan literature in the 1940s, it was to the francophone languor of poets such as Jean-Joseph Rabéarivello, anthologised by Leopold Sédar-Senghor in his influential *Anthologie de la nouvelle poésie nègre et malgache de langue française* of 1948 under the implied, and inappropriate, banner of *nègritude*. As Wole Soyinka has recently said of him (*Guardian*, 13 July 2002), the Rimbaud-obsessed Rabéarivello lived in a sort of internal exile on the island: 'A mixed up, identity-confused poet of genius, Rabéarivello occupied a creative habitation where the true indigenes were thousands of miles away in France. He applied again and again to be admitted and his frustration grew as the prospect grew more and more remote.' Eventually he killed himself. But he had achieved something astonishing: as far as the *rive gauche* of Paris – and most of the world beyond the island – was now concerned; this Romanised, Gallic though admittedly very accomplished school of writing represented Madagascan literature. If so, it had transformed itself so utterly since the time of *Ibona* and the medieval Malagasy writers in Arabic script that one cannot in retrospect entirely wonder at the expulsions of the early Victorian age or, indeed, at that latter-day suicide.

Print adaptation and the recovery of script

This, fortunately, is not the conclusion to the story. Print habitually adapts, when it does not subdue. Or, rather, alternative modes of communication adjust to print in copious and inventive ways. One is tempted to use the loaded term 'appropriation' here but wherever and whenever it occurs, the process is a mutual one in which each of the partners – print, script, speech – often gains. This is a major, perhaps the preponderant, fact in book history when viewed from a postcolonial vantage point. Indeed, one of the unexpected and beneficial effects of the proliferation of print during the long nineteenth century and the twentieth century was the inventive reclamation and reactivation of other, supposedly superseded modes of communication.

Indulekha's uncles were not the only people in India who evinced nostalgia for manuscript. Print had been held at bay for centuries; its staggered appearance had reinforced a perception of its inflexibility, a product in turn of the fact during the early decades of the nineteenth century that the invariable technique for printing books and newspapers everywhere was moveable type. This method was sturdy though inflexible, possessing a marked tendency to impose on literatures and cultures far and wide a certain uniformity of code and look. By 1830, however, print culture itself was changing, rendering it more sensitive to variant norms. The inception and then rapid diffusion of stereotyping from 1805 (the *Cambridge Stereotype Bible* appearing in that year), had led to certain economies of scale that were to facilitate mass consumption everywhere of textbooks and novels. The arrival of lithography in the 1820s had the countervailing effect of increasing diversity of method and means. Lithographic printing had been developed by Alois Senefelder in Austria in 1798, initially as an efficient way of reproducing sheet music.

Following the translation of Senefelder's book in London in 1819, it was avidly taken up in England as a cheap and effective way of duplicating illustrations, posters and maps (Twyman, 1970). It was India, however, that fully released its potential as a medium for text.

There is some dispute as to who introduced lithography to the subcontinent first (Shaw, 1994), the honours being shared almost equally between the British watercolourist James Nathaniel Rind, an assistant surgeon in the Bengal Medical Service, and the French artists M. Belnos and M. de Savighnac (Shaw, 1998). Be that as it may, by 1827 two lithographic presses had opened in Bombay, concentrating on illustrative work such as J. M. Gonsalve's *Lithographic Views* of that city, issued in 1826. That year further encouragement was provided by the discovery at Kurnool in the Madras Presidency of porous limestone of the right consistency for this kind of work, and within a very few years the technique was being adopted upcountry as far as Bihar. By the 1830s it was in use across northwestern India and the Punjab. It had soon crossed the border as far as Persia, where for several decades it was to drive out all other methods of printing (Browne, 1914: 9).

The reason for the rapid take-up of this new technology, especially in North India, was the perennial challenge of faithfully reproducing the exceptionally cursive Persian, and Persian-derived, scripts. Like Arabic Persian had been printed fairly crudely with movable type for centuries, in Europe as well as in Asia. By 1668 the Oxford University Press had acquired an Arabic font (Sutcliffe, 1978: xix); it was soon printing part-texts in Persian, as by the early nineteenth century were a number of London firms. By 1791 A. Upjohn of Calcutta had printed an edition of the *Works of Dewan* (the Persian poet Hafez) by the same awkward method, using a Nastaliq font struck four years earlier by the firm of Stuart and Cooper.

The unsatisfactory nature of many of these problems was the result of a technical impasse, the problem being that Persian, and to a lesser extent Arabic, characters are difficult to mint as pieces of separate type because of their exceptional 'joined-up'-ness; an excessive amount of kerning (in effect tucking letter forms round one another) being required to produce an effect acceptable to those used to reading handwriting. The technology of lithography surmounted this problem by one of two methods. Texts could be inscribed on stone slabs, then retraced in lithographic ink containing a heavy admixture of molten wax. When the stone was sluiced in acid (or, as in Lucknow, lemon juice), the text stood out because the acid bit into the bare 'hydrophilic' stone while the waxy 'hydrophobic' ink rejected it, providing a clear outline for repeated impressions. Some ingenuity was required from the start since the lines had initially to be written backwards on the stone so as eventually to produce a mirror image the correct way round (thus Persian right to left converted to left to right). Alternatively the words were written the right way round on paper first, and thence transferred onto the block. Indian printers were soon equal to both techniques, as by mid-century were those in Persia.

In India there was in consequence an efflorescence of new publishing houses in the upper provinces, many of them specialising in Urdu texts employing the Nastaliq form of the Persian script. Urdu had until that time been printed either by using relatively clumsy moveable type, the pieces of which fitted ill together and were liable to break off at the ends, or else by recourse to the more manageable Devanagari writing system, a solution which had the culturally ambiguous effect of underlining the language's affinity with its sister-tongue, Hindi. By 1796 John Gilchrist, to whom we shall return, had issued a tentative *Grammar of the Hindoostanee Language* employing this second solution; in it he argued that the two languages were so closely related as to constitute a common tongue. By the early 1800s the Serampore missionaries were publishing alternative letterpress versions of their 'Hindustani' New Testament in these two different scripts. The awkwardness remained. The way round it in North India proved to be the harnessing of what had been intended as an illustrative technique to mass produce whole texts, using what amounted to a careful, technologically enabled simulation of script.

In the earlier part of the century, North India had enjoyed no particular advantage in the print trade. A sampling of production at the time shows it to have been evenly distributed across the subcontinent, with a vigorous industry in the south. The arrival of lithography at mid-century, however, had the noticeable effect of swinging the balance of the industry northwards, so that by the 1860s the most flourishing centres of book production in India lay in Lucknow and Benares. A certain amount of this activity was in Hindi and other languages, but a large part was in Urdu using Nastaliq. In the Punjab it was the preponderant part, yielding a spectacular boost to the language, its literature, and the communities employing it as a mother-tongue (Shaw, 1979).

The characteristics of the Indian 'lithographic evolution', as I have termed it in Figure 1.4 (page 24), were arresting, whether viewed from the point of view of the skills involved or the cultural, even the political, repercussions of these processes. Urdu text was now being written backwards on prepared limestone in a procedure amounting to a virtual renaissance of handwriting, while compositors as such made way for a special kind of scribe. To modern eyes pages produced by this still popular method, or rather by the modern modifications of it called offset lithography (in which the text is transferred from the stone to a rotating rubber belt and thence to paper) or photolithography (in which a photographic plate is made from the initial impression) tend to resemble photocopying, since they do not have the depth of field associated with, say, letterpress. In the hands (literally in the hands) of masters of the craft, however, the effect was beautifully fluid, and it sat easily on the eye. Shaw for one sees in it evidence of a certain nostalgia for manuscript, and there is good reason to believe that for those who practised this tactile form of textual reproduction in North India during the later decades of the nineteenth century and the earlier decades of the twentieth, it possessed just this attraction. In the light of this observation the South Asian lithographic revolution may well be regarded as reactive, as a radical form of print adaptation to bring it into line with traditional aesthetic requirements, even in a sense as a form of resistance to modernity:

> Lithography was in essence a link with the past. It combined the cultural attributes of manuscript with the technical advantages of mass production. Lithography made the printed book no longer an alien artefact, but something visually more familiar and therefore culturally more acceptable. The mass-produced manuscript was, through lithography, a paradox realized.
>
> (Shaw, 1994)

The impact of these developments was, however, as relevant to the future and destiny of the subcontinent as to its past. The status of Urdu as a separate language was debatable up to the 1870s. Thereafter it was a fact of cultural alignment, because the burgeoning of Urdu literature enabled by the introduction of lithography had the marked effect of consolidating a separate constituency of readers (Orsini, 2002), especially in places where Urdu was the usual mode of colloquial discourse. For example in the year 1874, according to the Annual Report for that year, the Province of Oudh issued 134 titles in Urdu to 16 in Hindi, the province of Punjab 333 to 86. All were lithographed. A comparison with the rest of India is telling. In the south of India lithography was still reserved either for minority Urdu or Persian texts, or for illustrative work. The form these illustrations took could, even so, take the authorities by surprise. In July of 1870 Pasala Naidoo of Madras published a Tamil book entitled *Athmabothamritha Rasum*. The main text was hand-printed, but into it was tipped a vividly coloured lithographed sheet. A bewildered government inspector reported:

> There is a curious diagram inserted in the book for a play similar to a game at dice with figures of venomous snakes of various shapes and import, thereby to determine the evil disposition of each man who plays it. The diagram, however, is above the comprehension of the ordinary reader without some explanation from those acquainted with such diagrams.
>
> (*Madras Quarterly Report*, fourth quarter of 1870)

The game was called *Moksha-Patam*. When mass reproduced in Britain by the firm of Kismet from 1895, it became better known as Snakes and Ladders.

In northwest India the encouragement given by this new technology to political and cultural consciousness would prove even more arresting, and in several ways. Perhaps the most unusual facet of the scene to someone not used to the South Asian publishing environment is the proportion maintained between different literary genres. To illustrate it I have taken a cross-section from the output in United Provinces over a period from the last quarter of 1922 to the third quarter of 1924, chosen because it coincides with one of the notable peaks of European literary modernism, the time-span immediately following the publication in Europe of *The Waste Land*, *Ulysses* and *Jacob's Room* (Table 5.1). The figures are broken down by genre and cover production in Hindi, Urdu, Sanskrit and English, though it has to be said that the numbers in English were small, and those in Sanskrit even smaller. In 1922, the year when Eliot was drawing attention to classical Sanskrit in London by quoting the truncated conclusion to an Upanishad at the end of his poem *The Waste Land* and giving it a Christian wash in his accompanying notes, less than 5 per cent of the book production in this part of India was accounted for by works in that language. What is of especial relevance here, however, is that – with the exception of the very few English books produced, and in marked contrast to southern India – the medium of reproduction consistently specified in the records is lithography.

Table 5.1   Book production for the Upper Provinces of India, September 1922–August 1924, divided by genre.

Genre	4th quarter of 1922	1st quarter of 1923	2nd quarter of 1923	3rd quarter of 1923	4th quarter of 1923	1st quarter of 1924	2nd quarter of 1924	3rd quarter of 1924
Poetry	152	206	251	182	167	223	69	201
Fiction	67	46	79	52	35	61	52	46
Drama	15	21	21	12	5	20	20	14
Biography	3	9	7	5	4	6	5	6
Travels	1	—	1	—	—	—	—	—

Source: 'Quarterly Reports on Book Production in the Upper Provinces of India', 1922–4.

What will immediately strike readers unacquainted with this literary milieu is the preponderance of poetry. Much of this verse was religious, and all of it was cheap. A fairly typical example is Ajodhya Das's *Forty Poems to Shiva* produced in 1923 by Baijnath Prasad of Benares at a price of 1 anna, well within the pocket of the common reader. Its popularity is attested to by the fact that 4,000 copies were produced, considerably above the average of around 300 for many books of prose.

But these poetic productions were at the same time often political in a manner barely paralleled outside the South Asian environment. Ever since the Sepoy Rising of 1857–8 and the subsequent clampdown on subversive agitation by the colonial state, poetry had become for audiences across Northern India a natural organ for nationalist sentiment. Partly as a result, by the beginning of the twentieth century the most commonly reproduced text in this region was a lithographed religious or mythological poem, often with a coded political meaning. The authorities gradually caught up with this fact. As we shall see in Chapter 7, a fairly high proportion of the publications banned or seized by the government under successive Press Acts during the first half of the twentieth century were poetry books. In only 1922 the provisions had been amended to permit confiscation of suspect texts. The material seized included, inter alia, *Panjaba ka khuna va hatyare Dayara ki karatuta* (The blood of the Punjab and murderous Dyer's deed, BL PIB 56/16), a poetic protest of 1921 against the Jallianwalla Bagh massacre of April 1919 in Amritsar and the failure of the governor of the Punjab to condemn it; and *Poems of non-co-operation* (1939), a series published by Hindu Pustak Manda of Lucknow. Both appear innocuously in the quarterly returns in the safe-sounding category 'Poetry'.

They circulated for all that, and thus the lithograph presses of the period continued to fulfil a need that was social and political as much as it was literary and devotional. The community-building effects cannot be ignored. Political affiliations in North India increasingly centred as much around language as around religion. Since developments in textual reproduction had gradually given this language a new lease of life, a consolidation of awareness among Urdu-speaking Muslim communities ensued. When on 8 July 1935 Chaudhri Rahmat Ali, a student of Emmanuel College, Cambridge, composed a circular letter calling for the separate creation of a nation named after the acronym Pakistan, he stressed religious rather than linguistic factors (OIOC IOR L/P7J/6/689.ff. 494–5). The fact is that over large areas of northwest India the two went hand in hand. To an extent not always fully recognised, the nation-state of Pakistan (initially West Pakistan but, after its split with its Bengali-speaking eastern wing in 1971, a separate and largely Urdu-speaking demesne) is a child of the lithographic age.

Meanwhile lithography had made its way through Persia to Lebanon, whence traders carried it to West Africa. It reappeared in Senegal as a tradition of textual glass painting inspired by Shiite models and sustained by urban murids (local Islamic notables). Here too the purpose seems to have been to create and to preserve a zone of artistic expression free from the centripetal pressures of colonial print culture. As Mamadou Diouf puts it (2002: 120): 'In the city Murids appropriated the glass painting, the religious lithography introduced by the Lebanese, to narrate their own stories alongside and/or against the colonial civility.' By this method a local lithographic revolution was used to convey and to sustain traditional Arabic script.

When the enhancement of offset lithography arrived in the second half of the twentieth century, the liberation achieved was even greater. This was especially the case in places such as northern Nigeria where a vigorous script culture had been interrupted by the introduction during the early colonial period of print technologies ill suited to local writing systems. The pervasiveness of typesetting had meant, for example, that the *ajami* literature of Hausaland discussed in Chapter 2 was effectively marginalised; couched in the Maghrebi form of Arabic script, it existed uncomfortably in a new environment where the restriction of available typefaces meant that most printing of Hausa literature had perforce to be done in Roman. The result, as Graham Furniss explains, had been a plain alienation between self-expression and mass production, and the uneasy co-existence of separate but parallel printing conventions for the same language, neither of them adequate to the task. The arrival of offset lithography altered the score:

> With the introduction of printing presses in the colonial period there was the possibility of setting poetry and producing editions by the hundred or thousand. However, the first printing presses functioned primarily in roman script to produce government publications of one kind or another. A printing press established in Kano was able to set the standard Arabic scripts, and the early *Northern Province Newssheet* was produced in roman and Arabic scripts, but most *ajami* poetry was written in the Maghribi script, quite different from the standard typeset form. Nevertheless, handwritten manuscripts still circulated in the colonial period with the occasional printing undertaken privately in the Middle East or Egypt. As far as poetry was concerned, the key technical development came in the early 1960s with the arrival of offset printing both in government presses and into commercial presses in the Sabon Gari quarters, 'new town/strangers' quarters of northern cities. Offset printing meant that no special skills in setting type in Arabic script were required. Any original manuscript in any

script could be photographically copied and any number of copies reproduced, so long as the printer could read the order of the page numbers and knew which way up the pages were.

(Furniss, 1996: 12)

As in India a hundred years earlier, the fresh possibility of faithfully reproducing manuscript originals on a large scale restored a traditional, and much needed, balance between eye, ear and mind.

In India meanwhile the attempt to domesticate the book to subliminally retained script consciousness proved unremitting, and has remained a strong impetus behind much innovative print design to this day. Rabindranath Tagore (1861–1941), the bestriding colossus of Bengali literature during the first half of the twentieth century, never seems to have been entirely happy with the materiality of letterpress books, in which he seems always to have sensed a sort of alienation between eye and ear. The scholar and critic Swapan Chakrovorty for one has spoken of the 'radical discomfiture' experienced by Tagore with books of the sort printed in his youth by the Oxford University Press, Macmillan or their local imitators (2006: 124). Such a sensation seems to run beneath his curt and formal dealings with Macmillan in London (BL Add MS. 55004), when in 1913 – the year in which Tagore was awarded the Nobel Prize for Literature – they became his overseas publishers. The correspondence was conducted at one remove, through his nephew Sunerundram, and has none of the personal warmth usual with Tagore when writing to collaborators. Visiting the Great Temple of the Chariot of the Sun at Koranak in Orissa, Rabindranath is said to have remarked that the tumultuous, life-like and occasionally erotic sculptures adorning its walls represented a fuller book of Indian life than anything run off by printers. When in middle age he himself turned printer, setting up an active and intimately personal publishing concern to accompany his school and college at Santiniketan, departure from received norms of presentation became the order of the day. On its treadle-operated machines, no industrially manufactured paper was permitted. His first *Collected Poems* were overseen by his nephew in 1896; already they manifest individual peculiarities of typographic style, set out in double column with a range of paper shades, no ruling, and three separate fonts employed in the play scripts for dialogue, stage directions and names. By 1916 Tagore had introduced different colours for different editions of his works, struggling all the while to escape uniformity.

In 1926 Tagore discovered a satisfactory way of reintegrating print technology with the immediacy of the writing hand. While on a visit to Germany he was shown a newly patented Rotar Press machine in which the text was written out manually on thin metal sheets before being transferred to paper. Here is an eyewitness account by Nirmalkumari Mahalanobi, who accompanied him on this particular trip to Europe:

> When we were in Berlin that time, Prasanta Babu [her husband Prasanta Chandra Mahalanobi] said to the poet 'A brand new kind of printing machine has come on the market – an excellent thing. It's very small; there are thin aluminium sheets, the size of foolscap paper. One has to write on those by hand, and one's handwriting can simply be printed straight from them. It isn't very big or heavy: you can easily take one home with you if you want.'
>
> The poet was always very keen to try anything new. He immediately gave the order: 'Buy the machine tomorrow.'
>
> The next day the 'Rotar Print' machine arrived, with a sheaf of aluminium sheets to write on. My job was to sit and rule pencil lines on these sheets, to stop the poet's lines from going crooked.
>
> Whenever Rabindranath had time, he would write little poems to print on the Rotar machine. He was delighted that his dependence on the printing press would be considerably reduced.
>
> (Tagore, 2001: 171–2)

The technique delighted Tagore and, once the machine had been installed back home in Bengal, he was soon running off personally signed Bangla poems as gifts to friends. The summit of this particular ambition came in 1927 when Tagore was able to produce a complete edition of his volume of shorter poems *Lekhan* (Jottings) by this method, writing the entire text out by hand on aluminium before running off multiple copies. In an article published the following year in the autumn issue of the magazine *Prabasi*, he praised its liberating force:

> When I went to Germany I found out that a way had been invented of printing directly from handwriting. One has to write with special ink on a sheet of aluminium, and by printing from that with a special machine one can avoid the tender mercies of the compositor altogether.
>
> Then I wondered if those who did not regard tiny poems as literature would perhaps accept them in the poet's own handwriting. I was rather unwell at the time, and therefore had plenty of time on my hands; so I got on with writing these little English and Bengali poems on aluminium sheets … In due course these poems together with other brief poems [*kabitika*, 'poemlets'] of mine were published in the book called *Lekhan*.
>
> (Tagore, 2001: 163–6)

Such Gandhi-like passive resistance to standardisation remains a constant of Tagore publishing to this very day, though now undertaken by others. I have beside me a copy of a selection of Tagore's *Poems and Songs* 'transcreated from the Bengali' in 1995 by Sovana Dasgupta, issued from Professor Lal's Writers Workshop at 162/92 Lake Gardens in Calcutta, and picked up second-hand from a booth on the north side of College Street. The cover is hand-stitched, gold with a red, orange and green border. Opposite the title page stands a colophon that runs 'Hand-set in Times Roman typeface and printed on an Indian-made hand-operated machine ... on paper produced in India. Layout and lettering by P. Lal with a Sheaffer calligraphy pen. Gold-embossed hand-stitched hand-pasted and hand-bound by Tulamiah Mohiuddeen with handloom sari cloth woven and designed in India. This book is entirely handset, single letter by letter' (Tagore, 1995: 2). There are six 'hands' in that sentence, as many as Siva's. In other cultures, at other times, such an announcement would be redolent of some sentimental arts-and-crafts cosiness. In India it is suggestive of continuing adaptation, reflecting in turn a bracing cultural tenacity.

Print adaptation and the revitalisation of speech

However, it is not only scripted text that various print technologies have revived. In the regions in question, residual connections with, and the revitalisation of, orality has been equally, and in places more, significant. This is a phenomenon observable from either end: print assimilates speech, but speech may equivalently assimilate print. I shall deal with these two complementary trajectories in turn.

Among the most active publishing enterprises stimulated by lithographic developments in Upper India was the firm of Naval (or Nawal) Kishore, founded in Lucknow in 1858, the year following the rising (Stark, 2007). Munsi Kishore was born in 1836 and educated in Persian and Arabic through the teaching medium of Urdu. After further English-medium education at Agra College he trained as a printer with Koh-e Nur in Lahore before opening his own lithographic press in Lucknow and founding the Urdu-medium newspaper *Avadh Akhbar*. Kishore's was mostly an educational business catering to the growing needs of a rising social class resolved to assert themselves through formal instruction. The archives of the firm, now at the University of Chicago, and a detailed monograph by Ulrike Stark (2007) based on these archives, afford a bird's-eye view of its copious production. This was largely a lithographic press producing works in both Hindi and Urdu for the academic market. Though the language medium was different and the geographical reach more localised, it fulfilled in its own sphere the same sort of needs as those catered for on an imperial stage by, say, Thomas Nelson and Sons of Edinburgh, selling textbooks, primers, works of moral instruction and cheap reprints or redactions of the (in this case Indian) classics.

In one extraordinary respect was it distinct. Kishore's first book had been a reprinting of a version of an ancient Persian story cycle, *Dastan-e amir Hamzak* originally produced in 1801 at the College of Fort William in Calcutta using Gilchrist's letterpress. Soon, however, Kishore had decided to extend the cycle by drawing on the ever-present resource of the *dastan-gos*, live reciters of Hamzak narrative from the streets and compounds of Lucknow. First in 1871 he commissioned Abdullah Bilgrami thoroughly to revise text, producing a classic one-volume version in print to this day, in Urdu and latterly in English translation. Then, after producing a one-volume, 520-page edition set in Devanagari for his Hindi-reading public, he embarked in 1881 on his grand scheme. He invited three celebrated *dastan-gos* of the city – Muhammad Husain Jah, Ahmad Husain Qamar and Tasudduq Husain – to visit the press one by one on a regular basis, improvising elaborations on the legend which were taken down by hand and then copied mirror-wise onto the lithographic stone, and thence onto paper. The cycle was thus recited and copied relay-wise, with each narrator taking over the story just where his predecessor had left off, sometimes insulting him in the process, as scribes took down every word and the printers run the text off lithographically (Russell, 1970: 34). The volumes were issued successively, starting in 1881 and finishing with a fine flourish in 1905 with nineteen devoted to the adventures of Hamzah's descendants. Forty-six tomes were eventually produced by this method, a total of some 41,000 pages, making it in the opinion of the Urdu scholar Frances W. Pritchett 'the longest single romance cycle in world literature' (Bilgrami, 1991: xx). Its length was certainly remarkable; just as noteworthy was the fact that the method of transmission represented a complete and almost synchronous blend of the oral with scripted and printed text. For the readership, the pleasure afforded was extreme, though it may not have rivalled that of the great *ghazal* poet, Lothario and *bon viveur* Mirza Ghalib (1795–1869), who, on receiving just one volume of an earlier edition of the Hamzah cycle is reported to have exclaimed: 'And there are seventeen bottles of wine in the pantry. So I read all day and drink all night. The man who wins such pleasure can only wonder "What more had Jamshed? What more Alexander?"' (Russell and Islam, 1969: 255).

In Africa it is arguable that the contribution of print culture to the preservation of the oral tradition has been greater and more pervasive. In the opinion of scholars such as Isidore Okpewho, orality remains the very fount of African literature. It is likely to remain so, all the more because in future Africa may well come to rely less and less on the printed book, and more and more on digitalised resources in which visual and aural ingredients combine. But to stay with the printed book for the moment, there is abundant evidence that one of the principal effects of print culture across the twentieth century was to sustain oral memory. In the last chapter I alluded to one of the supreme adaptive achievements of print culture in mid-twentieth-century Nigeria: the issuing, in a standardised form of Yoruba, of the novels of Chief Fagunwa, a former secondary teacher of the language whose written work drew extensively on folktales that he had heard in the home. Fagunwa in turn provided the inspiration for Amos Tutuola, whose *The Palm Wine Drinkard*, published by Faber and Faber at the decision of T. S. Eliot in 1952, introduced a global audience to the resources of Yoruba oral narrative via a locally inflected English idiom. Early readers of Tutuola's stories noted an affinity with Bunyan, who was indeed pervasive in Africa through a plethora of different vernacular translations, as Isabel Hofmeyr (2004) has well illustrated. The true wellspring may have been in a common oral substratum on which both Bunyan and the Yoruba once drew.

But proverbs, as Emmanuel Obiechina among others has asserted, are the palm oil with which the novelist Achebe blends his food, and Yoruba songs are pervasive in the drama of Wole Soyinka, notably in *Kongi's Harvest* (1962). Igbo verse runs beneath the lyrics of Christopher Okigbo, published in Africa by Mbari of Ibadan and *Transition* in Kampala long before they appeared posthumously in England. The published epics of the South African Mazisi Kunene were based on Zulu originals; they were scribbled down as doodles during interminable committee meetings of the ANC before Heinemann, mindful of the difficulty of achieving publication in apartheid South Africa, offered publication in English in London. Indeed oral memory has shown a marked tendency to emerge in the most unlikely places, even where the formal context, or the author, seems to want to exclude it. Nobody was more contemptuous of village heirlooms than the Senegalese novelist, Marxist, cinematic director and one-time trade union activist Ousman Sembene (1923–2007). Sembene is on record as saying that the oral tradition was something that Africa should leave behind. His masterpiece *Les Bouts de bois de dieu* (1960) describes a titanic strike along the Dakar–Bamako railway line in 1947–8, and has frequently been compared to Emile Zola's *Germinal*. In fact, as Eileen Julien (1992) has amusingly demonstrated, in its epic might it owes just as much to the ancient epic *Sundiata* which describes the twelfth-century foundation of the Sahelian empire and dynasty of Mali. At one point in the narrative the connection becomes clear. The shop steward Tiémoko has persuaded the union to bring the blackleg Diara to trial: 'Buoyed up by his success, he sung out loud some strains from *Sundiata*' (Sembene: 1960: 147).

No less significant an aspect of this formal give-and-take is the oral assimilation of written – or more usually of printed – texts. To appreciate this phenomenon it is necessary to recognise just how frequently, in assemblies or informal gatherings, at rallies, in churches, temples, mosques or in the home – written or printed matter is absorbed by being read *aloud*. In India at least, such live rendition and aural absorption has been, and arguably still is, the normative condition for texts especially, as we have already seen, of the grand communal epics. Here is Anindita Ghosh describing a bilingual 'popular performative tradition' in late eighteenth- and early nineteenth-century Bengal, serving both the illiterate and semi-literate and persisting many decades after the Halhed 'moment':

> *Kathakatas* or collective narrative sessions, where religious works based on Hindu religious epics and mythology were read out by professional Brahmin narrators or *kathaks*, were in great demand during the period, and survived well into the print age. The texts were Brahminical in spirit and content, and almost invariably done in an ornate style of composition, with resounding alliterative words and elaborate metaphor. Not surprisingly, the reading event was divided into two sessions – morning and afternoon. In the first half, the reader merely read [in Sanskrit] from old tattered volumes, and sometimes more primitive wooden tablets. In the second half, the explanation of what had been read before was given in Bengali. The kathak retold the existing story, interspersing the narrative with suitable songs, poems, popular tales, and moral lessons, heightening the experience of listeners.
>
> (Ghosh, 2006: 40–1)

At such events written, and later printed, texts became the basis for oral exposition and improvisation, as again we observed in the case of the Tamil Nadu bow-songs. Newspapers have been treated like this for decades, even centuries, increasing their reach and influence well beyond their nominal 'circulation'. Books are employed in the same way, and none more so than the Qur'an, the Bible, and the prayer- and hymnbooks of various Christian denominations: Catholic, Presbyterian, Methodist, Anglican, Baptist or increasingly Pentecostal. The question arises, especially with the burgeoning syncretist churches across Africa, as to what extent such liturgical fare remains in any sense 'foreign'. To state the obvious, in sub-Saharan Africa, as for the most part in South Asia, nearly all Christian services are conducted through the vernacular. The Anglican Prayer Book currently in use in the Church of the Province of South Africa, published by Collins and distributed by David Philip, is issued in Afrikaans, English, Setswana, Sesotho, Siswati, Northern Sotho, Xhosa and Zulu, and in these languages (sometimes in two in combination) it is declaimed weekly, the length and breadth of the land. In the polyglot cities of West Africa it is customary for lessons to be read and sermons delivered in more than one tongue at any given celebration. In the Roman Catholic Cathedral of the Holy Spirit in the Adabraka district of Accra, the lessons and homily at Sunday morning mass are amplified in two or even three national languages in sequence – in Ga certainly, followed by Akan and sometimes too by Ewe – to much fanning of handkerchiefs and shuffling of feet. Given the literacy figures for Ghana (for which see p. 168) it is likely that up to 30 per cent of the very full congregation will be listening to words that they could not, or would be unlikely to, read from the page. Such utterances seep into the oral bloodstream. The tro-tro lorries that ply between the cities of West Africa frequently carry on their tailboards a half-verse from a psalm in Fante, say, or English or Akwapim Twi. The driver and passengers in the following vehicle may be expected to complete the half-quotation, relying much on the sort of oral recollection from verbal hints and fragments about which Karin Barber has written in connection with Yoruba *oriki*. The difference is that *oriki* memory is acquired orally and redeployed in the same medium. The memorisation of one of the many hundreds of African vernacular translations of the Christian scriptures derives by contrast from a printed and disseminated text, even if the one remembering has assimilated it by ear. If you ask the bead-seller haunting your compound what song she is cooing over her wares, the answer will most likely be a hymn she has heard in church.

Such scraps of music and verse are rehearsed, repeated, recycled and spontaneously re-deployed. In February 2007 I stood in the aisle of the Methodist church in Cape Coast, a building whose foundation goes back to 1838 (Bartels, 1965: 32), and listened as a circle of women in the chancel improvised in Fante, antiphonally and with lifted hands, led by a matron in red Java prints. At first it sounded like extemporary prayer. Closer attention revealed it to be an *abididwon*, a fairly recent form of improvised choric supplication based on the traditional *kurunku*. Structured around a Bible narrative, such performances also draw liberally on the Fante hymnody of the Methodist church, which again has roots going back as far as 1830. On the campus of the University of Ghana at Legon nowadays large numbers of evangelically minded students will stand on the playing fields from dusk until dawn indulging in the practice known as 'speaking in tongues' – extemporizing verbally under the pressure of spirit possession. The result, continuous and polyvocal, sounds at first like proverbial babble, before the ear adjusts to detect snippets of the Book of Revelation in Nzema, or Acts of the Apostles in Ewe. In both of these instances, the reality is a hybridised performance, oral in mode, literary in content.

The consequences of such diffusion are sometimes incalculable. The Cory Library in Grahamstown, South Africa (Cory Ms. 16,430) holds the minutes of a town hall meeting in King Williams Town on Thursday 29

November 1928, the purpose of which was to select the 326 hymns and 33 chants in a new missal intended for 'the Bantu Church, the Congregational Church, and the Presbyterian Church of Africa'. At the last moment the committee decided to slip into an appendix a Xhosa number entitled *Nkosi Sikelel' iAfrika*, originally composed in 1897 by Enoch Sontonga, a teacher at a Methodist mission school in Johannesburg. Seven verses had recently been added by the Xhosa poet Samuel Mqhavyi, and five years previously the first recording of the hymn had been made by Sol Plaatje in London. This internationally known song was to be adopted as the rallying call of the ANC during the long, dark days of apartheid. Currently it supplies the national anthems of Tanzania (as *Mungu ibanki Africa*), of Zambia (as *Lumbanyini Zambia*) and of liberated South Africa, sung, in modulating four-part harmony, by tens of millions of patriotic souls, most of whom will have absorbed the words – and sometimes the music too – initially from print.

6 Communication and authority

Peddlers of power

The interplay of power across the field of communications is perhaps best observed through the attempts of various parties to control it. It is to the several communities involved in this process – and to the divers sorts of leverage they seek to exert – that I would like therefore now to turn. As before, I shall not be privileging the print medium above any other. To do so is tempting; in the context of the present argument it is, however, a temptation that should, I believe, be resisted as liable to lead to over-simplification. What we shall find instead, I think, is that in each communicative dispensation – script, say, or print – an eightfold balance of power operates between producers, priests, pundits, politicians, policemen, protestors, publishers and punters. I shall be looking at the influence of the last of these groups – with the public, in fact – in my last chapter. In this and the following one I am concerned with the behaviour of the literary police force, and in particular with three constabularies who do not always recognise one another's uniforms. These are respectively scholars, editors and censors. The power of the last is well attested, especially in colonial dispensations, and I shall be dealing with it in Chapter 7. In the present chapter I want to urge the possibly paradoxical proposition that scholars and editors have frequently exercised an equally decisive, though possibly a more subtle, influence over the ways in which peoples communicate, especially on paper. Such control, I wish to maintain, is all the more penetrating since, though censors and other legal agencies aim to control entire texts, editors and scholars habitually guard the very gateway to textuality itself, and even exercise some managerial sway over antecedent items such as language and script

The policing of speech

Ever since the Tower of Babel, people have been worried about the promiscuity of human speech. In Chapter 4 I offered some tentative figures for language spread in West Africa, based on two different criteria used by David Dalby (1977): either by counting every language group that recognises itself as separate, or by extending each grouping as far as it went before its speech becomes unintelligible to its neighbours. The first tally was, I noted, larger than the second. Dalby's criteria have proved useful in the African context. They were not, however, quite original, based as they were on guidelines used in fieldwork undertaken sixty years earlier in South Asia. Between 1903 and 1918, the Irish linguist George Grierson published a seven-volume *Linguistic Survey* of then-imperial India, appropriately based on locally collected versions of the biblical parable of the prodigal son. It was Grierson who first thought up the two criteria mentioned above. Applying them to the subcontinent as a whole, his figures were 544 as against 179, though these were almost certainly underestimates.

Grierson was a civil servant, one-time opium agent for Bihar, the local languages of which locality especially absorbed him. The *Survey* was the love of his life, but it was also a government publication, and the research team that conducted it were on the official pay-roll. In effect, they were philological equivalents of the Land Survey Department for which the fictitious Kim, amongst others, worked, and which operated as a well-known cover for spying. No espionage activities have ever been attributed to the large, and lumberingly witty, Grierson. His project was none the less another of those 'maps', like censuses and museums, which in chapter 10 of the 1991 edition of *Imagined Communities* (163–86) Benedict Anderson highlights as mechanisms of imperial information-gathering and control. The Press and Book Registration Act of 1867, mentioned in Chapter 3 above, was yet another.

Now turn to a modern hundred-rupee bank note. Printed down a column to the left of the obverse side (the other side to the image of Gandhi) are the

Figure 6.1   A hundred-rupee note showing the fifteen official languages of India.

words 'One Hundred Rupees' in the languages of the nation-state of India as recognised by the Reserve Bank, fifteen in number. This modest total is practically circumscribed: a note exhibiting all of Grierson's 544 tongues would be unwieldy, or else the specimens given of each would need to be minuscule. Apart from practical considerations, however, the list also makes a political statement about unity and diversity. It has its origins in another official document: the Constitution of India of 6 November 1949. Signed by Jawahurlah Nehru and thirteen other founding fathers, the constitution had listed the languages to be used by the regional states of a nascent administration, alongside the federal language of English. Fourteen in number, these were Assamese, Bengali, Gujurati, Hindi, Kannada, Kashmiri, Malayalam, Marathi, Oriya, Punjabi, Sanskrit, Tamil, Telegu and Urdu. The number has now risen slightly to the twenty-three represented on the Language Commission of India. A question remains as to how Grierson's totals have shrunk so. The available answers have much to tell us about imperialism, and that related phenomenon nation-building. They furthermore shed much light on different modes of verbal transmission, the primary subject of this book.

Imperialism is a term often confused with colonialism. Though they sometimes go hand in hand, and though their cultural consequences are often similar, they are not invariably the same. Imperialism is the imposition of political authority from outside; colonialism a process of immigration and settlement. The Greek communities on ancient Sicily and the Bangladeshi presence in London's East End have both been referred to as 'colonies'; the presentation of Burma to Queen Victoria as a New Year's Day gift on 1 January 1886 was a manifestation of imperialism as its most presumptuous. What happened in India was that – imperceptibly at first, and then abruptly – the first turned into the second. Bengal had been treated by the British as a trading settlement, though from 1813 onwards the East India Company gradually assumed the reins of government, including responsibility for education. Again, it is easy to slip into simplification. The decision of the Committee for Public Instruction in 1835 to concentrate its resources on the dissemination of English had the long-term effect of turning this imported (in that sense 'colonial') tongue into the official code for administration throughout the Raj ruled, following the Sepoy Rising of 1857–8, directly as a 'Crown Colony'. But there never was any attempt at the hopeless task of introducing English throughout society. Alongside it, and at every social level, Indian languages thrived.

The linguistic effects of imperialism have mostly been like this, except in places like Canada and Australia where the colonisation swamped the local languages and cultures it found in its path. In India and Africa a dual linguistic policy operated. Just as the Romans had introduced Latin as the code of official discourse throughout Pax Romana, leaving the local vernaculars (the tongues of *vernaculi*, the slaves) to be spoken in the market place, so the British in India or Nigeria made government an English language reserve, and permitted the populus at large to speak as was their wont. This distinction of attitude, however, should not blind us to another complementary policy with far deeper effects. Though government was now conducted in the language of governors from overseas, its application throughout society could only take place through the languages of the indigenous governed. There accordingly emerged a process of what I will call secondary linguistic imperialism: the marshalling and regimentation of the swarming fecundity of local speech into a fit channel for persuasion and governance.

Though frequently at loggerheads with government, and banned in British India until 1813, the missionaries, for example, were of necessity implicated in linguistic regulation at a micro-level in their capacities as translators and publishers (Grierson, 1903). For Christian proselytising to take effect, the scriptures had to be printed in languages the recipients understood. In South India, back in the sixteenth century, the Jesuits had printed the devotional classics of Catholicism in Tamil. In Bengal in the very early nineteenth century, the Baptists printed the Bible. Such was the linguistic complexity of the region, however, that several language groups needed to be identified and mapped out, and an arduous publishing programme undertaken aimed at the constituencies thus crudely constituted. In his correspondence William Carey (Angus IN/15) repeatedly refers to these different readerships as 'nations'. By 1815 thirty-three were being catered for. The prolixity of the scene, and the cost of the publishing operation it required, frequently worried Carey, so he started work on a *Universal Dictionary*, never published, which would bring this wilderness of self-expression under one unifying net.

In 1813, missionaries were at last allowed into Bengal. Thereafter printing was carried on both in Calcutta and Serampore. The anxieties over language, however, remained. The hardest nut to crack, as it happened, was Hindi. Were it and Urdu, both of which were spoken across a wide swath of northern India, one language or were they two? Hindi was conventionally written in the Devanagari script, and Urdu in the Persian. This divagation, however, was far from universal; in the early 1800s the Baptists were printing their Urdu (or, as they called it in conformity with the Gilchrist-influenced terminology of the time, their 'Hindustani') translation of the New Testament in both, at some inconvenience to themselves since, as Carey loudly complained, the Persian script version had to be separately commissioned and funded. It caused his typesetters agonies.

The temptation to regularise and, in print terms, to economise, had long been apparent. In the late 1780s the Scotsman John Borthwick Gilchrist (1759–1841), then an assistant surgeon with the East India Company's regiment serving in Upper India, had noted how many of the troops drawn from various regions employed Urdu as a lingua franca. Determined to standardise it for administrative use, he travelled to Lucknow, where with the help of local munshis he enlarged his vocabulary, to the extent that in 1786, eight years after Halhed's Bangla grammar, he felt able to advertise by public subscription *A Dictionary* (of) *English and Hindustanee*. The title was partly explained by his Preface, in which he announced that Urdu – or, as he called it, 'Hindustani' – represented the 'grand living popular speech of all Hindustan' (Gilchrist, 1787: iv) – that is, potentially of much of India. Held back by Gilchrist's improvidence, the book did not appear in full until 1798 when the Calcutta firm of Stuart and Cooper issued it in three parts, and inevitably in letterpress, for a price of 40 rupees. Since, as already explained, the Nastaliq Persian script was difficult and expensive to reproduce by this means, its Urdu sections were set in a Devanagari font designed by Wilkins, and probably struck by Karmakara. Controversially, Gilchrist had attached to its third volume an appendix called *A Grammar of the Hindoostanee Language*, in which he strongly argued that Hindi and Urdu were distillations from a common stock. He continued urging this view when in 1801 he was briefly appointed Professor of 'Hindustani' at Fort William College in Calcutta, which he had just persuaded the company directors to set up as a training ground for newly arrived civil servants (Carey taught Bengali there). He withdrew in high dudgeon to Edinburgh in 1804 after attempting unsuccessfully to get his students to debate the motion that, given a free choice, all Indians would choose to become Christians.

In the irascible Gilchrist, his whiskers, according to the Edinburgh bookseller (and early exponent of evolutionary theory) Robert Chambers, 'as white as Himalayan snow', his face as striking as a 'Bengal tiger' (Chambers, 1832–5, ii: 107), the standardising tendency reached an apogee. It is symptomatic of his reputation and fraught legacy that Hindi scholars have since accused him of causing an Urdu secession, while Urdu scholars blame him for holding the two languages together in an artificial hoop of steel. His influence on Indian writing was paradoxical to a marked degree, more especially on the Urdu side of the mooted divide. The Urdu of the *ghazals* and *qwallis* is floridly pretty; Gilchrist wanted to render it as relatively straightforward and serviceable. To this end at Fort William he gathered together a team of local experts with the plan of publishing local folktales in a forthright, manly style. Amir Khusraw Dihlau's (1253–1325) classic *Bagh o bahar* (The Garden of Spring), for example, is a cycle of stories from the Persian reminiscent in form – though far shorter in scope – of the *Arabian Nights*, which in the early years of the nineteenth century were newly becoming popular both in India and Europe. In 1804 Gilchrist supervised an edition that was, of course, set mechanically in Devanagari. Stylistically, too, it conformed to the college's prosaic norms. The pandits of Lucknow scorned the lacklustre result, so it is hardly surprising that later in the century they threw in their lot with Nawal Kishore and his lithographed Persian–Urdu script. Kishore, needless to say, would exist well outside the government's sphere of influence even if, along with other presses by that time, his firm was subject to formal surveillance. Hence, in the very long run, lithography released Urdu, as it was at last becoming generally known, from an official straitjacket that had been both typographic and stylistic. It was Gilchrist, the whiskered superintendent of the language police, who had woven this constricting garment.

In West Africa, meanwhile, Samuel Ajayi Crowther was attempting to convert his own Yoruba people to Anglicanism. With this end in view in 1843, whilst on the Niger expedition with Schön, he started to draw up a word list, using the Lepsius orthography. By 1848 both his list and his Yoruba Book of Common Prayer had been printed in this newly standard form. Nor did Crowther's communicative and standardising ambitions stop there, since he then applied himself to the study of the northern lingua franca, Hausa. In the 1850s, following a British expedition to the Niger delta, he turned his attention to Igbo. In the 1860s, Nupe followed. By New Year's Eve 1891, when the now Bishop Crowther died at the age of eighty-four, he had realized his ambition of seeing the whole of his translation of the scriptures into Yoruba through the press.

All of this, however, had been achieved at some linguistic cost. Crowther was originally from the ancient town of Oyo, where he had grown up speaking that locality's distinctive dialect of Yoruba before being transported to Sierra Leone, where at college he had learned English, Latin and Greek. He learned to read and write these foreign languages long before he attempted to reduce the Yoruba tongue to writing. As a result, when he set about rendering Holy Writ into Yoruba it was, not surprisingly, the Oyo language that he used, enshrined in the Roman script modified along lines recently suggested by Lepsius (Crowther, 1867–84; Hair, 1967: 1–15).

The consequences for Nigeria's now twenty million Yoruba-users have been far-reaching. Since it was the first of the many Yoruba dialects to be printed, Oyo soon became the basis for Standard Yoruba or Yoruba koiné, the language used for local administration over a large area, for the publication of all literature, including in the 1940s the novels of Fagunwa, in schools and on radio and television (Ajayi, 1960, 2002; Fagborun, 1994). This compromise language, which takes Grierson's criterion of self-description at its word, yokes an Oyo vocabulary to idiom from nearby Ibadan. It also retains a literary flavouring from Crowther's New Testament, including expressions he had literally translated from the Greek. Politically, too, the ramifications of Crowther's choices could hardly have been foreseen. It was around his standard that, in the early twentieth century, a corporate sense of Yoruba identity, absent until that point, began to coalesce. According to Crowther's biographer and namesake, Jacob Ajayi (1999): 'It was in the process of translating the Bible into Crowther's Oyo dialect, which he and his colleagues adapted and standardized into a written form of the language, that Yoruba nationalism or ethnicity was born.' Needless to say, the original object of the exercise – and the main agent of the resulting standardisation – was less writing, as such, than print.

Likewise, when he focused on Igbo, Crowther's sources of contact were from the areas of Igboland the British expedition of the 1850s had reached. In reducing the language to writing in his primer of 1857, it was therefore the Onitsha dialect he reproduced, and again the Lepsius orthography that he used. That vocabulary and spelling system accordingly became the basis for Igbo literature right up to 1941, when Ira C. Ward, a British linguist who had worked with Westermann, proposed changes based on the language as spoken around Owerri that were then incorporated into so-called Central Igbo. The efforts to squeeze this multifarious regional tongue into a single mould did not cease with independence. In 1972, shortly after Biafra was absorbed back into Nigeria after a disastrous civil war, the Society for Promoting Igbo Language and Culture proposed yet another, supposedly more inclusive, compromise that came to be known as Standard Igbo. The language wars that resulted have enjoyed no armistice, outlasting the civil war itself by decades, and several of Nigeria's leading authors, including Achebe, have been in the front line. We have already observed the fondness of Achebe's fictitious catechist Isaac Okonkwo for an Onitsha-dialect translation of the New Testament published in his youth. In this he is a sentimental heir of Crowther, just as surely as he is a reluctant victim of the 'Central Igbo' modernisers of a later decade. His creator has at times distanced himself from both. In his universally loved novel *Things Fall Apart* (1958), it is the Idemili dialect that Achebe prints (spoken a few miles up the Owerri–Onitsha road, but distinctive for all that). In 1999, reverting to Isaac's preferences, he launched a strongly worded vocal attack on Standard Igbo delivered throughout in fluent Onitsha dialect, leaving many of his audience floundering. Few interventions have so dramatically illustrated the pulsing interplay between the printed, the written and oral at the heart of Africa's cultures.

The policing of scripts

The meddling of Lepsius and Westermann represented two phases of an ongoing debate in both India and Africa as to how languages should be printed. The issues at stake were slightly different in each location, but there are interesting shared elements. Universality and accessibility were the primary issues at stake. The Serampore missionaries, for example, would have preferred to reproduce the thirty-three languages into which they were translating the scriptures in one identical font. By this means they would, they believed, save on materials and founders' wages, even if obliged to keep a cohort of translators on their payroll. Soon after establishing the press in 1801, Carey is to be found looking around for a candidate for normative use among India's many scripts. His eye fell on Devanagari. In 1816, in a Memoir addressed to 'the Society in Serampore', he and his colleagues have this to say about the Babel of India's tongues:

> Some of them have a peculiar character of their own, as the Orissa [*sic*], the Kashmeer … the Goojaratee etc. In the greater part of them, however, the Deva-nagree is familiar to most of those who can read, and as this alphabet [*sic*] is perfectly complete, while some of the local alphabets are greatly deficient, it seems desirable to extend the Deva-nagree as widely as possible. It would greatly facilitate the progress of knowledge, if it could have that extension given it in India, which the Roman alphabet has obtained in Europe … It is our design ultimately to publish an edition of most of these in the Nagree character.
>
> (Baptist Mission, Serampore, 1816 [Angus IN/21, 15])

The policy failed because it did not recognise the intimate relationship existing in readers' minds between script and regional identity. No self-respecting Bengali of the *bhadralok* class was likely to prefer taking in his literary or biblical diet through the print medium of a script as intimately connected with Upper India as was Devanagari, so with mixed feelings the saints of Serampore continued using the Bengali typefaces that Panchanan had so carefully devised for them. By 1818 newspapers were being produced in this Bangla font, sowing the seeds for the intense politicisation of the middle class. A printed literature in Bangla soon followed, flourishing alongside a growing literature in English. The scene was now set for the split cultural personality that would mark the bilingual intelligentsia or *bhadralok* of Bengal up to the time of Kipling, and well beyond it. An early exemplar was Raja Ram Mohan Roy, founder of the reformed Hindu church known as the Brahmo Samaj. Roy was a convinced advocate of English-medium education, complying in this respect with the policies of Bentinck and Macaulay. At the same time he founded and contributed to journals in Bangla, and is properly recognised as a leading forerunner of the Bengali Renaissance, an event that would almost certainly not have occurred in the manner and with the force it did, had Devanagari ever held sway.

The fruits of this fortunate assertion of typographic independence, nourished by the *babu* class, have been described by Partha Chatterjee:

The crucial moment in the development of a modern Bengali language comes ... in mid-century, when this bilingual elite makes it a cultural project to provide its mother tongue with the necessary linguistic equipment to enable it to become an adequate language for a 'modern' culture. An entire institutional network of printing presses, publishing houses, newspapers, magazines, and literary societies is created about this time, *outside* the purview of the state and the European missionaries, through which the new language, modern and standardised, is given shape.

(Chatterjee, 2003: 7)

The dynamics of power, however, are seldom simple, and few are more likely to compromise the autonomy of others than those who have just established their own. The standardisation of Bangla language and script, so dearly bought, was to prove the bane of Assam, Bengal's immediate neighbour to the northeast, with its related, though emphatically distinct, language and written characters. In this region the equivalents of Serampore's acts of enabling had been achieved by the American Baptist missionaries at Sibsagor in Upper Assam. By 1813 they had published the first Bible in Assamese, *Dharmapustaka*, and from 1846 were to print the first newspaper in the language, the *Orunodi*, a vigorous organ of local aspiration and opinion. The urgency of their directives, however, entailed a double bind: the men of God assumed the dialect of Sibsagor to be a model for all Assamese usage: this is therefore what they reproduced. And with an eye to the purse, they chose to represent Assamese through a Bangla font copied from Carey's thriving concern to the west. The ramifications of these decisions were exacerbated when, following the Yandaboo Act of 1826, Assam was absorbed into British India. According to the provisions of Act XXIX of 1837 the administrators of a newly created region were to be drawn from the population of the area concerned. In Assam, however, the assumption of Bangla communicative norms, and a shortage of qualified local manpower, meant that *pukka* Bengalis took up a disproportionate share in the new administration. The aggregate impact of these developments has been stigmatised by Hemjyoti Mehdi (2008) as one of 'sub-imperialism', and was in the twentieth century to provoke an 'Assamese Renaissance' centred on an autonomous print industry. The upshot is to suggest that our process of 'secondary linguistic imperialism' produced in practice a sort of internal domino effect, as larger groups successively imposed themselves on smaller with the assistance of freshly established hegemonies of print, only to stimulate in their turn fresh ripples of cultural – and typographic – resistance.

In Africa the interventions of the script police were, if anything, more drastic, since in regions purportedly devoid of any existing writing system, they believed themselves to enjoy *carte blanche*. Since the interlopers seemed agreed that only the Roman script would do, they set about, at various times and places, adapting it phonetically to local typographic use. The problem was that nobody could quite agree how this should be done. Across black Africa, missionaries frequently preceded administrators: they flung themselves at the body of local speech with reckless and rancorous abandon. In Buganda, in what would later be Uganda, and among the Gikuyu of future Kenya (Ngugi, 1986: 67), rival writing systems arose at the behest of Protestant and Catholic churches. The Kabaka, traditional ruler of Buganda, was amused by this dissension, and set about playing the two groups against one another, to the delight of his subjects but the confusion of would-be literates. Anglican missionaries from the Church Missionary Society had arrived in his country in 1878 in response to a letter posted in the *Telegraph* by Henry Stanley encouraging Christians of every persuasion to enter this new field. They tempted the royal appetite with eloquence and Huntley and Palmer's biscuits. Hot on their heels came a community of Catholic White Fathers sent from Algiers by Cardinal Lavigne. The rival groups severally set about bending the ear of Mutesa I, who inquired with some puzzlement 'Has every nation of white men another religion?' (Mullins, 1904: 24).

This ruler's equivocation was later described with amused pride by his great-grandson, Mutesa II: 'His diplomacy was like a juggling act and all the coloured balls were in the air at once.' The monarch summoned the factions to debate their respective claims before him. The Catholic spokesman was Father Simeon Lourdel, the Anglican, the Scottish engineer-turned-clergyman Alexander Mackay. 'Lourdel spoke in a mixture of bad Arabic, Swahili, Luganda and French … The padre was really, to say the least, not guilty of using too much native politeness' (Mutesa II, 1967: 36). A period of competitive evangelisation ensued, with rival crash-courses in literacy. To this day the collective noun in Ganda for Christians is the same as that for 'readers'. Under Mwanga, who succeeded in 1884, they were resisted hard. Ham Mukasa, a founding father of Ugandan literature who was later to become a revered public figure, recalled an incident from his youth:

> One day as I was going to see my friend, a Roman Catholic named Fuke who lived at a place called Kitebe, as I left the house I heard him grumbling that so many people had learned to read. On the very next day I heard that the King had caught about 80 of the readers and many of them had been put to death.
>
> (Mullins, 1904: 183)

Mackay, the Protestant engineer, had soon reduced Ganda to his own system of Romanised typography. He personally maintained an Albion

Press, manufactured by Frederick Ulmer of London and installed by him at Natete, for which he cut wooden characters with his own hand (Yule, n.d.: 131). By 1887 he had turned out St Matthew's gospel on it, done from the Greek. Twenty years later, not to be surpassed, the White Fathers set up their own press at their Junior Seminary at Bukalasa, later moving it to Kisubi. To 'counter the influence of the Protestant presses' (Page, 2008) they launched the periodical *Munno*, typeset in their very own Ganda spelling, also Roman-based. Soon, in a masterly internal balancing act, Buganda possessed two *katikiros* or Chief Ministers – a Catholic and a Protestant – two different translations of St Matthew, and two scripts for the national language. Bodies of competing literature began to appear in each. The sectarian-based writing systems were not to be reconciled until 1947.

In the Gold Coast meanwhile the Methodists, installed at Saltpond by 1835, made early noises about translating the scriptures into local Fante, employing a version of the Roman script supplemented with additional characters for unfamiliar vowels and diphthongs. Fante is a member of the Akan language group, quite as variegated as Yoruba or Igbo, ranging from Nzima in the far west to Akwapim Twi in the east. For how many of these variants should a separate literary apparatus be provided? What system should be used and, between neighbouring dialects, where did one draw the line? In 1875 the Basel Mission at Akropong issued Christaller's uniform dictionary for both 'the Asante and Fante language' using Lepsius's system, the basis for what came to be known as the 'Old Orthography'. Unsurprisingly, Fante patriots resented being subsumed with their upcountry cousins in this abrupt manner, an insult compounded by the German lexicographer's designating both communities by the same term 'Tshi'. The ensuing fracas held up orthographic standardisation for the Akan linguistic family for over a century. Thus while the Ga, the relatively cohesive population of the capital Accra, acquired their own Bible in 1888 by obligingly embracing the Lepsius system, the Fante people, exposed to missionary activity for far longer, were not to receive a complete version of their own until 1935.

In 1927, conscious of these embarrassments, the government invited Westermann to visit the colony and propose a common way. The purpose of the exercise, it was carefully explained to the various parties involved, was to smooth the way towards a relatively homogenous local print culture, partly for the sake of aspiring authors. As explained in a pamphlet *The New Script and Its Relation to the Languages of the Gold Coast* (NAG Education Files 10/5/31), a compromise of some sort was felt to be desirable if literature was to flourish and be published at a reasonable cost, since 'if dialects are unified in spelling, a writer writes for a larger public, and is therefore encouraged to publish his work, and can produce it at a cheaper rate' (Government of the Gold Coast, 1931a: 23). The scheme ran into difficulties immediately. In 1932 the Governor announced with barely concealed irritation:

> As Professor Westermann consulted various prominent Africans before devising a common script for the Fante and Twi dialects for the Twi language, there was reason to believe that his proposals would meet with acceptance by the people. Such was not to be the case. Protests against the new script were received from the Provincial Councils, as a result of which I decided to ask them to select experts in which a separate dialect is spoken, and to submit proposals for the standardization for the dialects of the Akan language and generally with regard to the scripts to be used.
>
> (Government of the Gold Coast, 1919–57: 1932, 61–2)

Alas, the Methodists would not conform, and the Fante people, 300,000 strong, still insisted on their own script. If … Fante does not come into line with the other languages', thundered the Education Department, 'it will probably die in due course' (NAG11/606/31; Government of the Gold Coast, 1931b). Despite these pressures, alternative writing systems for the three main branches of the Akan tree – Asante, Akwapim and Fante – continued to be used side by side for over forty years. An acceptable orthography for the whole cluster was not finally agreed until the 1980s.

Undeterred or perhaps prompted by such examples, the Progressive Writers Movement of India, the literary arm of the nationalist movement, resolved in the 1930s that India should abandon its historic scripts, and universally adopt Roman for the sake of unity and mutual intelligibility, a view that they ironically shared with the architects of liberal imperialism such as Charles Edward Trevelyan (1807–86) a century before them. The writers of the 1930s, however, cherished a further, polemical intent: that their liberating and nationalist sentiments should be more readily available in printed form to all communities in India (Gopal, 2005). Their case got nowhere. To this day, India, having contented itself at Independence with a modest tidying up of Devanagari to produce so-called 'New Hindi', communicates with itself through an intricate filigree of printed and written codes. Intercommunication between them is maintained on a modest but still valuable scale through the inter-translation programme of the Sahitya Academi, established in 1954, whose publications have to date made available over 2,000 parallel versions of chosen works in the different official languages of India. In the meantime the Roman script is reserved for what the British poet W. H. Auden once called 'good, mongrel, barbarian English'.

The policing of repertoires

The distinction introduced in Chapter 2 between repertoires and texts is one that possesses a discernible connection with authority. There I suggested that in certain contexts a fluid repertory, either oral or written, is more common than definable texts that are fixed and then handed on. In the framework of our present discussion, we should now be able to perceive that a text is a repertoire that has been edited, or one might say policed.

Again, it would be tempting to account for this difference through the vicissitudes, or perhaps the inexorable logic, of cultural history, as if the inception of the editorial function coincided with the introduction of script, or else of print. Varieties of this doctrine have been advanced by McLuhan, Ong and Eisenstein amongst others, though somewhat against the evidential grain. In fact control or flexibility in varying degrees have been, and are, characteristic of all communicative dispensations, oral or scribal, on the printed page or in cyberspace. The balance in all cases depends less on prevailing 'technologies of the intellect' than on realities of social power, on cherished views of authentication, and on the varying ways in which societies choose to embody the prerogative of individual choice.

Oral repertoires are manifestly both stable and unstable. The apparent permanence of many of their imaginative productions is, it is generally now agreed, the result of memory and repetition acting as guarantors of continuity. Homeric epic abounds in phrasal formulae that assist memorisation, and probably served as buttresses against verbal mutation in the centuries before this much-prized repertory was consigned to writing. Much the same may be asserted of the *Rig Vega*, of the *Ramayana* (which, in contrast to the *Mahabharata*, appears to have been conveyed by word of mouth long before it submitted to the pen), of the *Puranas*, and of much of the *orature* of ancient India. A high proportion of this, whether didactic, mythic, scientific or therapeutic, took the form of verse, a widely recognised mnemonic. It was in verse that it was then written down, though it was the oral backdrop that was widely believed to render it authoritative. The reason was that the formulaic nature of oral performance had – or was believed to have – served as a breakwater against error. To that extent at least, oral artists acted, and act, as their own editors and watchdogs.

Their vested interests, however, have not always lain in the direction of fixity. Ruth Finnegan (1970: 96–7) describes the panegyric activities of the griots of the Mandinke and related communities in Senegambia. Entrusted with the retention of long genealogies, they would deliver these pedigrees before the powerful and affluent in swelling paeans of praise, and in expectation of financial reward. Should their expectations be unrealised, however, they would readily extend their performances, adding a moiety of vituperation that rose in intensity until proper remuneration was forthcoming. Nor was their opportunism unique. Shakespeare's Feste, an able stand-up comic, practised much the same custom: he praised and blamed in proportion to his wages. Griots and clowns have this in common: holy pariahs, their stigma confers on them an ability both to flatter and to wound. As Finnegan remarks of her griots (97), both are 'set apart from those to whom they addressed themselves and not unexpectedly met with a somewhat ambiguous attitude among members of society – at once feared, despised and influential'. The transvestite artistes who ply the trains of contemporary India have much the same effect. Their repertoires are bargaining procedures, their weapons gratification or else humiliation. In southern Africa the same may be observed of praise-singers among the Sotho (Daniel Kunene, 1971; Hodza, 1979) or the Zulu (Mazisi Kunene, 1970, 1979); in West Africa to some extent, it may be asserted of the male and female *henos* of the Ewe people of Togo and eastern Ghana. Their poetry is both pre-prepared and occasional: they edit on the hoof. Nor is this tradition dwindling. Several Ghanaian poets active in the twenty-first century are from an Ewe background and are in effect *henos* of the book. Kofi Anyidoho, from Wheta in the Volta region, both publishes and records his poetry. Like his countryman, the slightly older Kofi Awoonor, he thus straddles the theoretical divide between the literary and the oral. Awoonor, adapting an indigenous tradition of improvised invective even in some of his English-language verse, has not baulked at airing his very own humorous 'Songs of Abuse' – published though displaying all the vigour of live vituperation – in the flagrant shop-window of print (Awoonor, 1973). The all-important differences, of course, are that as readers we cannot observe the embarrassed or resentful reactions of those traduced, nor, just as long as a printed 'edition' lasts, can the author adjust his praise or insults in response.

Scribes of all cultures are similarly torn: possessed of a seemingly enhanced editorial prerogative, in practice they often look to the spoken tradition for legitimisation of what they write down. The Christian gospels were conveyed by word of mouth for several generations before being entrusted to papyrus, where the effort was to recapture faithfully what had once been told (Streeter, 1924). In much the same way, the *grantha* of pre-modern India, whether in Sanskrit or the vernaculars of the vulgates, frequently harked back to oral originals believed to have been consistent in form and wording and thus, potentially at least, in 'text'. Manifestly, with the growth of the written domain, a marked potential existed for newly codifying what had been, and was still being, spoken aloud. In practice, during the vernacular revolution of the early second millennium CE, exactly the opposite seems to have occurred in India. Released from the hegemony of Sanskrit by the proliferation of regional scripts and newly authenticated literary codes, the scribes of the period revelled in their freedom. They diversified what they had inherited, introducing episodes adapted to the tastes of local readerships, many being unrecognisable elsewhere. Thus the Oriya-medium *Mahabharata* of Sarala Das elaborates in versatile fashion on the putative Sanskrit original of its purported author, Vyasa. Nor has variation stopped there, since, as Sumanyu Satpathy (2005) explains, 'several palm-leaf manuscripts of [Sarala's] text exist in thousands of households, and many printed versions of these are available in the book market'. Equivalent cases of regional, and scripted, adaptations of the oral classics may be recounted all over South Asia. The transformations involved in this divagating domestication of a common narrative stock proved far more extreme than the phenomenon in medieval Europe to which Eisenstein has given the name 'textual drift'. In India, drift was irrigation, as work after ancestral work was diverted towards local fields of receptivity through the industrious input of copyists. Thus oral 'texts' turned into written 'repertoires', at the hands of local elites.

The press could also be ambivalent in its effects. Karmakara's technological adaptation of calligraphy to the purposes of a print culture might be seen as the turning of the tide, though in practice it benefited mainly the lifeguards. With print arrived a certain anxiety stemming from an increment in distribution and, with it, perceived dangers of multiple textual erosion. The watchmen sat up in fear. In Pune, as we have already seen, the one-time mathematician V. S. Sukhankhar headed a team of custodians minding over the *Mahabharata*, whose apparent textual integrity they were determined to ensure. For them the diversifying influence of the vulgates spelled not variety but corruption, whose malign influence they were resolved to dispel with iron editorial fist. They spoke not of standardisation – their true endeavour – but of the 'restoration' of what had once been whole. Regularisation of volume two, the *Sabhā-parvan*, for instance was part-entrusted to a classically trained American, Franklin E. Edgerton of Yale, who thought that he had discovered a reference to Rome in its second line. Of the forty manuscripts collated from a range of local sources, seven contradicted this reading. But, as Edgerton carefully explained, with due deference to his director, 'six of these are very inferior manuscripts of the vulgate devanagari recension which in my experience (confirming Sukhankhar's) has shown to have very minor value for the reconstruction. (The seventh is a Ms of the Kashmirian recension K2, which has obviously been contaminated from a vulgate source.)' (Edgerton, 1938: 262). So out the variants went, and Rome was once more victorious.

Once the notion got about that local variation spelled corruption and the textual wholeness might be restored through intervention, there was no stopping the pandits. In Benares in the 1980s a committee of Brahmins, the Kashi Raj Trust, met over an equivalent task: the publication through the sifting of all local variants of an 'authorised version' of the *Garuda Purana*, another of Vyasa's supposed works, concerning that most intimate of concerns for Benares citizens: mortuary rites. Their 'scientific' deliberations appealed to a great number of sources both oral and written, since if tradition honoured *shastrik* – that is the heritage of Sanskrit documents – it had also to take into account *sruti*, that which had faithfully been retained through verbal repetition. The committee was also prepared to consider such embellishments as certain of their own members might voluntarily propose, since to do so would be to draw on just the sort of retrieval from spontaneous memory the convention of *sruti* required. The resulting 'authorized version' was thus to a high degree paradoxical, especially as the existing redactions of the work, once collected, proved to have very little in common. As the anthropologist Jonathan Parry was to remark of the work-in-progress:

> What we have, then, is an attempt to restore something that probably never existed. Yet for the Brahmin Pandits it is a matter of faith that it did exist, and that it was actually composed by Vyasa whom they regard as an historical individual rather than as a generalized symbol of tradition. In other words, the whole apparatus of the critical edition is directed ... to the essentially religious purpose of recovering as nearly as possible the divine inspiration of a purely mythical character. The objective result, however, is a completely new recension of the work.
>
> (Parry, 1985: 213)

What appears to have occurred in both these instances is a conspiracy between a particular technology and a particular myth, though a myth in Roland Barthes's sense of the word: an enabling social perception rather than something merely untrue. We might call it the Myth of the Text. Both the Pune team and the Benares Brahmins were working on myriadic repertoires of expression supposedly once composed by the same author, and both were attempting to haul them into a seamless verbal net. In this laudable project they were energised by notions of textual integrity stemming partly from ancestral notions of divine authority, and partly from traditions of textual scholarship bred by the very print culture that would later enable them to replicate their findings. Thus print, or print-based scholarship, may distil a 'text' from out of its raw materials, like rum from crude molasses. With the help of the press, it may then reproduce the same endlessly, in neatly labelled bottles.

A text under these circumstances is, therefore, a bottle for processed repertoires. For it to attain widespread currency, however, a third element is required: an exam-regulated academic system. This is less of a modern phenomenon than is sometimes believed. The Manchu emperors, who were

obsessed by exams, instituted regular editorial authorisations of China's volu-
minous printed literature, accompanied by purges of undesirable reading
matter conducted in a spirit of censorship, a subject to which we shall turn
presently. The most celebrated was the edict of 2 February 1772 CE by which
the Emperor Ch'ien-lung caused 10,680 printed titles to be listed in a grand
catalogue comprising four 'treasuries' or subject areas (classics, history, philosophy and *belles lettres*). Of these, the 3,593 most acceptable were then recopied
by hand into 36,500 *chuan* or bound volumes, with the imprimatur of the
Hardin Academy, or Forest of Quills (Guy, 1987: 5). The interesting difference here, however, was that it was the woodblock-printed books that varied;
once an orthodox version was selected, it was carefully written down.

The latterday Manchus of imperial India enjoyed a similar turn of mind.
Not content with producing edited texts and translations of the ancient
Indian classics, they turned their attention next to Macaulay's pet, English
literature. Unavailable as a subject in the British university system until the
1890s, this was first examined formally in entrance examinations for the
Indian Civil Service in the 1870s, and then reimported back into England.
The examiners examined the students, who in turn examined the texts. For
this protocol to work, texts were necessary that were uniform enough to be
examined by both. Thus there arose texts that were set in a double sense:
by the syllabus, but also as jelly or molten metal is set, that is in stable and
immutable shapes.

Over the later years of the nineteenth century substantial publishing
emporia arose, in India and later in Africa, to service this bureaucracy-
driven need. Metropolitan companies of the ilk of Macmillan (from 1886),
Longman (from 1890) and Oxford University Press (from 1913) set up
branches in the colonies largely to supply edited 'textbooks', together with
'readers' or linguistic graded anthologies culled from the same standardised
fare. The development coincided with an anxiety over – and elaboration
of – copyright designed to safeguard the integrity of 'texts', and with it the
rights, including royalty payments, of authors and their affiliates. At the same
time, a multitude of local enterprises set up shop in places such as Dakha in
eastern Bengal to provide school texts, including 'set' texts of the British or
Indian classics, together with an accompaniment of scholia, commentaries,
cribs and cribs upon cribs (Mamoon, 2006). Nor has this business in the
least abated. In present-day South Asia several firms make a decent living
catering for this very market. Around the purlieus of Calcutta University, or
outside the gates of neighbouring Presidency College, may still be found a
cluster of minor *al fresco* outlets such as the 'Success Book Stall' or the 'Binoy
Book Stall' selling sets of past question papers for the entrance examination
to the West Bengal Civil Service, in which *babus* of the twenty-first century
are invited to answer multiple-choice questions such as:

Paragal Khan helped in bringing the first ever Bengali translation of:
(a) Ramanayan
(b) Mahabharat
(c) Upanishad
(d) Brahma Sutra

At the same time firms such as Worldview in Delhi, or Wilco in Mumbai, survive almost entirely by producing, for the student and general market, editions of English-language classics, many of them 'set texts' provided with helpful, and examination-driven, notes.

As Europhone literatures from relevant parts of the world came into being, they too were drawn into the educational nexus. No body of writing in human history has made it so rapidly from publisher's specimen to examiner's rubric as the 'postcolonial literature' of the late twentieth and early twenty-first centuries. In some cases the interval involved has been a few months. This is partly a matter of fashion, but it has also been a product of a well-intentioned alliance between publishers, lecturers, teachers and educational administrators. Among the high-profile instances has been the African Writers series marketed throughout Africa and elsewhere by Heinemann Educational Books between 1962 and 2003. The series was a paperback operation, which cleverly duplicated the orange covers of Penguin fiction for its mostly brand-new titles to suggest an instant classic appeal. Promoted as quality literature, these books were none the less marketed as textbooks with a standard educational discount of 15 per cent (Currey, 2003). A close eye was kept throughout on the needs of colleges and schools. The *entente* was a natural one, since the salad days of the series coincided with the accession to independence of a procession of former British colonies, and the recently Africanised ministries of education in nation-states such as Zambia or Tanzania were naturally keen to indigenise their syllabi, including their literature courses. Many leaped at the chance of adopting newly outdoored African authors and 'texts'. As the archives of the series at the University of Reading confirm, many of its eventual 365 titles were snapped up by an eager examination system, almost as soon as they were published.

7 Licensed snoopers and literary protestors

Policing the text

The Emperor Ch'ien-lung was an imperialist of sorts, though his empire was a very old one. The emperors of China had sought to monitor literary expression and production for a very long time, and there had been a sequence of purges going back to the tenth century. What was remarkable about Ch'ien-lung's exercise was its thoroughness. There seems to have been a double purpose in view. Rulers situated in the fastness of Peking wished to know what opinions and views were being voiced through the vastness of their dominions, so they sought to gather in, and to store, evidence of such widespread self-expression. But they also wished to sift the results, and to root out everything that called their administration into question. Not content with destroying copies of any subversive material, they wanted to eliminate the sources of that contagion. In the early days of xylography this was easily achieved by publicly burning the offending woodblocks. Later on, they attempted to discipline and punish the individuals concerned in the dissemination of offensive publications. What seems to have worried the imperial Chinese authorities in fact was not so much the existence of subversive literature as its duplication.

Censorship, book registration, copyright regulations and the like are all ways of controlling the seemingly unlimited potential for dissemination unleashed by proliferating technologies. There is little sign, however, that such methods control the flow of literature itself; indeed they often produce the countervailing effect of diverting that flow into ever more vigorous – if occasionally more circuitous – channels. Repression – a mode of resistance to promiscuous communication – provokes the reactive form of counter-resistance known as protest, and with it further efforts at control, in widening cycles of confrontation. In this chapter I will be examining the configurations of such friction across South Asia and southern Africa. Readers sometimes wonder why so much postcolonial literature to date has been adversarial in tone. The contents of the present chapter may go some way towards explaining why this has been the case.

The dread of free diffusion

Even as the Emperor Ch'ien-lung was pursuing his literary inquisition in Peking, similar developments were afoot in India. Two categories of print-monger proved especially abhorrent to the early government of British Bengal: missionaries and journalists. From the standpoint of the twenty-first century it may seem ironical that one was then regarded as being as dangerous as the other. To understand this attitude, it is necessary to bypass the intervening consensus of the Victorian age and enter the mindset of the late Enlightenment. Christianity was viewed as a stabilising factor in eighteenth-century England because it was traditional, and sealed the social order. To men like Wilkins and Hastings (and initially to Halhed as well, though he was later to convert to a millenarian form of Christianity), it appeared that in India the equivalent pacifying role was most credibly performed by the culture's own religions: Hinduism, Jainism, Islam. By inducing conversions and introducing the Bible, missionaries were, it was feared, likely to deracinate the prevailing system. Thus they stood accused in September 1807 of 'issuing publications ... of a nature offensive to the prejudices of the natives, or directed to the object of converting them to Christianity' (Priolkar, 1958: 112) The East India Company dealt with this menace initially by banishing the missions to places like Serampore that were beyond British administration; later by restricting their activities to religion and education. Journalists posed a far tougher challenge. Indeed, they were to prove a thorn in the flesh of successive administrations right up to independence, and well beyond.

No sooner had newspaper editors set up shop in Calcutta than the civil authorities moved to control them. Habituated to regarding newspapers as a menace – an impression strengthened in official minds by the gagging in Britain of such organs as John Wilkes's *North Briton* (1762–5) – the East India Company was rapidly on its guard against sedition. Indeed the very ubiquity of printed matter – its ability to materialise in different places at one time, to be absorbed by the many who could read or listen – represented a state of affairs relatively new to the Indian context that itself gave rise to disquiet. Two years after James Augustus Hickey had founded his two-page weekly *Bengal Gazette* in Calcutta in 1779 – the first English-language peri-odical in India – he was arrested and fined for exposing corruption among Company officials. In London his revelations would eventually contribute to the impeachment of Warren Hastings. In Calcutta meanwhile Hickey was again prosecuted the very next year, his press was confiscated, and he served a prison sentence of nineteen months. Charles Bruce, who launched the *Asiatic Mirror* in the same city in 1791, fared little better. After castigating the administration of Lord Wellesley, Governor-General from 1797, he was branded by his Lordship a 'hazard'. 'If you cannot tranquillize the editors of this and other mischievous publications', fumed Wellesley to his deputy shortly before leaving on a tour of Madras, 'be so good as to suppress these papers by force, and send the persons to Europe' (Marshman, 1859: 119).

Information-gathering proved especially sensitive during the governor-generalship of Lord Minto (1807–13). In between acquiring Mauritius and Singapore, his Lordship grew nervous that the newspapers might scupper his plans for outflanking the Russians and French in Afghanistan. At this period, lamented J. M. Kaye in his *Life and Opinions of Charles Lord Metcalfe*, 'the dread of the free diffusion of knowledge became a chronic disease, which was continually affecting the members of the government with hypochrondrical day-fears and night-mares in which visions of the Printing Press and the Bible were ever making their flesh to creep and their hair to stand erect with horror' (Priolkar, 1958: 247). Curbs on press freedom were therefore imposed in 1810, though relaxed in August 1816 by Minto's successor Lord Hastings, who held a comparatively enlightened attitude towards the press. With the turning of the tide in favour of Evangelical Christianity in the 1810s, missionaries were suddenly let off the hook. However, when the *Calcutta Journal* pilloried the appointment of a personal favourite as garrison chaplain in February 1823, pressure again mounted for further restrictions on newspapers. It resulted in Press Acts in both Calcutta and Bombay, requiring affidavits from all editors swearing to their loyalty and good behaviour.

The following year, and 6,000 miles away on the Cape of Good Hope, the Scottish poet William Pringle (1789–1834), an associate of Sir Walter Scott and later a campaigner against slavery, found himself in deep trouble. Pringle is sometimes regarded as a pioneer of South African poetry, though during his stay in the country he suffered very ill luck. Arriving as one of the English settlers in Albany (now the Eastern Cape) in 1820, Pringle found his way to Cape Town, where, eating one evening at the table of the die-hard Tory Lieutenant-Governor Sir Charles Somerset, he was praised by a fellow diner as 'a good Staunch Whigg' (Pringle, 1973: 65). This description did not endear him to the governor, who appreciated neither his views nor his verse. When in January 1824 he and the printer George Grieg started a newspaper, the *South African Commercial Advertiser*, they soon ran foul of Somerset, who suppressed it after two issues. Pringle was summoned to Government House, where Somerset 'opened upon me in the following terms, "So, Sir, you are one of those who think it proper to insult me, and oppose my Government"' (ibid.). Disconsolate, Pringle and his family left for London. Grieg, though, successfully appealed and the paper started up again, but not for very long. In January 1826 P. S. Buissanne, 'late Receiver of the Land Revenue', was accused of embezzlement and ordered by Somerset to be deported. *The Times* of London covered the case, pointing out that the condemned man's place of temporary confinement was to be Robben Island – later even more notorious – 'where all the convicts are kept' (*The Times*, 25 January 1826: 3). Four months later, when the mails arrived, Grieg reprinted the article in full, whereupon by a 'Circular' dated 10 March 1827 (NLSA AC Fol/968703 CAP) the *Advertiser*'s licence to publish was once more revoked. This time, the ban was final.

Such fluctuations in the fortunes of one short-lived periodical reflect in miniature a much broader imperial picture. Anti-colonial rhetoric might like to maintain that the attitude of the authorities to dissenting opinion was uniformly unsympathetic, but in practice until fairly late in the nineteenth century, when the demands of subject populations grew more vocal, it fluctuated quite markedly. The result was a kind of concertina effect by which editors were squeezed one year and released from pressure the next. In India, for example, the acting governor, Charles Theophilus Metcalfe, Calcutta-born and a former student of Gilchrist's, proved relatively friendly to free speech. On September 15 1835 he brought the pioneering era of print censorship in South Asia to a close by repealing the existing Press Acts at one impressive stroke (Priolkar, 1958: 127). Somerset's draconian measures in South Africa were repealed the very same year, paving the way for what was to become a distinctively liberal Cape Colony tradition.

Thus far, in any case, the authorities had concerned themselves exclusively with the printing and dissemination of material in English. Increasingly from mid-century on, however, publishing in India was to entail both the English-medium and the vernacular-medium press, two constituencies into which the print industry was increasingly to be divided, in Africa as well as India. It was not long in South Asia before the second would dwarf the first in diversity and scale. Official reactions to this development were mixed at first. Officially there was a recognition that cognisance should be taken of the energetic vernacular sector; in practice any such initiatives ran foul of the absence of a proper system of enforcement, and of an increasing indifference to writing in local languages among government circles, where the tide had long since turned against orientalism.

Besides, it was widely recognised that monitoring literary output throughout an expanding imperium would be a Sisyphean undertaking. Copyright in the empire, for example, was almost non-existent before the late 1830s. In January 1806 the Asiatic Society of Bengal had contacted their representative in London to ask whether their publications – specifically their journal *Asiatick Researches* – might be protected from piracy as all British books and journals were, by being entered at Stationer's Hall. He replied that such a move, while feasible, would be 'wholly ineffective … Nothing less than printing from the manuscript in England would guard against unauthorised impressions' (Nair, 1995–2000, ii: 783–4). From the 1830s onwards the East India Company accordingly took desultory steps to assume for the subcontinent the responsibilities that the Stationer's Company had long exercised in Britain. Thus in February 1837 we find the company insisting that copies of any book published in an Indian language be deposited in its library in London. This was followed by successive Copyright Acts in 1842 and 1847. The mechanism for managing the literary scene therefore existed, but it was very casually deployed until pressing political events highlighted its necessity.

Protest phase one: the *Nil Darpan* affair

Indeed until 1860 book registration was by and large voluntary, and sedition where it existed was subject to very haphazard redress: a state of affairs vividly illustrated that very year by a *cause célèbre* in rural Bengal. For several decades concern had been expressed over working conditions in the indigo-growing industry. It was a staple trade, but an unhealthy one, and the side-effects on the eco-system and social fabric were dire. After culling, the crop was matured in large open trenches where it was shredded on treadmills by poorly paid husbandmen or *ryots*, whose lands had often been requisitioned to make room for the businesses for which they were now obliged to work. But in 1860 in the district of Champaran, a mission-boy turned postmaster, Dinabandhu Mintra (1830–73) wrote *Nil Darpan*, a five-act play whose Bangla title literally translates as *The Indigo-Planting Mirror* (that is, the indigo industry held up as a glass to social injustice). Its protagonist Goluk Chunder Basu is arrested for complaining against land sequestration and hanged in prison. His tormentors are resident British indigo planters rather than the colonial order a whole; nor was the play ever interpreted in general as an anti-colonial work. As a District Officer called in to investigate the incident is made to remark, 'Now the ryots say to each other "All bamboos are of one tuft, but of one is made the fan of the Goddess Durgah, and of another the sweeper's basket"' (Mintra, 1861: 69). Missionaries and planters, in other words, are of the same stock, but of a very different turn of mind. The second group got very short shrift. When at the play's eventual performance an enraged member of the audience, Iswar Chandra Vidyasagar, threw a shoe at the factory manager, the actor playing the part caught it in mid-air and salaamed.

But alarm bells were ringing at Government House, and the secretary to the Bengal Government, Seton-Carr, asked for a translation to be prepared and printed. The playwright contacted his friend and former teacher James Long, a noted defender of press freedom and author the previous year of a *Report on the Native Press in Bengal*, who undertook to see it through the press. A translation was commissioned from the pandit Michael Mudhusudan

Datt, and 500 copies were run off with the government seal, some of which were sent to the newspapers and others to the planters' organisation, the Landowners' and Commercial Association. The planters were not pleased. Taking action against the printer on two counts, they succeeded in obtaining judgment against Long, who, despite the vocal protests of his mission and other supporters, was gaoled for twelve months. Seton-Carr was sacked.

The official correspondence relating to this case is held in the National Archives of India (NAI June–August 1861, Pub 34A–12B) and it makes rewarding reading. At no point, it seems, was serious consideration given to banning the play or the book, or to prosecuting the author, the translator or indeed the theatre management. Nor did the means for taking these steps exist at that date. The sole recourse of the planters was to the common law of libel, appropriately enough as it happens, since sedition as such did not concern them (it was they and not the government, after all, who had been maligned) so much as the tarnishing of their good name in the eyes of the business fraternity and the Anglo-Indian community in general. Seton-Carr had exceeded his brief, and botched the entire operation. Long the liber-tarian had simply broken ranks.

As Partha Chatterjee (2003: 22–5) has remarked in a recent discussion of the *Nil Darpan* affair, the whole case had reeked of double standards, a point made nearer the time by George Cotton (1813–66), Anglican Bishop of Calcutta, former public school headmaster and known humorist. Possibly, opined the bishop, the publication of the play had been libellous:

> But we must say that, as this is the case, it is very fortunate for Mr Dickens that Yorkshire schoolmasters, Chancery barristers, clerks in government offices, and masters of workhouses did not know that this was the state of the law when he published his various tales directed against their real or reputed malpractices. The planters of *Nil Darpan* are certainly not worse than Mr Squeers, and the twists and intricacies and delays of Chancery are represented in another novel [*Bleak House*] to be no less fatal to the happiness and sanity of suitors than Indigo advances, according to *Nil Darpan*, are to the welfare of the *ryots*.
>
> (Long, 1861: 5)

The age of surveillance

The cataclysmic event that was to transform official attitudes had in fact occurred some three years earlier. The Sepoy Rising of 1857–8 was to have a deep and long-lasting effect both on the practice of governance in colonial India, and on its underlying logic. As Chris Bayly has effectively demonstrated (1996, *passim*), the revolt had unearthed an extensive informal network of local communications of which the authorities had been largely unaware. Such obliviousness was not to last for long. Within twenty years a system for the registration of books and newspapers, tighter copyright rules, provisions for the censoring of stage and page and fines for infringement had all been put in place, amounting overall to a comprehensive network of literary surveillance.

By far the most comprehensive and far-reaching of these measures was the promulgation, as Act XLV of 1860, of the Indian Penal Code. This vast body of law affected every sector of Indian life: the coinage, rules of evidence, 'rash driving on a public way', assault, slavery, prostitution, even (in Article 377) the first legal prohibition against homosexuality in India, a law incidentally still in force. Few of these provisions dealt with literature directly, but several could be cited to silence an aberrant publication. Under 'Of Offences against the Public Tranquillity', for example, Section 153 outlawed behaviour likely to cause a riot, while Section 292 outlawed the sale of obscene books, and Section 293 forbad readers from possessing one (except 'for any religious purpose', a sub-clause which legitimised, say, the *Kama Sutra*). In the next few decades a series of amendments tightened the net, notably 124A, added in 1870, which defined sedition. These provisions were to remain on the statute book for generations, eventually to be incorporated into the legal systems of the independent nations severally carved out of the body of colonial India, entering by this means the penal codes of free India and Pakistan (in 1947) and Bangladesh (in 1971). In a number of recent high-profile cases of censorship in these countries, the relevant articles in this inherited century-and-a-half-old body of colonial law have continued to be invoked.

The underlying logic behind the code was as revolutionary as any of its single provisions. Hitherto, as we have seen, governance in the colony had taken the form of managing competing interest groups – the civil service, the planters, the missionaries, a vast and varied population – and addressing grievances arising amongst them. Henceforward resolves were to be made in the name of the imperial system as a whole, regarded as vested in the institutions of the Raj. From now on indeed it was possible to argue within a given colony that an individual threat from a given source compromised the body politic as a whole. Hence was born the rationale of corporate responsibility or collective security in support of which successive colonial regimes – and, following them, successive national governments – have seen fit to intervene in literary expression, as in other spheres. The survival of this logic of supervision from colonial governments to the national states of our own world represents one of the starkest instances of continuity in twentieth-century history.

It is possible to argue that the increasing regimentation of the book trade also played a role in this general tightening of surveillance. The first inkling of change in that direction occurred in a letter of 1863 from the Asiatic Society of London, forwarded to Bengal by Charles Wood, then Secretary of State for India (a post which had then existed for a mere five years):

> It is doubtless well known to you that, of late years, the Hindus have shown great literary activity, partly by editing numerous texts of their ancient literature, partly by translating English and Sanskrit books into the vernacular dialects, and partly by producing original compositions of a political, scientific, and religious character. But, though these books are very numerous, and in many respects important, and though they have an extensive circulation among the natives of India, only a very inconsiderable portion of them is at present accessible to European scholars, and the knowledge of these few is in most instances due to chance, or to the goodwill of disinterested persons residing in India. It is unnecessary for us to dwell on the serious hindrance which has arisen from this circumstance to a proper appreciation of the actual condition of India and its inhabitants, equally from a scientific as from a political point of view; and to some degree we may add to the proper administration of the country itself. Frequent attempts have indeed been made by scholars and booksellers in this country to remove the impediment, but they have proved altogether unavailing. It is, therefore, our conviction that there is here an urgent necessity for the *authoritarian assistance* of the government, and that *by this means alone*, the claims of oriental studies in England can adequately be satisfied.
>
> (NAI Home Dept 1863, no. 32, fol. 3; my italics)

The phrasing of this communication was exemplary. Here was new-style inquisitiveness masquerading as old-style orientalist learning. The surface text implied 'We are scholars and gentlemen; we need to scrutinise more carefully our sources.' The sub-text whispered 'If you want to keep these chaps in order, with respect, sir, you need to learn a little more about them.' On both levels, the message enjoined, 'Listen in!'

The measure that resulted from this initiative, Act XXV of 1867, known as the Press and Book Registration Act, implemented the recommendations of the Asiatic Society almost to the letter, even adopting the very pro-forma for the registration by publishers of titles that the Society had laid out in their memo. Its purport and effects have, however, been the cause of some disagreement among book historians. Robert Darnton, for example (2001), is in little doubt that the intention was to monitor self-expression in delayed reaction to the Rising. Priya Joshi by contrast comments 'the temptation to cry censorship is strong, except that the job of summarizing was often left to Indian scribes, who either through blindness or insight provided notably bland abstracts for volumes that were in fact marked by their anticolonial sentiments' (2002a: 49). The fairest decision between these viewpoints is that Joshi is by and large correct about provisions for book registration, while Darnton's approach proves to be far more relevant to the scrutiny and selective translation of vernacular newspapers that went on at the same time, reaching fever pitch at moments of national crisis, such as that ensuing in 1905–6 from the temporary partition of Bengal, the subsequent press campaigns, riots and famine (Fraser, 2007b). In the National Archives in Delhi, the *Reports on Native Newspapers* for the several provinces of imperial India fill one very large room.

The more important fact is that all of these measures, widely imitated throughout the empire, provided a basic framework onto which makeshift extensions could be added at times of emergency (Barrier, 1974). In 1876 a Dramatic Performances Act banned plays of 'a scandalous and defamatory nature' and ones 'likely to cause disaffection to the government' or to 'deprave or corrupt'. Following the establishment of the Indian National Congress in Bombay in 1885, anxieties markedly increased in the subcontinent. Four years later the anti-rioting clause in the Penal Code was extended to include any fostering of inter-communal resentments. After a series of attacks on governmental officials in 1907–9 an Indian Press Bill of 4 February 1910 required all newspapers registered under the 1867 Act to deposit a security of 5,000 rupees, to be forfeited on the publication of any 'objectionable matter'; troublesome periodicals could now be silenced, and a specific clause strengthened an existing provision in the Post Office Act for the seizure of suspect publications at ports of entry. At the same time, a circular to schools prohibited 'crude teachings' on the deleterious effects of Crown rule.

Protest phase two: literature and nation

As we enter the modern period, the interplay between suppression of opinion and articulate protest becomes increasingly plain. The literature of societies in transition towards independence came to be orchestrated by a reiterative counterpoint in which laws were framed specifically to prevent forms of articulation that promptly rose to challenge them. Literary culture as a result came to be shaped, and sometimes narrowed, by a desire to speak the unspeakable, a process realised more frequently in political terms than in those of personal morality, though in practice the two were often linked. Within this vast and convoluted field of interaction I intend briefly to compare five contrasted regional or cross-regional histories that, chronologically speaking, run almost end-to-end. The first concerns the standoff between the authorities of the British Raj and the intelligentsia of India between 1900 and independence in 1947; the second the complicated application of censorship laws in South Africa during the years of apartheid (1948–1994). The third involves the colonial repercussions of the *Lady Chatterley* trial of the early 1960s; the fourth the perpetuation of colonial censorship provisions in postcolonial Africa. The fifth and last is the Salman Rushdie affair.

In early twentieth-century India, the stress on collective responsibility in successive amendments to the Penal Code provoked a countervailing flood of texts in the vernacular, less frequently in English, expressive of a popular national will. The Press Act of 1910 was largely used to control newspapers, a measure easily achieved by strengthening penalties provided for by the Registration Act of 1867. It also, however, netted a shoal of suspect literary publications: from political verse like *Svadesa kavya* of 1922, a Bengali anthology celebrating Hindu identity and castigating the colonial government, to harangues like *Panjaba ka khuna, va hatyare Dayara ki karatuta* (The Blood of the Punjab and Murderous Dyer's Deed) of 1923 protesting in Hindi against the massacre that year of 379 civilians in the Jallianwalla Bagh in Amritsar. Much of this literature addressed local emergencies and needs, often viewed as grist to the mill of a nationalist cause. A certain amount of this polemic, however, was undoubtedly inter-communal, and as such prophetic of tensions that have arisen in 1947 and since. When in the 1920s the Muslim-owned newspaper *Paigham-i-Sulah* accused the Hindu pantheon of loose morals, the Anrya Saraj cleric Pandit Kalicharan replied with a pamphlet entitled *Vichitra Jivan* claiming that the Prophet himself had been no paragon of virtue. Both were prosecuted. A Muslim favourite was to criticise the Hindu institution of the sacred cow, but Jains and Christians were also targets from all sides. All these fell foul of section 153A forbidding the stirring up of sectarian hatred (Jones, 2001: 1170–1). As we shall see, this was the very provision that, absorbed into postcolonial law, was later to be invoked against Salman Rushdie's reputedly anti-Qur'anic novel *The Satanic Verses* (1987).

The government strove to dampen such passions, and at the same time to stem the tide of controversial material flooding in from abroad. Sikh communities along the west coast of America were a ready source of propaganda; in 1915 copies of the San Francisco-printed and Punjabi-language *Ghadara di gunja: Desha bhagatam di bani* (The Thunder of Rebellion: The Voice of Those Who Love Their Country) were seized, some aboard an ocean-going vessel bound for Canada, others from a Sikh battalion re-entering the Punjab bent on an uprising (BL PP Panj D13). English-language publications were likewise watched, sometimes on superficial pretexts. The fact that the compassionate social novels of the Peshawar-born Marxist Mulk Raj Anand were issued in London by the left-leaning publisher John Wishart was enough to place them on a list of material confiscated by customs at any port of entry (Barrier, 1974: 126). Prominent among them was *Untouchable*, Anand's book of 1935, remodelled and simplified on the advice of Gandhi, depicting a day in the life of a latrine cleaner blighted by caste. Soon Gandhi's own works were proscribed, notably *Quit India*, the transcript of a speech made to the Indian National Congress on 8 August 1942 in opposition to the war and demanding prompt British withdrawal (OIOC MSS Europ D 670/7). The Second World War, naturally, produced a crunch-point in India. The pamphlets and posters of the Indian Nationalist Army, recruited by Subhas Chandra Bose from prisoners of war in the Far East with the purpose of invading Bengal and setting up an independent Indian state, were naturally forfeit, as were their manifestos and even pay-books. When the constitution of India was promulgated shortly after independence in 1947, it contained a ringing declaration of freedom of speech, immediately followed by a much longer clause limiting the freedom thus proclaimed to such publications as did not imperil the sovereignty of India, or its friendly relations with other states, public order, decency or morality and did not involve contempt of court, defamation of character or incitement to an offence.

In South Africa, following the country's accession to Dominion status in 1910, a number of initiatives had been taken in the spirit of the Indian imperial codes. The Native Administration Act of 1927, for example, had contained a 'hostility' clause that authorised the government to intervene to safeguard race relations, thus paving the way for more drastic provisions of information control such as the Riotous Assemblies Act of 1930 with its clause 228A against incitement to racial hostility, and the Entertainments Act of 1931 which outlawed scenes in which Europeans mixed with non-Europeans (Jones, 2001: 2283-6). The position grew markedly more tense with the election in 1948, one year after Indian independence and much against the mainstream of developments elsewhere in the world, of an Afrikaner-dominated Nationalist government bent on the maintenance of racial supremacy and a public life conforming to the Puritanical doctrines of the Dutch Reformed (or, as satirical bystanders had it, the 'Much Deformed') Church. It is impossible to understand the literary politics of South Africa between 1948 and 1994 without appreciating the fact that throughout this difficult period it operated in essence as an internal colony (much the same may be said of Rhodesia between 1964 and 1981). The cornerstone of its information policy was the Suppression of Communism Act of 1950, empowering the government to ban suspect organisations wholesale, notable the Communist Party itself and, after 1960, the African National Congress. The provision was extended into the sphere of self-expression by the Internal Security Act, also of 1950, proscribing the propagation of opinions by members of banned organisations, and by those who attended their meetings or had fled the country to evade the new laws. In 1963 the 1931 act was broadened through the setting up of a Publications Control Board empowered to scrutinise all books and if necessary to declare them 'undesirable', and thus to ban them (van der Vlies, 2007: 56). Taken together these measures abolished most cultural activity in South Africa tending towards dissent. The poet Dennis Brutus, an ANC member, was incarcerated on Robben Island from 1963–4; on his release he quit the country, beginning a personal exile shared in the mid-sixties with Ezekiel Mphalele (in Kenya), Peter Abrahams (in Jamaica), Alfred Hutchison (in Ghana) and a gaggle of revolutionaries in London, including Bloke Mondisane, Alex la Guma and Lewis Nkosi (de Lange, 1997: 13–14). Most of these found publishers abroad, though the books they produced were subject to official scrutiny before they could be imported into, or marketed within, South Africa – a test many failed. Though more middle-of-the-road writers such as the novelist Nadine Gordimer managed to stay on and produce reputable work, to a large extent the South Africa of these years threatened to become a literary desert.

Though the laws were draconian, in practice they were modified subtly in response to changing conditions, and their mode of application was often capricious. A chorus of moral and artistic disdain abroad also made the authorities in Pretoria increasingly sensitive to accusations of philistinism. As a result a new Publications Act in 1974 allowed literary merit as a minority consideration that might under certain circumstances be invoked to outweigh majority censure (van der Vlies, 2007: 58). The not infrequent result was a cat-and-mouse game between writers, publishers and censors in which the first two continually harried the defences of the third. While some authors like Nkosi seemed perpetually to be off-limits, others such as La Guma and J. M. Coetzee frequently needed to fight their corner on an almost text-by-text basis.

La Guma was first banned, and then after 1974 progressively unbanned (van der Vlies, 2007: 56–61). Coetzee's first publishers meanwhile were Ravan, a small independent outfit with roots in Christian social activism, which was constantly on the edge of the law. On 11 January 1974 Peter Randall, the firm's director, wrote to Coetzee while putting his first novel *Dusklands* through the press, 'We are proceeding with your book as best we can in between court cases, visits from the police and other unsavoury matters' (NELM 98.8.1.1–29). The novel was never in danger, but while working on his second book, *In the Heart of the Country*, the following year Coetzee warned that it might attract the attention of the censors; he asked Ravan whether under these circumstances they would need to submit it to the Board. Randall replied that he would never do this on principle, and would be prepared to go ahead provided the text did not obviously infringe existing laws on obscenity, libel or state security. In the circumstances preparations proceeded apace, with Ravan preparing a South African edition in English and Afrikaans, and Secker and Warburg in London a British and Commonwealth edition in English only. In June 1977 the book was published, and the USA rights were sold to Harper and Row. On 19 July Ravan wrote to the author 'I am afraid that the censorship boys have already struck on *In the Heart of the Country*, and the book has been embargoed or banned, as you will know' (NELM 98.8.1.16).

By October, on a plea of merit, the ban had been lifted. Indeed considerations of excellence were often to spring to Coetzee's defence, since what the incumbent chairman of the board, the lawyer J. C. W van Rooyen, was wont to call 'the likely reader' (Coetzee, 1996: 188) of such masterpieces of understated realism was deemed to be a rarity. As Elizabeth Lowry has remarked, 'during the Apartheid years Coetzee's novels were regularly passed by the South African censors not because they did not deal with material that might be construed as critical of the state, but because their threat was thought to be ameliorated by their sheer literariness' (*London Review of Books*, 14 October 1999). This caveat did not, however, protect the personnel of Ravan itself, who were never to be entirely out of trouble. In the very month of the novel's ungagging a swath of organisations was placed under a new restraining order; in December Peter Randall himself was personally banned under the terms the 1950 Act.

His successor at Ravan, Mike Kirkwood, was highly conscious that the embargo in October that year had hobbled eighteen other organisations. However, two recent commissions, the Wiehahn and the Riekert, had questioned the application of the laws, thus creating a loophole Kirkwood was determined to exploit. The result was *Staffrider*, a magazine that deliberately courted risk from the very beginning, deriving its title from the adolescent joy-riders who regularly took their lives into their hands on the country's railway system. As the editorial to the first issue announced 'A staff rider is, let's face it, a *skelm* of sorts. Like Hermes or Mercury – the messenger of the gods in classical mythology – he is almost certainly as light-fingered as he is fleet-footed. A skilful entertainer, a bringer of messages, a useful person but … slightly disreputable. Our censors may not like him, but they should consider putting up with him.' At its height the magazine had a print-run of 10,000 and from the beginning it favoured a policy of allowing joint submissions by means of which a whole community, a township, might find a voice. Thus *Staffrider*, itself born out of protest, served in effect as a seedbed for a fresh flowering of independent publishing houses, mostly small and African-owned that, in the face of constant state repression, were to advance the cause of liberation during the 1980s. Prominent among these was Skotaville, founded in 1983 by Jaki Seroke, a former Ravan employee, and Mothobi Mutloaatse. When in September 1987 Seroke was detained under the Internal Security Act, he was replaced at the helm by Nokwanda Sithole, under whom a prize was initiated for writing in African languages. Skotaville went on to publish *Hope and Suffering* by Desmond Tutu, the large-hearted Archbishop of Cape Town. Perpetually harassed by police, it survived well into the 1990s, by which time the superstructure of apartheid censorship was tottering, finally keeling over with the enfranchisement of a full African electorate in 1994.

The argument from autonomy

Though out of synchrony with the rest of the formerly imperial world, apartheid South Africa was in one respect far from unique. Superficially it put into effect an exaggerated form of the information control imposed elsewhere in Africa immediately prior to self-rule. When challenged from overseas, however, it rapidly fell back on a species of defensive logic increasingly used by a number of freshly independent countries in Asia and Africa determined to keep their ideological houses in order. This recurrent rationale depended on a threefold logic, and it was fast becoming the fallback position of discipline-conscious states throughout the Third World. The first of its elements was the old colonial argument for collective internal security. Increasingly, however, two further strands were added to this classic plea. One was autonomy of jurisdiction, by which newly established legislatures carefully distanced themselves from enactments framed in the former metropolis. (Until 1910, after all, South Africa had been a British colony; it was not a republic until 1961.) The second, frequently related to it, was a preoccupation with autonomy of standards, by means of which many non-Western governments now sought to induce, sometimes to enforce, a literary, moral or spiritual culture suited to their own particular historical background and circumstances.

One can trace the beginnings of this logic from the early 1960s with the differential judgments reached in various jurisdictions across the world in the face of Britain's decision in 1960 to license for sale an unexpurgated paperback edition of D. H. Lawrence's novel of sexual liberation, *Lady Chatterley's Lover*. On 1 August that year David Philip, a 33-year-old South African English graduate then working for OUP in Salisbury, Rhodesia, dispatched a six-page submission to the South Rhodesian Censorship Board, of which he was then a member. The question presently before this committee was whether Lawrence's book should be allowed to go on sale in the then Central African Federation. Philip's opinion was that it should:

in setting out his reasons, he none the less let slip the causes for the Board's concern. These were subtly different from those aired at the Old Bailey:

> On the other side I fully appreciate the sincerity and the validity of the doubts that many people (including at times myself) may have about the effect of this book on our mixed community. If I have stressed positive merits more than the harmful effects that the detailed description and the four-letter words may have on young and immature people, that is because I believe that the quite considerable merits of the book, and also the author's intentions, may be lost sight of in the surprise of the subject matter.
>
> (NELM 423.1)

The novel, one need hardly add, depicts in graphic and candid terms the liaison between Constance, wife of a landed aristocrat crippled in the Great War, and her husband's gamekeeper. Anxieties had clearly been expressed that this passionate infringement of class barriers might, in the volatile circumstances of a colony on the brink of independence, be interpreted by readers as an incitement to – or at least a token of clemency towards – violation of the racial hierarchy on which that society still then rested. Such worries had been vivid enough in Central Africa in 1960, the year of the Sharpeville Massacre and the banning of the African National Congress in nearby South Africa. They did not, however, win the day in Central Africa, where the book went on sale throughout the Federation on 30 November.

Ten years earlier, matters had stood somewhat differently when the novelist Doris Lessing, who had grown up in Rhodesia, offered her recently completed *The Grass Is Singing* to several local publishers. The book described no sex, featured no expletives and was distinguished throughout by its delicate treatment of difficult subjects, especially the progressive derangement of Mary Turner, lonely wife of an unsuccessful white tobacco farmer, and her reliance on her domestic servant Moses for practical help, and possibly for emotional consolation. Mary is murdered, the servant is suspected. We never find out the exact nature of their relationship. So troubled, however, were editorial reactions to the whiff of an affair, not just on this occasion between a highly placed female and a male employee, but between European mistress and African servant, that the novel had proved impossible to publish in Southern Africa. When issued by Michael Joseph in London in 1950, it had immediately been banned in South Africa, as had its author.

The relative leniency with which Lawrence was treated, the embargo on Lessing, strongly suggest that, where hegemonies of class and race were in question, considerations of power were likely to weigh more heavily than prudishness. Indeed, many of the same concerns were to be rehearsed thirty years later when Nkosi's much-delayed novel *Mating Birds*, dealing with the purported rape of a white woman by a black man, came before the South African censors (NASA PCB P87/08/15). Once more the argument put was that the delicate state of local inter-race relations rendered publication inappropriate.

That autonomy of social and ethical standards was no parochial concern of the South African system, however, is amply illustrated by continuing international twists to the international *Lady Chatterley* saga. In 1965 New Zealand (McCleery, 2007: 200–2) licensed the paperback edition for sale, but in ways that made clear its independence from the British decision. In the India of 1964 a bogus buyer – in fact a police spy – purchased the book from one Ranjit Udechi, proprietor of the Happy Book Stall in Bombay, who was duly hauled before the courts and fined. At the appeal hearing the novelist Mulk Raj Anand appeared as a defence witness, urging much the same points about the book's quality as had been voiced by British experts at the London trial, but further arguing that despite appearances the book was morally clean, thus echoing E. M. Forster's Preface of 1935 to his own novel *Untouchable*. In a prolix and learned judgment, Justice Mohammad Hidayatullah cited Dean Swift, Dr Johnson, John Middleton Murry and J. B. Priestley, but he also invoked the aforementioned provisions of the Indian Penal Code of 1860. Blaming the book's message on the primness of Lawrence's sisters, and its coarse diction on his ignorance of Latin, he found for the prosecution, because he could discern no preponderant social gain to compensate for the novel's crossing the 'permissible limits' of 'our community standards' (*Ranjit D. Udeshi* v. *State of Maharashtra*, 19 August 1964). National 'authenticity' had won.

Elsewhere the triple logic of collective security combined with autonomy of jurisdiction and standards was soon being deployed to far more devastating effect. Most starkly, in the precarious circumstances of many of Africa's independent states, it was the writer, with his or her tireless personification of the popular will, who very often bore the brunt of political insecurity and consequent clampdowns. In 1969, despite international protests, the Nigerian playwright, poet and novelist Wole Soyinka was locked up for two years and four months by the Federal regime of General Yakubu Gowon. His crime was that at the turning-point in the Nigerian civil war of 1967–71 he attempted to negotiate between breakaway Biafra (whose secessionist cause had been espoused by Achebe) and the federal authorities in the capital Lagos, thus questioning the right of the federalists to speak for the nation as a whole. His account of his incarceration, *The Man Died*, was written between the lines of Paul Radin's *Primitive Religion* and Soyinka's own poetry collection *Idanre* (Soyinka, 1975: 9), both smuggled in by well-wishers. In the following decade the Malawian poet Jack Mapanje was exiled and later imprisoned, his misdemeanour being to question the absolute right of the country's ageing leader Dr Hastings Banda, an elder of the Church of Scotland, to unchallenged power, and his relentless control over all organs of opinion. In the 1970s and 1980s censorship in nominally free Malawi was every bit as drastic as in nearby apartheid South Africa, and, though the country's stock of creative writers was smaller, most of them were embargoed. In 1977 in Kenya, Ngugi wa Thiong'o wrote and co-produced in Gikuyu a play *Ngaahika Ndeenda* (I Will Marry When I Want), a satire on the neo-colonial antics of the then president, Arap Moi, and his plutocratic government. Imprisoned without trial in Kasimi maximum security prison, Ngugi wrote his next book, the novel *Caitaani mũtharaba-Inĩ* (Devil on the Cross), on the prison's toilet paper. In the Nigeria of the 1990s the novelist Ken Saro-Wiwa and eight others were imprisoned and finally executed for championing the communal property rights of the Ogonni people of the Delta creeks against the depredations of international petroleum corporations on whose profits, during that oil-rich decade, the prosperity and corruption of the military government depended. One year after the institution of majority rule in Zimbabwe, *Black Sunlight*, a novel by the country's most enterprising writer, Dambudzo Marechera, was banned using a censorship law inherited from Ian Smith's minority white regime (Veit-Wild, 1992: 290). In a sequel reminiscent of what was happening in South Africa at the same period, the book was then reinstated on appeal, after submissions by expert witnesses. No insult to the regime was ever intended; the only reason for suppression having been potential offence offered to the country's many Christians by the book's scatological vocabulary. In the early part of this century, during the later years of the regime of Robert Mugabe, newspapers were banned, writers driven into exile. All of these actions were overtly taken in the interests of collective national security yet, when challenged by international organisations such as Pen International, Amnesty International or *Index on Censorship*, the governments concerned regularly fell back on the supplementary rationales of autonomy of jurisdiction and autonomy of standards. These were the very arguments used in the new millennium by the government of Sudan over internal and external dissent to its policy over famine-stricken Darfur, until in July 2007 the wishes of the United Nations Security Council prevailed. These, too, were the arguments deployed by Mugabe's government against mounting pressure to step down to forestall bankruptcy in Zimbabwe. As one beleaguered minister put it, 'We do things our own way here.' Appeals to freedom of speech emanating from Western Europe were welcomed just as little as repressive measures originating from the same quarters half a century earlier. Indeed the formerly colonised were the more likely to fling the charge of hypocrisy back in the face of these do-gooder sons and daughters of former colonisers. *Plus ça change, plus c'est la même chose*. The muzzling of the national press in such countries, the stifling of writers, depended on much the same thinking.

In every one of these instances of personal muzzling, a centralised state did not hesitate to cite in support of its actions the inherited paraphernalia of colonial laws, incorporated into their constitutions at independence, sometimes with minimal change. The appeal to autonomy of standards, however, occasionally now complicated the argument, since its field of cultural applicability sometimes transcended the borders of the nation as such. Religious affiliations and taboos, in particular, proved no respecters of boundaries. In the closing years of the twentieth century a cross-national dimension thus appeared in the imposition of censorship. It is with two victims of this new dispensation, both authors of novels entitled *Shame*, that I wish to close this survey.

Messages and mullahs

Sometimes a single scene can cause trouble. At the end of book two of Salman Rushdie's novel *The Satanic Verses* the prophet Mohammed is attacked by a trio of high-flying cranes that 'fall upon him from the night sky, the three-winged creatures, Lat Uzza Manat, flapping around his head, clawing at his eyes, biting, whipping him with their hair, their wings' (Rushdie, 1988: 124). The birds are traditional female deities of the city of Mecca, *Gharaniq* in Arabic, whose intercession Mohammed has momentarily been persuaded to recognise in verses appended to the fifty-third Sura of the Qur'an, known as Al-Najm. These verses he has since expunged, persuaded they are of the devil: for this reason in the nineteenth century they were dubbed 'satanic' by the Glaswegian Islamicist, colonial servant (and head of intelligence in Agra during the Sepoy Rising), William Muir. The pecking goddesses, briefly admitted into the canon and just as rudely expelled, are outraged. 'He struggles against them, but they are faster, nimbler, winged.'

In the years following its publication Rushdie's novel gave rise to the most celebrated case of censorship of the closing years of the twentieth century. Banned in Pakistan and Bangladesh and briefly, too, in India, it provoked a *fatwa*, a judgment of exclusion and potential death sentence, against its author, delivered by the head of Iran's Shia community. It is less often realised that the novel itself deals with censorship, or perhaps with the bowdlerisation or excision of a tabooed text. Rushdie's fundamentalist enemies had attempted to shame him, but his own theme in this and other books is shame itself, or rather the textual humiliation occasionally inflicted by censors. In a novel he had written some years previously called – explicitly – *Shame*, Rushdie had defined this very quality as a wound self-inflicted by victims of social or personal outrage (Rushdie, 1983: 115–16). *Sharam* is the term in

Urdu (ibid.: 139), etymologically related to *haram*, the Arabic term for what is forbidden (or perhaps banned), a noun related in its turn to *harem*, a place most men may not enter.

Five years later in northern India, in December 1992, the 450-year-old Babri mosque in Ayodhya, southeast of Delhi, was rased to the ground by a crowd inspired by the Hindutva ideology of the reigning BJP Party, themselves purgers of history textbooks that did not reflect the viewpoint of Hindu supremacists in this nominally secular country (Sen, 2005: 62–9). The incident was followed by a number of reprisals against Hindu communities elsewhere, most poignantly against the 12 per cent of the population of Bangladesh still Hindu by affiliation, despite the abrogation of its secular constitution by a country officially Islamic since 1978.

When the novelist, liberal journalist and medical doctor Taslima Nasrin depicted some of the outrages inflicted against Hindus in Bangladesh in her novel *Lajja*, widespread disturbances and book-burnings again followed, together with a *fatwa*. The book was rapidly banned in both Bangladesh and the Indian state of West Bengal. In both instances the statute used was 153A of the Indian Penal Code of 1860, severally incorporated into the constitutions of both nation-states, a law originally framed to suppress activity that 'promotes or attempts to promote feelings of enmity or hatred between different classes of Her Majesty's Subjects'. Nasrin's case was much taken up abroad by organisations such as Pen International. When her novel was translated into English by Kankabati Datta, the title *Shame* was chosen, perhaps in deference to Rushdie's earlier book, though it is a fair translation of the Bangla word. Protests continued on both sides of the argument, and so did the bans. Unrepentant, Nasrin wrote her autobiography in several volumes, also successively banned, and turned up smiling to sign copies at the Kolkata Book Fair. Hundreds of copies were sold; asked why they were buying them, the purchasers replied that it was largely because the book was proscribed. In 1997 the English translation was reissued in London by Prometheus Books in association with the *Independent* newspaper as part of their series of banned books, alongside *Lady Chatterley's Lover* and William Burroughs's drug-filled saga *The Naked Lunch*. 'Not', cried the blurb 'since Salman Rushdie's *Satanic Verses* has a book provoked such mob violence, public outcries and calls for the author's death.'

Both of these high-profile cases demonstrate just how self-defeating a ploy it can be to muzzle a book of any description. They also, however, raise a number of issues relevant to our general argument. Though Rushdie and Nasrin's novels were quite different in subject matter and style, they clearly both chafed at a similar nerve. Rushdie's intentions were primarily comic, Nasrin's polemical; yet both in their various ways challenged particular readings of other and earlier texts: in Rushdie's case the Qur'an as literally construed, in Nasrin's case the body of Sharia law as rigorously applied. Both were judged and found offensive in certain parts of the postcolonial world, and at two different levels. First at the level of national jurisdiction, where the laws invoked to silence them were precisely those which, one and a half centuries earlier, had been introduced as measures of domestic discipline in what had then been colonial possessions. At the supra-state level, however, both were confronted by bodies of traditional law pertaining initially to pre-colonial dispensations: that is to Umma, the worldwide community of believers.

Six years before either case hit the headlines, V. S. Naipaul, British novelist of Trinidadian East Indian provenance, wrote a travelogue entitled *Among the Believers: An Islamic Journey* in which he warned that the rise of literalist Islam was compromising freedom of expression. His jeremiad was widely derided at the time by cultural relativists, but we might legitimately inquire whether the issues it broached are not best discussed in the frame of book history. Our theme has partly been the co-existence and interpenetration in our world of oral, written and printed norms. This is not a point about the 'survival' of previous phases of communication: in the world that we presently inhabit, texts – sacred or otherwise – are subjected to widely different habits of reading almost in equal measure: recited aloud or else *sotto voce*, written out, printed, perused and then again recited. Viewed against such a backdrop the Rushdie and Nasrin affairs both represent clashes between certain kinds of 'writer' and certain categories of readers. Both are enthusiasts for authenticity, and both honour text. The author does not wish his work to be tampered with, altered, censored or expunged; some readers do not wish new reading experiences to override or occlude their understanding of, or reverence for, other and sacred texts.

In Chapters 5 and 6 we spoke of resistances between alternative dispensations of the word. Orality, we thought, reinforces memory. It also predisposes the reading process towards mnemonic modes, while encouraging imitation and fidelity to what is absorbed. Throughout the world, day in and day out, the Qur'an is learned through recitation. Meanwhile, sometimes suspended aloft in aeroplanes, people read the novels of Salman Rushdie. Many a woman and man knows the Qur'an by heart, few if any *The Satanic Verses*. This is a judgement on neither, but it is a measure of their difference. The tensions that rend our world are sometimes viewed as resulting from a clash between different international alignments, ideologies or value systems; sometimes as the expression of opposing 'civilisations'. In the present context they are more helpfully interpreted as reflections of divergences between various sorts of text, various protocols of reading and various constituencies of readers.

8 The power of the consumer

Reading masses and high-minded elites

And so finally to the punters: in other words to you, the readers. I want to start this discussion of readerly power with two assessments: one forty years old, the other more recent. Both focus on West Africa, both address the phenomenon of a 'reading culture', and both – so it seems to me – illustrate just how deeply the assumptions of Euro-American book history and criticism have sunk into the minds of commentators on literary reception in the wider world, sometimes at the very points at which they seem most determined to resist them.

In 1972 Chinua Achebe was asked by *The Times Literary Supplement* to write a short journalistic piece in response to the query 'What do African intellectuals read?' The first sentence of his essay was arresting: 'The temptation is indeed strong to answer that question in one word: nothing.' He then went on to qualify his statement, and to set out his findings:

> In 1958 or 1959 I did a little crude research in a small British Council library in Enugu, where I lived at the time. From that little exercise, I proved to my statistical satisfaction what I had always known instinctively. I discovered that European residents of Enugu read fiction, poetry, drama, etc., while Africans read history, economics, mathematics, etc. My research was easy enough because the library had the interesting and convenient (if somewhat unconventional) system of recording in pink and black on the borrowing card according to the colour of the borrower. (I hasten to add that no racism was ever intended: the system was developed out of genuine curiosity to ascertain the reading habits of the two communities.)
>
> It was clear that the Africans who went to the library did not go in search of literary pleasure.
>
> (Achebe, 1975: 38–9)

Let us therefore examine the private reading habits of one particular imagined Nigerian at a period half-way between Achebe's mini research project and the publishing of his diagnostic essay. In 'the early sixties', Ugwu, servant to a lecturer in mathematics at the University of Nigeria at Nsukka, is proudly showing off to his colleague Harrison some reading matter he has salvaged from his employer's waste-paper basket:

> Harrison touched the pile of journals on the table. 'You are reading all of these?' he asked in English.
> 'Yes.' Ugwu had saved them from the study dustbin; the *Mathematical Annals* were incomprehensible, but at least he had read, if not understood, a few pages of *Socialist Review*.
>
> (Adichie, 2006: 210)

The episode is drawn from the novel *Half a Yellow Sun* by Chimamanda Ngozi Adichie, daughter of a professor of statistics at Nsukka who once occupied the campus bungalow in which Achebe had formerly lived while teaching in that college, at a period a little after that at which her novel is set. Ugwu the enthusiastic autodidact, it has to be stressed, is not preparing for any examination. He reads at night, for the same reasons as most autodidacts: out of a mixture of curiosity, pleasure and a desire for self-improvement. His preferences – mathematics, politics and economics – coincide precisely with Achebe's recorded observations. The trouble is that, by Achebe's own preferred standards, Ugwu is not simply imbibing lesser materials – lesser because factual and non-literary – but can scarcely be said to be reading authentically, that is for its own sake. His activity is instrumental towards some practical goal, as apparently is that of his mathematician boss. Such a verdict is not quite as dismissive towards this category of readers as it might perhaps seem. It is, however, a little short-sighted over the bibliographical significance of, say, texts on maths or statistics: the very skills on which Achebe seems to have relied for his piece of home-grown library research.

Almost half a century later, in her book *Bearing Witness*, the American sociologist Wendy Griswold addressed the vexed question as to whether Nigeria possessed what she called a 'reading culture'. Griswold's approach was distinctive. Confining herself to novels, she excluded all fiction not in English (and thus anything published in one of Nigeria's 521 indigenous languages) and everything under 60 pages in length, on the grounds that anything shorter was a pamphlet, or perhaps a novella. 'This rule', she averred, 'excludes most chapbooks of the Onitsha sort' (Griswold, 2000: 22), thus banishing at a stroke the burgeoning of shorter fiction and plays and self-help books in English from the early 1960s in one locality in eastern Nigeria, categorised by the Igbo critic Emmanuel Obiechina (1973: 1) as 'an integral … part of the West African literary scene'. In the course of her research Griswold took a KLM flight from Amsterdam to Lagos and, passing down the aisle, noted that few of the black passengers seemed to be immersed in a book. On the basis of such impressionistic evidence she inferred that Nigerians do not possess an ingrained habit of leisure reading, unlike the commuters she had earlier observed on a suburban bus in Washington, most of whom had their noses in Saul Bellow or the equivalent. Griswold's overall conclusion was that, although Nigeria possessed 'a reading culture in the strict sense' (that is, some people read some books), it did not possess one 'in the more general sense' (118), by which she apparently meant that the custom of getting lost in literary fiction was not widely diffused in the population as a whole. It should be clear from this summary that Griswold's conclusions were largely predetermined by her own arbitrarily chosen definitions. She did not deny that a significant proportion of the local middle class studied self-help books, or tracts on business or management, or that the Muslims of the north applied themselves to the Qur'an, or the Christians of the south to the Bible. Yet she did not regard these activities as pertaining to a 'reading culture' as such, a term about whose application – at least in her own cherished 'general sense' – she seems to have made up her mind well in advance.

It is obvious that, in the case-studies cited, neither Achebe nor Griswold was working as objective or unprejudiced book historians. Both had absorbed a hierarchy of evaluation from the milieu of literary criticism, and imported it into what should have been quantitative inquiries. Their approach to these questions was, moreover, orchestrated along generic divides: between 'non-fiction' and 'fiction' (and within that category between 'literary' and 'popular' fiction), between the humanities and maths, science, business and what-have-you. It should be manifest from the arguments set out in earlier chapters that boundaries between such divisions are drawn along historically over-determined lines. They are, for example, largely meaningless in the worlds of orality or manuscript lying behind so much reading practice in Asia and Africa. Griswold's neat distinctions were products of print culture and its affiliates: librarianship (where they orchestrate the Dewey classification system), publishing (with its separate 'lists') and the kinds of bookselling in which different subjects are laid out in dedicated 'sections'. Interestingly many street-level booksellers in Asia do not set out their wares in this way but, in accordance with the practice known in New Delhi as *lala*, acquire and set out their merchandise – sometimes horizontally, more usually vertically – in undifferentiated bulk. Achebe and Griswold by contrast tend to take classifications for granted, despite the former's avowed devotion to the far less segregated oral tradition. They also both reflect, perhaps subconsciously, a conviction that has no place in book history as such: that literature (and, even more narrowly, fiction) in the academic sense of the word represents the most appropriate, perhaps the highest, occupation of the reading mind. Let us now survey the universe of readers and readerships, unclouded by such thoughts.

A world of readers

How would Dr Odenigbo, Ugwu's master and master-statistician, approach the phenomenon of reading in Africa and Asia today? Presumably, as Achebe once did, through statistics, although with a little more impartiality. What would he notice? First that there are wide discrepancies in reading facility between different populations, second that these discrepancies are not entirely predictable and, third, that there flourish many kinds of reading.

Even within India there are local and other divergences. The overall literacy rate for citizens aged 15 or over is usually placed within the range 61 to 64.8 per cent, depending on whose tables you employ. Inside these overall estimates there exist divergences of both gender and region. A recent British government report puts male literacy in India at 75.3 per cent and female at 53 per cent (Allen and Jessee, 2007: 7–8). The figures are more impressive in some states than others: in certain parts of North India they stand way above the national average, and in the southern state of Kerala they are well over 90 per cent (Sen, 2005: 157). It has to be stressed, mind you, that ability to read is here being construed according to average competence in one of the twenty-two recognised languages of India. Minority groups are therefore likely to have lost out in the statistics, and two large disadvantaged populations – the Dalits or Scheduled Castes and the Adivasis or Scheduled Tribes – are very scantily represented. Another factor not reflected in the official statistics is what one might call parallel literacy. Very many Indian nationals read and/or write more than one script. A middle-class adult born in the Punjab but resident in Delhi may well be comfortable with three distinct writing systems – Devanagari, Nastaliq and Roman – and in this respect would be far from untypical. Judging by this hidden factor of 'parallel literacy', South Asia is a more densely literate region than the USA: that is to say more people read more codes. Reading ability in English as opposed to Indian languages, on the other hand, is very difficult to assess apart, since it is so seldom tested separately. Most approximations hover around 5 per cent, but one Delhi publisher put it for me as low as 2 per cent (Fraser, 2007a: 12). This 2 per cent of 1.1 billion is still 22 million, a reputable enough target group. It nevertheless represents a small minority in national terms, even of the reading public.

In Africa the discrepancies are even wider. The largest nation-state on the continent, Nigeria, has overall figures comparable to India's, as do Kenya,

Table 8.1   Comparative literacy figures for fifteen representative African nations (percentages)

Angola	67.4	Ghana	57.9	Niger	28.7
Burkina Faso	21.4	Guinea	29.5	Nigeria	67.0
Burundi	59.3	Kenya	73.6	South Africa	82.4
Chad	25.7	Lesotho	82.2	Tanzania	69.4
Cote d'Ivoire	48.7	Malawi	61.1	Uganda	66.8

Source: relevant national entries in United Nations (2006).

Uganda and Tanzania. Other countries show up more favourably, though there is quite a noticeable tail, as the sampled national aggregates in Table 8.1 may indicate.

A number of ancillary points may help to make sense of this information. Once again, the official figures are based on an ability to read a moderately taxing text in a recognised national language, and again some disadvantage necessarily accrues to smaller linguistic communities. Because of the nature of the schooling system, however, there exists in most cases a far closer correlation than in South Asia between ability to read in the language of the erstwhile coloniser – in most instances the language of government and official discourse – and the declared overall figure. This differs from country to country, but in the francophone Sahel where, owing to the highly selective nature of the academic system in former French West Africa, literacy figures teeter at around a quarter of the population, a very high proportion of this educated echelon will be literate in French. And in a country like Ghana the situation is fast changing. Throughout most of the twentieth century instruction in state schools was conducted through the vernacular for the first six years, and thereafter in English. Since 2000 it has been conducted in English throughout the Ghanaian school system. Within a few decades all citizens who are capable of reading at all will be able to read in English. Indeed an ability to read in English alone, though to speak at least one indigenous language fluently, is far from unknown across anglophone Africa as a whole.

These are the sorts of figures that preoccupy governments, international agencies and NGOs. A book historian, however, is more likely to finesse such inquiries with further questions. How much time do people spend reading – for what purpose and where – and what is their reading matter of preference? Information on such matters is not easy to come by, but rewarding when obtained. India, for example, comes almost top of the world league for the number of hours spent reading each week, according to a global NOP survey conducted in 2005. On average this found that literate citizens of India spend 10.7 hours per week at their books, almost twice as long as the

5.7 spent weekly among citizens of the United States. The global average is 6.5, slightly above America's. But it is the kind of reading that is striking in South Asia. Novels of any kind come very low down the list, and literary novels by major Indian writers still lower. *How to Help Your Child Excel in Maths*, however, is extremely popular, as are encyclopaedias and *Your Essential Guide to Career Success*.

In Africa as a whole reading preferences are fairly comparable. A recent survey made by the Lumina Foundation across Lagos, Enugu, Oyo, Edo, Kogi, Kaduna and the River States confirmed that, in southern and middle-belt Nigeria at least, reading habits display a remarkable consistency with tendencies noted by Achebe in Enugu in 1959 (Kalango, 2006). The survey confined itself to newspapers, but even so the results are revealing, with 59 per cent of respondents replying that they read as a matter of course. When asked what kind of periodicals they saw on a regular basis, 29 per cent replied that they enjoyed 'soft news', 22 per cent that they read what would prove of practical use to them and 13 per cent that they read a national newspaper every day. Only 2 per cent said that they had time or money for what was termed 'leisure reading', which presumably included most fiction. When asked why they did not read more, 41 per cent replied that they could not afford to. Once again, however, one notices that these inquiries were conducted with an eye to predetermined categories of reading matter. A more realistic impression might well be possible if one learned to think outside this prepared grid. Once again, therefore, I turn to the tyranny of genre.

Reading before genre

The Kolkata Book Fair is the largest in South Asia, timed each year to coincide with the *puja* of Saraswati, the goddess of learning. The thirty-first such event was held on the spacious plain of the Maidan in February 2006, despite a banning order from the High Court against public meetings at this congested spot. The following year it moved to nearby Salt Lake City, but still the punters poured in, since this is less a trade fair as such than a festival for book buyers, over 14 million of whom turn up each year, many returning every day. Among the marquees are food stalls, ice cream vans, playgrounds and crèches. Families attend in their hundreds of thousands. An area is provided for creative writers, resourcefully named Montmartre. Indeed, a visitor might be excused for thinking the exercise savoured less of publishing than fun. Or perhaps of the very fun of publishing, in this self-designated City of Joy.

To walk round the marquees is as good a way as any to inform oneself about the spread and balance of India's book trade. The offerings are extremely various, catering for every language group, age group, profession and clique. Ananda publishers, M. C. Sarkar and Dey's are amongst the local firms displaying their many books in Bangla across the generic range, but the large multinationals also have stalls – Oxford University Press, Orient Longman, McGraw-Hill and Penguin India – as do the learned associations: the Asiatic Society with its editions of the classics, the National Book Trust with its collections of English, Bangla, Hindi, Urdu and Oriya. The Zoological Survey of India, the Botanical Survey of India, the Geological Society of India, the Bible Society of India all have tents. The major national newspapers set out their merchandise, as do a number of small magazines. Niche publishers such as Permanent Black with its scholarly monographs or Worldwide with its friendly texts for students are a marked feature of the scene. Feminist presses such as Zubaan and Women Unlimited put on a good show. And then I noted Frank Educational Association specialising in early schooling, Seagull with its innovative list of controversial non-fiction, Manohar with its range of Indian interests. If you want propaganda, the Communists and Naxalites will happily provide it. The Flat Earth Society was very glad I called. Despite the labels, how helpful, though, is it to think of all this wealth of interest as divisible into genres?

The first attempt to squeeze the cornucopia of India's bustling book trade into the straitjacket of generic categories occurred in the 1870s with the implementation of the 1867 Book Registration Act. Reports were compiled each year in Calcutta from the returns compiled locally in each Presidency. They make painful reading now, since government had decreed that all books produced in India's many languages should be tabulated under the following headings: Arts; Biography; Drama; Fiction; History; Language; Law; Medicine; Miscellaneous; Philosophy (including Mental and Moral Science); Poetry; Politics; Religion; Science (Mathematical and Mechanical); Science (Natural and other); and Travels and Voyages. Take for example a decade in which the forces of modernisation and nationalism made marked strides in India: the 1890s. The first fact one notices from the surviving reports (OIOC IOR MF 1/I98) is that nobody seems to have travelled, or if they did, were silent about the fact, since the space for Journeys was mostly left blank, or occupied at most by one or two titles. The next surprising fact, already noted in Chapter 3, is the almost total lack, in this most agitated of periods, of books nominally about politics. In 1890 the Bombay Presidency produced six, the Punjab five. The very next year Bengal, that hotbed of unrest, owned up to none at all. Manifestly political titles were being tactfully hidden under other headings, for political reasons. The third observation of substance is the relative scarcity in most regions of India of self-declared fiction. In the year 1894 Madras fielded 28 novels out of a total production of 887 books, a thirtieth of the whole. That year the Punjab managed 37 out of a total book run of 967, the following year the Punjab declared a mere 55 fictional titles out of 1,304. (Unsurprisingly perhaps the Presidency most proud to proclaim its output of novels at his period was Bengal: in 1891 it declared 63.) The fourth striking feature is a large bulge in the Miscellaneous department, into which were scrambled books a hard-pressed bureaucracy found it difficult to classify. In 1994 the Punjab listed 218 miscellaneous titles out a total production of 967; in 1989, Bombay 132 out of 745. Clearly, generic classification was already proving something of a strain.

What were the stalwarts? Law and Medicine both fared well as training grounds for two of India's leading professions. But the two overwhelmingly large categories were those that might surprise some onlookers: poetry and religion. In the Presidency of Bombay in the year 1890 115 books of poetry were published along with 341 devotional texts. In the following year the Northwest Provinces and Oudh produced 70 books of verse and 306 religious works, almost a third of the total. In the same year the neighbouring Punjab managed 328 books of poetry and 292 of religious matter, making up between them more than half the book production in that region for the year 1891.

What these figures tend to show is, not simply that the South Asian book mart at that period was utterly distinctive in its tastes, but that the modes of book classification routinely applied to it by librarians trained in other traditions made very little sense. If at the turn of the twentieth century one had approached a citizen of Bubaneswar in Orissa squatting on her haunches over an edition of Sudramuni Sarala Dass's metrical redaction of the *Mahabharata* (one such was published in Cuttack in 1898–9), and asked her what manner of text she was reading, how could she have answered? Poetry? Well, the work is in verse. Fiction? Of course it is fiction. Drama? Well, it is strongly dramatic. Religion? The *Mahabharata* is indeed one of the great devotional classics of India. Science? It has plenty of it. Maths? Like so many ancient Asian repertoires, it draws on that too. Politics? Our reader might well have baulked at that question, but there is many an admirer of that epic who would claim that, in the broadest sense of that term, the *Mahabharata* is a profoundly political work. It is also cross-generic in its readership appeal, or maybe – just maybe – pre-generic.

Arguably African literature, too, has always been markedly cross-generic in its orientation. Take a work produced in the early twentieth century on the Gold Coast of West Africa. *Ethiopia Unbound* was published in 1911 by Joseph Ephraim Casely-Hayford, a Fante who read for the Bar in London and returned to the coast to lead the fledgling nationalist movement. The book was sub-titled 'Studies in Race Emancipation' and followed the adventures of one Kwamankra as he rubs shoulders with the intelligentsia of Cambridge and London, argues through much of the night on issues of the day, and returns to the Coast to carve out not merely his own destiny but that of his people. The book began as fiction sure enough, with an unforgettable evocation of the Bloomsbury of the *fin-de-siècle*, but well before it shifted scene back to Africa it had evolved into an essay, or rather a series of chapters on subjects of pragmatic or ideological interest: the relations between the races, the character of African life, the nature of traditional political institutions, the way forward for such a colony. In its 300-odd pages it embraced religion, gender studies, social anthropology, propaganda and much that we might now band together loosely under the banner of Cultural Studies, all this while never quite ceasing to be a story. Was this diffusion, diversification or, as some genre-obsessed critics might conclude, artistic degeneration? Certainly Casely-Hayford's book conformed to few of Griswold's 'rules'.

The same is true of much African 'fiction' of later periods. In the 1970s the Bureau of Ghana Languages launched a series of titles aimed at the general market and incorporating short works in the major languages of the country. The list was undifferentiated by genre, and featured novellas alongside tracts on agriculture and health. Its catalogue for 1971–2 included twenty-six books in Akwapim Twi, forty-one in Asante Twi, twenty-three in Dangme, twenty-two in Ewe, forty-seven in Fante, twenty-five in Ga, thirteen in Kasem and thirty-three in Nzema, a total of 231 titles. All of the fiction was strongly didactic, devoted to social problems, individual moral choices and questions of conduct. Among the Twi titles was *Amba Nyansawa* by A. C. Nkrumah, depicting two girls, one respectful, the other arrogant and insubordinate. Both make journeys across country, in the course of which the polite girl is rewarded for her good manners, while the arrogant one discovers that rudeness does not pay. Among the Fante novellas was *Etsuo Fe Neke* by E. A. W. Engmann, the life history of a child spoilt by the deleterious influence of an over-indulgent mother. These tales were as overtly moralistic as *The Pilgrim's Progress*, an important and frequently translated missionary text whose nonconformist, self-respecting ambiance several of these authors seem to have absorbed. Other influences were folk tales, locally staged musical dramas (such as the 'concert parties' popular on the Gold Coast since the 1930s) and the films produced in the 1950s by the Gold Coast Film Unit. Among the latter had been the Venice Biennale Award-winning *Amenu's Child* of 1950, about a mother who, believing her baby's fever is caused by the spirit of a child she has earlier lost, consults the medicine man rather than a doctor, and watches the infant die. Two years later *The Boy Kumasenu* was produced to a score by the British avant-garde composer Elisabeth Lutyens. It told of a boy cast out of his fishing community as a result of false accusations of spreading bad luck who migrates to the city, where, triumphing over a multitude of petty temptations, he ultimately thrives. Clearly these were self-help books in the guise of fiction aimed at the needs of survival, above all economic. In which respects, of course, they drew fairly directly less on the novel than on a domestic tradition of practical advice.

In such Asian and African scenarios we are confronted by an apparent elision of modes. These elisions in turn, I would suggest, are dictated by publishing policies shaped by anticipatory responses to known patterns of receptivity. Emmanuel Obiechina (1973) long ago illustrated such factors at work in the Onitsha-market literature of eastern Nigeria, and Stephanie Newell (2000) has performed much the same service for Ghanaian popular fiction in English across several decades. The readers created the genre. But similar pressures were operating at much the same period in the realm of what some commentators might wish to separate out as 'literary fiction'. Probably the most respected Ghanaian novelist of the twentieth century, for example, both inside the country and outside, was Ayi Kwei Armah. This once famous writer began his career with a vivid if gloom-ridden political parable set during the declining years of Nkrumah's government, whose title, *The Beautyful Ones Are Not Yet Born*, was drawn from a motto observed on the back of a mammy lorry. Two accomplished but essentially conventional novels followed before in *Two Thousand Seasons* he forsook social realism, some would say the novel form itself, and produced what was virtually a sermon in fictive guise decrying the betrayal of the peoples of the West African hinterland by self-seeking middlemen. All of his subsequent books adopted this admonitory tone, carrying fiction well into the realm of polemic. A lesser-known work of the 1990s, *Osiris Rising*, mixed anthropology, archaeology, comparative religion and a story line with a marked political and feminist edge. Bypassing the large publishing houses, it was issued by Armah's own imprint in Senegal.

Over the other side of the continent Ngugi wa Thiong'o, still Kenya's best-known author, commenced by producing well-crafted books in a social realist vein. After the impressive achievement of mature books such as *A Grain of Wheat* and *Petals of Blood*, he changed his manner of writing, his language of literary expression and, at the same time, the terms of his publishing contract. *Devil on the Cross* was an overtly moralistic and political tale first written in Gikuyu as *Caitaani Muthuraba-Ini* and published in that language by Heinemann East Africa in 1980 before being translated into English by the author himself and issued for an international audience in the African Writers series in 1982. Ngugi has continued to reach audiences both African and international, while making his own publishing arrangements. And, as we shall soon see, his ambitions, style and content have been increasingly audience-driven.

Counter-interpreting romance

So far I have been concerned to show how the cross-generic tastes of certain audiences have created climates of expectation confounding the expectations of middlemen, and encouraging writers to meet the needs of readers directly. I now want to explore the more radical proposition that readers possess a further power of dismantling hierarchies of merit, and of redirecting tradition. Such readerly independence of mind can be traced from the recent past. It also exists at the heart of what we have come to know as the 'postcolonial'.

To return to Ngugi, then, what was the reading that formed him when young? In 1982 he told a story about his literary generation that is well worth attending to. Thirty years earlier, shortly after the beginning of the war of independence known by the British as the Mau Mau Emergency, his contemporary and friend Mĩcere Mũgo, then a schoolgirl, was frightened by a witch. The apparition's name was Gagool, and Mũgo had found her in Rider Haggard's adventure romance *King Solomon's Mines*, an 'old hag' variously compared to a vampire bat or a snake, and last met 'fighting like a cat'. 'I was so terrified', Mũgo confessed twenty years later, 'that for a long time I felt mortal terror whenever I encountered old African women' (Ngugi, 1986: 18). The reference, and the incident recalled, are recorded in 1986 in Ngugi's change-of-heart essay *Decolonising the Mind*, where it is offered as characteristic of the reading habits of a certain Kenyan generation fed on a mixture of British literary classics and thrillers (12): Dickens and Stevenson alongside Haggard, Elspeth Huxley and Nicholas Monsarrat, then more Haggard, John Buchan and Captain W. E. Johns of *Biggles Flies West*.

Such early preferences of his, the middle-aged and now much published Ngugi insists, smacked of one-time cultural subordination: a revealing judgement since he is analysing as much his chosen leisure-time reading as the academic syllabi of Kenyan schools at the period. Ngugi *recognises* that Haggard has at one time been popular; the point he wishes to make is that he should not have been. There exists a clear division in this radicalised writer's mind between reading practices and reading priorities: between what people, including children, actually read, and what they should be reading. I want in this section to take a hard look at this view and, in a wider context, to consider its appropriateness.

The case of Rider Haggard is not a bad place to begin. Ngugi calls him a 'genius of racialism' (1986: 18) but does not deny his one-time appeal. How come these future writers and firebrands once took to so politically sensitive a text as *King Solomon's Mines*, first published in 1885 and a runaway success ever since? Viewed from the point of view of publishing logistics, the answer would seem to be obvious. Haggard, after all, was a literary darling of the empire. *King Solomon's Mines*, for example, was much translated, as were its companion pieces *Allan Quatermain* and *She*: unsurprisingly into Afrikaans (1938), but also into Swahili, Zulu (into which, significantly, during the years of apartheid, *King Solomon's Mines* was translated thrice) and Sotho, and by 1959 into the click language, Xhosa. Haggard's African tales appeared in abridgement, as language readers and as illustrated classics; and then of course there were the films.

But the popularity of such literature among black Africans involves the awkward problem identified by Ngugi, and reformulated by Edward Said in his *Culture and Imperialism*. 'Almost without exception', Said confidently asserts (1993: 227), 'these narratives ... far from casting doubt on the imperial undertaking, serve to confirm and celebrate its success.' If he and Ngugi are right, the Haggard cult was the result of brainwashing. Yet in 1956, four years after the introduction of circulating libraries in the Gold Coast, and a few weeks before the country's independence as Ghana, a survey was taken of reading preferences in the capital Accra. Haggard's books came third, just after the ever-popular Marie Corelli and Shakespeare, beating Dickens into fourth place (Newell, 2002: 104–5, 112). And Haggard's works remained a sort of ideological and cultural litmus test. An episode in Achebe's fourth novel, *A Man of the People* of 1966, suggests how it could be applied. The demagogue of the novel's title is Chief the Honourable M. A. Nanga MP, minister in the first post-independence government of a country strongly resembling Nigeria, whose partiality for public speaking has earned him the sobriquet Grammar-phone. The story is told by his soon-to-be-disillusioned assistant Odili, who at one point makes an inventory of his employer's bookshelves (Achebe, 1966: 61–5). They are, he says, 'not quite to my taste', containing an American encyclopaedia, the self-help manual *How to Make Speeches* and Haggard's *She* and *Ayesha: The Return of She*, both in simplified versions made by Michael West, former educationalist and doyen of the New Language Teaching Method. So reliant for his personal reading is this dignitary on what were in effect schoolroom texts that he seems incapable of distinguishing between author and editor. When asked whom he considers the most significant writer of the day, West's is the name he offers. The narrator's – and by implication Achebe's – verdict is unsparing: the minister is a vulgarian, unworthy of his post.

Yet if Mũgo, Ngugi, Achebe and Said are all justified in regarding a fondness for authors such as Haggard as a symptom of intellectual and political backwardness, where does that leave the popular audience who once received them with such relish?

Here other factors came into play, notably, I suspect, the willingness of common readers to disassemble such texts and reassemble them according to a logic – often a political logic – of their own making. There is plenty in the novel of *Solomon's Mines*, as opposed to the Hollywood filmic version of 1950, that might enable the average reader to do this. In the film the British protagonist Allan Quatermain is a dashing, raven-haired hero; in the book he is a garrulous runt, who, having failed in his career as a hunter of elephants, sets out in to the wilderness in search of will-o'-the wisp legend, without much idea where he is going. His companions are similarly risible: Captain Good with the full set of false teeth with which he amazes the locals, Henry Curtis with his homoerotic crushes. The desire present in the novel, and most of the approval, is directed towards the accompanying Kukuana people, stand-ins for the Zulus, whose cause Haggard was championing at the time he wrote it. It is precisely this sort of historical counter-logic in Haggard's fiction that Sol Plaatje seems to have picked up on when he recast *Nada the Lily* in his own novel of counter-romance, *Mhudi*. That the average colonial reader could and did much the same is suggested by the even more remarkable case of a romantic author banned from most academic syllabi: Marie Corelli.

Corelli (alias Mary Mackay, 1855–1924) was despised by the chattering classes of Britain. She none the less acquired in the eyes of colonial readers the status of a near-deity. 'So high was the admiration for Marie Corelli [throughout Africa]', Achebe notes (1975: 38), that 'in a little book just published in Nigeria ... she is numbered among the world's superwomen, in the company of Joan of Arc and Mary Magdalene.' Achebe refers to Corelli's widespread popularity with dismay, an attitude he shares with the Bloomsbury set of the 1930s, who consigned her work to a rank equivalent to 'middle-' verging on 'lowbrow'. When in 1926 the young Indian novelist Mulk Raj Anand, a committed Marxist, mentioned to Virginia and Leonard Woolf that he had partly modelled his prose style on Corelli and Haggard, they reacted with shock to his taste (Anand, 1981: 105; Joshi, 2002a: 210). But Leonard Woolf was aware of a fact of which his wife was ignorant: in India and Ceylon (where he had once served as a junior colonial official) Corelli's didactic romances *Vendetta* (1886), *Barabbas* (1893), *The Sorrows of Satan* (1895), *The Treasure of Heaven* (1906), *Thelma* (1887), *Temporal Power* (1902) and *The Soul of Lilith* (1892) were extensively imported, locally reprinted and stocked in most libraries as well as being multifariously translated, adapted and abridged. She was just as universally appreciated in Africa and the Caribbean.

There was nothing passive about this cult. Through diverse strategies of interpretation, colonial societies took their pick from Corelli's writings and from her moral and social attitudes, explicit or implied. In this they were assisted by the vehemently – and in European terms anachronistically – allegorical nature of her writings, and by her usefully contradictory ideas on questions such as marriage, the place of the woman in the home, fidelity and infidelity and the uses of money. Different societies, of course, extracted different qualities from these lurid and satisfying writings. As Stephanie Newell has demonstrated (2002: 98–118), in the Christianised coastal areas of Nigeria, the Gold Coast and Sierra Leone by far the most popular of Corelli's many books was *The Sorrows of Satan*, in which Lucifer cuts a swath across English society in the shape of a foppish and decadent aristocrat of dubious continental extraction. From this tale of indulgence and repudiation African Christians seem to have imbibed a satisfyingly self-righteous distrust of a metropolis they had never visited, a consoling distrust of privileges and enjoyments they were never likely to enjoy and certain bracing nostrums of sturdiness and *petit-bourgeois* self-reliance. One clue to the local popularity of the book resonates in its opening sentence, a rhetorical question posed by its narrator, an indigent novelist who is about to succumb to Satan's power 'Do you know what it is to be poor?' Well, West African readers by and large did, and seem to have interpreted the remainder of that book in the light of that indignation and that knowledge, relished all the more because it was robed up as a Protestant parable of Good and Evil, sin and repentance.

Newell arrives at her reconstruction of African responses to this novel though her knowledge of colonial society of the period, while conceding that any such exercise in community mind-reading is at best hypothetical. The same cannot be said of Corelli's impact on multi-faith India, where direct evidence of prevailing patterns of interpretation is available through multiple translations into different languages, often with discreet interventions or not-so-discreet interpolations by editors and translators (Bhattacharya, 2007: 219–44). Among the most translated Corelli blockbusters was *Barabbas* (Hindi and Gujarati 1895, Oriya 1954, Malayalam 1955), a book whose heretical approach to the biblical crucifixion story had caused Corelli to break with her first publisher, George Bentley. Most translated of all was the misogynistic tale *Vendetta* (Sindhi 1920, Bengali 1922, Hindi 1954, Oriya 1963, Bengali again 1970), recounting the blood-curdling revenge taken by an outraged Neapolitan husband on his unfaithful wife. In India *The Sorrows of Satan* came third (Bengali 1903, Gujarati 1958, Bengali again 1960), though what appears to have exercised Indian as compared with African readers was not the book's anti-hedonistic bias but its unsympathetic portrayal of the New Woman, the aptly named Lady Sybil Eaton: her disastrous and wavering marriage to the novelist narrator compounds his many troubles, and her apposite sermonising on the marriage market is highlighted in all these versions. Probably the two Corelli texts which tell us most about the complex Indian obsession with her legacy, however, are a couple of novels reflecting her vacillating stance towards the Suffragette movement and woman's role in marriage. In *Thelma* (Marathi 1911, Bengali 1960), the Norwegian heroine decides to stick by her husband despite rumours of his reputed affairs with other women. In *The Murder of Delicia*, translated into Bengali by Begum Rokeya Sakkawat Hossian in 1922, the rumours are authentic, and the forgiveness is lacking.

Most Indian admirers, unlike her African or West Indian fans, had little time for Corelli as a vehicle for Christianity. The wife in *Thelma*, for example, is held out as a role-model of chastity, yet the publishers of the (Western) Bengali text promise the book's readers that they will be 'enchanted and overwhelmed by reading a reflection of Hindu ideals and culture in the character of this Norwegian girl' (Bhattacharya, 2007: 226). Passages extolling the importance of loyalty to one's spouse are dwelt upon, both in the text and in the translator's Preface. It is Corelli the social conservative, not the iconoclast of capitalism, that the readers are here invited to contemplate – almost Corelli the Begum.

Reading and readers today

Ever since the publication in 1989 of Ashcroft, Griffiths and Tiffin's iconoclastic *The Empire Writes Back* there has been an understandable emphasis in critical circles on postcolonial writing as an 'abrogation' of imperial norms and influences. It is not always recognised, however, just how securely this rejoinder is earthed in a communally shared habit of critical assimilation, amounting at times to textual subversion. Plaatje and Ngugi have already been mentioned, but the supporting evidence is abundant: from Salman Rushdie's reconstruction of *Tristram Shandy* in *Midnight's Children* to Achebe's reaction against the paternalism of Joyce Cary in *Things Fall Apart*, to Walcott's rewriting of Homer, Soyinka's of Euripides (and in *A Dance of the Forests* of Shelley), or Anand's recycling of the social realism of H. G. Wells. These are high peaks in a range that runs across the spacious tracts of the reading world once covered by empire. But the habit itself is widespread and common to readers and writers. It flourishes still.

Take, for example, just one articulate constituency: West African undergraduates. At the University of Ghana at Legon stands a neo-Italianate bookshop catering for the tastes of local academics and general readers, together with the requirements of the university's syllabi. Here you will find the texts prescribed for the university's departments, consisting in the case of literature of classics home-grown and foreign: Achebe, Soyinka, Dickens, Lawrence. (In February 2007 there were seventy-two copies of E. M. Forster's novel *Where Angels Fear to Tread*, a recently abandoned set text.) Beside them sit productions by Ghana's small but resilient band of independent publishers. Offerings by Woeli stand near those by South Saharan, which include *The African Predicament*, a recent and well-publicised volume of essays by the Ghanaian poet and novelist Kofi Awoonor. Titles from Infram and Ayebia are also present, including the latter's *Between Faith and History*, a biography of the Ghanaian president John Kufour launched in December 2006 at a ceremony presided over by Soyinka. There are a number of Mandeliana, including Mandela's own *Long Walk to Freedom*, almost – though not quite – as many as you would find in a bookstore in Cape Town or Durban. Mandela, Kufuor, Soyinka and Awoonor are manifestly role-models in a fairly direct sense. You will also come across a scattering of professional self-help books from India such as P. K. Madhavan's *Careers in Publishing*, together with books for that year's secondary school exams. On a recent visit these were *Hamlet*, Athol Fugard's *Siswe Banze Is Dead*, Elizabeth Gaskell's *Wives and Daughters*, Robert Bolt's *A Man for All Seasons*, George Eliot's *Silas Marner* and Peter Abraham's *Black Boy*.

Meanwhile, outside in the sunshine, cluster a number of independently owned stalls at which one discovers what students enjoy reading when unsupervised. New Point Publications is fairly typical of the sort of one- or two-man outfit seen all over Accra that manifest a West African version of India's *lala* tendency, while servicing the general trade in leisure reading. It stocks stationery, pens, a range of American periodicals, *Ebony*, the *National Geographical Magazine* and a lot of pulp fiction: Sue Grafton, Lawrence Block, Ed McBain. By far the most popular author represented, however, is Francine Pascal (1938–), a New York graduate who since the 1970s has produced a stream of novelettes aiming at high school and junior high school kids in the USA and selling to date 260 million copies worldwide. They are set in East Coast institutions and portray the ups-and-downs of adolescent existence: 144 Sweet Valley High novellas; 118 Sweet Valley Twins; 76 Sweet Valley Kids; 61 set in Sweet Valley University and 30 in Sweet Valley Junior High. The presence of these titles in large numbers at the university suggests that in Africa they are enjoyed by an age group four to five years older than in America. The proprietors of New Point tell me they do a steady trade, mostly among girl students. By far and away the popular series is Pascal's *Fearless* depicting the adventures of one Gaia Moore, a young woman mysteriously born 'without the fear gene'. A little research among the women on campus discloses that these short books are deconstructed and reconstructed in much the same way as readers of an earlier generation did Marie Corelli. Of course, the social and personal ideals projected onto the characters are updated. Separating story from context, such readers adopt the doughty Gaia as a channel for their own assertive and proto-feminist aspirations. In Africa at least, Pascal – whatever one may think of her (largely ghost-written) prose – is the Corelli of her time.

A similar set of contrasts may be obtained in New Delhi nowadays by visiting any of the 'high-end' emporia around the city. The flagship Oxford Bookshop on Rajiv Chowk with its terracotta tiles, metal and wood bookcases, its glass-encased Cha Bar and titles from Thames and Hudson, OUP and Penguin India, as well as from local niche publishers like Tara, Katha, Zubaan and Women Unlimited; Fact and Fiction in Vasant Vihar with its range of travel titles; Eureka on Narmada Market with its red-painted bricks and children's literature. Then walk out into the sunshine and patronise one of the street vendors who have set up their stock, average price 30 rupees, along the pavement in serried, mostly unclassified, ranks. By far the greater proportion of what is on sale here is in English, yet even within this sector, representing a little over 20 per cent of the book production in the subcontinent, there is a remarkable variety of appeal. It may reasonably be sampled by taking a look at the catalogue of just one major supplier of such modest outlets. Named after the Buddhist concept of material form, countrywide in scope, wholly Indian owned and supplying the paperback needs of a large swath of the growing middle class, this is 'Rupa'.

Rupa operates out of Ansari Road in what has since the 1970s become the major publishing neighbourhood of New Delhi, indeed of India as a whole, Daryaganj. Its prices seldom stray above 300 rupees compared to the 500 one might easily pay for a Penguin hardback in, say, the New Book Depot on Connaught Place; the average is 95 rupees, or the equivalent of £1.50 sterling. All 2,520 of its offerings, except for twenty-eight Hindi titles, are in English. Its catalogue lists them by genre, though the divisions are roomy and capacious. There is a partiality for biographies, currently eighty-nine in number, drawing on a tradition going back at least as far as OUP's nineteenth-century Rulers of India series. Mostly they are Indian in subject, pre-eminently scientists and national leaders, with Pandit Nehru and Mother Theresa alongside Homi Bhabha, architect of India's nuclear programme and uncle of an internationally known critic more familiar outside India. There are seventy-eight children's books, mostly by Indian authors, but including three by Kipling. The business management section looms large, and the 'Indian interest' section features omnibuses on 'Dance', 'Hindu Gods and Goddesses', 'Monuments' and 'Musical Instruments'. Tagore is almost alone among Indian writers in enjoying a whole section to himself, an honour also bestowed on William Shakespeare, P. G. Wodehouse with his pseudo-Edwardian japes, Henry Cecil with his courtroom sagas and Richard Gordon with his farces of hospital life. The most prominent novelist by far is the British-born, though long-time Indian resident, Ruskin Bond, a depicter of Indian solitudes praised, amongst others, by Naipaul.

Rupa does not declare sales figures, but is candid about its bestsellers. These include *The Dancing Democracy*, Prakasha Ray's amply illustrated study of the turbulent politics of neighbouring Nepal, alongside Anurag Matar's *Inscrutable Americans*, a humorously fictitious account by an Indian engineering student of his visit to the States couched mostly in Indish (or

'Indian English') as letters back home. It is a popular and alertly witty work, soothing middle-class professional anxieties with the syrup of mild jokes. Much the same, I think, may be claimed for Rupa's runaway fiction best-sellers, both by Chetan Bhagat. In *One Night at the Call Centre,* the staff at one of Delhi's many international exchanges receive an incoming message from God. *Five Point Somebody* by contrast deals satirically though affection-ately with the *angst* of low score achievers at one of the subcontinent's highly competitive institutes of technology. This is a literature of identification and displacement, and it sells well, spotlighting the lives of those with whom its readers perceive themselves as locked in a common Darwinian struggle: doctors, lawyers, engineers or technicians. It highlights achievement, while laying anxiety to rest with a balm of consoling levity. Outside India it is almost unknown.

The great tradition poco-style

So much for the popular end of the market. But what of great, what of modern classic writing? How, for instance, do we place in a book-historical context the emergence over the last half-century of acclaimed, star-studded postcolonial literatures, almost all of them framed in the international, and formerly colonial, language of English? A top-down account, of which there have been too many, would see these as products of the intervention in the market of mainly overseas publishing conglomerates. Once again, however, I think they are much more effectively viewed as reflections of the evolution, the ramifying tastes and – supremely in this case – the diversifying location, of their audiences.

Interpreted as a series of publishing initiatives, they are quite easy to date. The wholesale internationalisation of African literature began in 1962 when the London firm of Heinemann Educational Books under its managing director Alan Hill reissued in paperback, and as number one of their newly initiated African Writers series, Chinua Achebe's first novel, *Things Fall Apart*, published four years earlier in hardback by the parent firm William Heinemann. The series would survive as a commissioning enterprise until 2003. Over that period it brought out 365 titles, a few of them reprints or translations, most of them brand-new. It published literature in most genres – here at last the term seems apposite – though fiction predominated over poetry and plays, thirty-one of the first fifty issues being novels. Among their authors were some of the most illustrious names in international anglo-phone African literature including Achebe himself, soon to be appointed the series's Founding Editor, and Ngugi, who entered the series in 1964 with its seventh title, *Weep Not Child*. Peter Abrahams and Alex La Guma came from South Africa; Bessie Head from Botswana; Buchi Emecheta from Nigeria; Nurrudin Farah from Somalia. Francophone novelists saw the light of day in English translation, notably two satirists from Cameroon, Mongo Beti and Ferdinand Oyo; the Senegalese syndicalist and novelist-cum-film-director Ousman Sembene; the angry Guinean polemicist Yambo Ouologuem; the Senegalese mystic and educationalist Cheikh Hamadou Kane. Tayib Saleh's intriguing contra-Conradian fable *Season of Migration to the Far North* was translated from Arabic, Okot p'Bitek's verse by his own hand from Acholi. Male authors predominated to begin with, but increasingly, as after 1990 Heinemann bought up rights to several women writers' work, the gender balance shifted, with Doris Lessing, Ama Atta Aidoo and Veronique Tadjo of the Ivory Coast coming in to join the inimitably truth-telling Bessie Head.

By the time of Head's death in 1986, however, the series was fast changing. At first 80 per cent of its sales had gone to Africa, then seen as the target audience, with 10 per cent each going to Britain and the United States. However, as some African economies declined – the closure of the Nigerian stock exchange in 1984 being an especial blow – less and less money was available to purchase books from over-stretched national budgets. As the core African market lapsed, a fresh element rode to the rescue. Consequent upon the civil rights movement in the USA, black studies programmes had opened in colleges all over the States, each of which was anxious to place Europhone African literature on its syllabi. Gradually the balance of trade shifted towards this market, so that by the end the quotients had almost reversed, with over 50 per cent of sales being absorbed by a new and diasporic constituency, and only about 20 per cent by Africa itself. Within that reduced ratio, the African market had also of course spread out, catered for by branches in Nigeria and Kenya, the managerial staff of which, notably Henry Chakava in Nairobi, were allotted a growing role in the selection of texts. Despite this internal diversification, eventually the word 'African' in the African Writers series logo, envisaged at the outset as a description both of content and of appeal, came to refer to its authors in a literal and localised sense, but to its readers in a far more extended and vicarious one. It became a series for the black world, and for all of those in a global context interested in its genius.

The series enjoyed an enviable reputation in its heyday, but stirred up resentment in some quarters: from commercial rivals, rejected authors, academic ideologues and a number of authors uncomfortable at appearing in so glossy – and reputedly so inauthentic – a showcase. There have been critics of late who view the enterprise as some sort of neo-colonial commercial plot, such as Camille Lizarribar (1998), or who regard it as having pandered to an almost pornographically inaccurate, and certainly an outdated, view of Africa, such as Graham Huggan (2001). All such assessments have ultimately to take into account the nature of the list: its economic base and its limitations. First, these were not trade books in the usual sense of the term. From the very beginning these were educational titles marketed in the same way as school textbooks, with a standard educational discount of 15 per cent. They were intended for school syllabi, and, as time went on, were increasingly successful in being adopted for them. At the outset a cunning decision was made to appropriate the orange cover tone of Penguin's lucrative fiction list with its prestigious authorial stable of Lawrence, Waugh and Huxley. Something of the cachet attaching to such well-known metropolitan authors soon started to rub off on the series as well. The international world of letters, which (with the freakish exception of Amos Tutuola's *The Palm Wine Drinkard* accepted by T. S. Eliot at Faber and Faber in 1952) had until then taken very little heed of Africa, suddenly sat up and paid attention. In the academy meanwhile a secondary critical literature burgeoned with surprising haste. Some groupies were to proclaim in retrospect that they had watched a 'new literature' being born. I have already said enough in this study to convince you that claims of this sort were sadly misplaced. What had occurred in actual fact was the outing of a literature that until that time had addressed its formidable energies inwards.

The wholesale internationalisation of South Asian literature began nineteen years later, again in London, when Salman Rushdie's second novel *Midnight's Children*, issued by the firm of Jonathan Cape, won the Booker (later the Man Booker) Prize for fiction in 1981. This was very late indeed in the evolution of Indian writing as a whole, and some half-century after the Indian novel in English first created ripples in the wider world. Yet until 1981 the only Indian author to benefit from widespread international acclaim had been Tagore, an earlier beneficiary of the prize system, since W. B. Yeats had ensured he won the Nobel Prize for Literature in 1913. But the fiction of the Marxist realist Mulk Raj Anand, of the mystical polymath Raja Rao and of the whimsical satirist R. K. Narayan, much read and translated within the subcontinent, had been known only to select coteries beyond it. Anand had approached seventeen different London publishers before Edgell Rickword, the Communist sympathiser and former editor of the influential *Calendar of Modern Letters*, had accepted his first novel *Untouchable* for John Wishart in 1935. The book had been much revised on the advice of Gandhi, appearing with a slightly patronising Preface by E. M. Forster. It is a marked symptom of the relatively low esteem with which Asian literature was regarded in the cosmopolis until the early 1980s that several of this earlier generation of anglophone writers had needed British literary figures to endorse or 'puff' their books. Narayan was taken up by Graham Greene, and, even as late as 1971, a reprint of G. V. Desani's Shandean masterpiece *All About H. Hatterr*, a welcome influence on Rushdie, had required a pugnaciously defensive Foreword by Anthony Burgess.

After Rushdie there occurred an instantaneous surge in India's international literary visibility. Amitav Ghosh, Vikram Seth, Rohan Mistry and Kiran Desai were just some of the writers to benefit from a global artistic vogue that proved productive of substantial profits for British and American publishing houses and the global conglomerates that owned them. It turned some authors into international celebrities. The *fatwa* delivered against Rushdie on Radio Tehran in September 1989 in the aftermath of his fourth book *The Satanic Verses* was as productive of celebrity as of notoriety. By 1990, in the West at least, for everyone who had read one of his books, a thousand had heard of him. In Asia, where his work was subjected to widespread bans and censorship, the discrepancy was still more extreme.

The Rushdie case serves to open up some larger queries that have hovered around these highly glamorous, highly innovative literatures, as steeped in experimentation as they are in tradition. The *fatwa* crisis stirred hearts and minds in Asia, and disturbed pieties with deep cultural roots in the East. Yet the first riots against the novel occurred in Bradford, and it was in the West, his place of long-term residence, that Rushdie sought refuge. These facts, and the burgeoning cult surrounding a generation of authors who in figurative terms seem like Rushdie's children, have perpetuated quibbles in certain resistant minds. Written in the West in English by authors intermittently – or sometimes permanently – resident in the West, published, praised and rewarded in the outside world, are these not in some sense literatures *of* the West? Questions of this sort continue to nag in some quarters. As we shall soon see, they badly need rephrasing.

'Canons to the left of them'

One perspective on such problems is afforded by the activities of publishers. In her provocative and well-researched study *Postcolonial Writers in the Global Marketplace* the American theorist Sarah Brouillette has recently set out the logistics of this particular approach. Rushdie's British publisher is Cape, part of the Random House group; in the USA, too, his publisher is also now Random House, purchased in 1998 by the German-based media giant, Bertelsmann. Bertelsmann is calculated to control approximately 10 per cent of the communications network worldwide and in 2000, two years after the takeover, Random House's 2 billion dollars of worldwide sales contributed 12 per cent of the consortium's total income (Brouillette, 2007: 50). It is thus a fair guess that Rushdie's growing body of fiction has contributed more than a mite to the 40 billion euros of revenue the company declared in 2004. Sales of translation rights for more than forty languages have boosted the proceeds. The economics of this equation derive from the size of a consortium that enables it to practise calculated economies of scale. Within its large worldwide audience it identifies clusters of readers with common interests. The teenage girls who supply Simon & Schuster with a market for their *Fearless* titles constitute one such constituency. Readers of literary fiction constitute another since, though a minority everywhere, in global aggregate they amount to a respectable, nay a desirable, market. Within this sophisticated catchment of readers the publishers are further able to identify a more specialised taste for what you might call, in the broadest sense of the term, 'postcolonial fiction'. An investment in titles of this kind clearly reaps respectable rewards.

For Brouillette, facts like these do not simply relate to context; they also constitute an important element in a writer's self-positioning. Though a taste for postcolonial fiction is widespread, relevant economies of scale work only if it is comparatively self-consistent, that is to say if 'postcolonial fiction' as a brand is more or less recognisable everywhere. It is in the interests of those controlling the purse strings that the gap between literary fiction in general and 'postcolonial fiction' in particular should prove as narrow as can be, that is to say that as much contemporary fiction as possible should ideally nestle within an identifiably postcolonial brand. (Within the contours of such an argument the apparent domination of international prize lists by authors perceived as 'postcolonial' comes as little surprise.) The pressures on individual authors to conform to certain expectations of setting, theme and style are accordingly intense. Such writers must draw on an exotic background, but do so accessibly in English; they must speak for the deprived without themselves seeming deprived; they must be victims, though glamorous victims. For Brouillette much of the mature work of South Asian and other artists caught in this trap can be construed as a meditation on the resulting personal and artistic dilemmas, the limitations on originality they threaten to impose, the sovereign need to counter such cramping celebrification through sorties into the creatively unpredictable and unknown.

This is a cogent style of analysis, though from my point of view it leaves one vital element out of the equation. From the perspective of Delhi, Dakha or Cape Town, a more frequently applied litmus test is an author's relationship, less with her publishers than with her readers. The crisis of the postcolonial author, by this standard, is one not so much of commodification as of audience. Doubtless there exists a lacuna in this respect between reality and perception. *Midnight's Children* has continued to sell reasonably in India, both in its legitimate Penguin imprint and in pirated editions marketed at a fifth of the price. Yet he has never been consistently in print there, and Rushdie and his successors are far less translated locally than were their far less internationally renowned predecessors. A sensitive and well-attuned Hindi translation of Seth's *A Suitable Boy* has famously been made by Mahatma Gandhi's grandson Gopal. The firm of Vani Prakashan has issued Hindi versions of *Midnight's Children* and *Haroun and the Sea of Stories* and Roy's *The God of Small Things*; Bengali translations have been made of Ghosh's novels. Yet a perception persists in many quarters in South Asia that these are Western authors, simply because most of their readership is believed to lie in the West. This is an illusion because the 'West' no longer consists of a culturally or ethnically homogenous location. Like virtually everywhere else nowadays, it is a hotchpotch of co-existent, and sometimes conflicting, sometimes co-operative, sub-groups, many of whom pertain to diasporas originating precisely from the 'here' of the 'here and over there' divide. Readers are frequently diasporic beings whose tastes have been formed by travel, social change, disparities of social outlook and the multiple ironies springing from these ubiquitous facts. The last spectre of traditional book history we need to exorcise is the assumption that as objects of possible inquiry readerships stay put, either in the sense of social stability or in the more literal – but here more trenchant – sense of clinging to place. Readerships actually move, and so correspondingly do interpretative communities, reading practices, even varieties of repertoire or text. Why therefore is there this continuing perception among readers of world literature of some sort of a rift?

One possible answer is that, as defined by their readerships, postcolonial literatures have tended to split into two camps: one largely for domestic, the other for diasporic consumption. Within the comparatively small circle of English-language readers in India, for example, favourites and ready sellers include the satires of Chetan Bhagat and graphic (that is illustrated, comic-style) novels such as Sarnath Banerjee's *The Barn Owl's Wondrous Capers*, the appeal of which in the diasporic world is for the most part dwarfed by the more grandiose – and perhaps more heroic – tomes of Rushdie. There are, of course, exceptions that bridge this gap: the filigree, and subtly felt, stories of Kiran Desai's mother, Anita, for example, appeal to both constituencies, as do the books of Arundhati Roy. My point is that such coincidences of taste stem from shared responses in respective readerships rather than any collusion between publishing groups or lists, much as the latter may have enabled them. The ultimate driving force behind literary configurations of this kind, and the affinities that underlie them, really is the power of the consumer.

Arguably a similar split has begun to open up in the field of African fiction. The bitter honesty of John Coetzee's work, for example, has won him the Man Booker Prize twice. Though widely read in South Africa, north of the Zambesi it is hardly known. And one of the few authors from sub-Saharan black Africa to have enjoyed international publicity on the Rushdie scale is Ben Okri, winner of the prize in 1991. Okri's roots are firmly located in the Nigerian midwest; his masterfully realised. themes are as authentic as those of any other African author. Despite this, a perception lingers in West Africa that he is an overseas writer: not because of his chosen language of self-expression, which in common with both Achebe's and Soyinka's is English, nor because of his place of residence in London (both Achebe and Soyinka, after all, have spent long periods in the USA, as has Ngugi), but on the grounds that he is an artist much read and fêted outside the continent who frequently tackles broad themes of relevance to the diaspora. In February 2007 I sought opinions on my friend Okri from a postgraduate class in 'Postcolonial Literature' at the University of Ghana. Their knowledge and awareness of African literature in general was both alert and informed. Yet only one student had heard of the author of *The Famished Road*, and none had heard of the Booker. By the same token there are African authors such as Armah or Elechi Amadi who remain almost unknown among general readers abroad.

There are short- and long-term solutions to this hiatus. In the short-term the movement into local markets of the large internationals, and the co-existence of semi-autonomous franchises such as Penguin or Routledge India, promises to ease up the field, because it makes a similar range of titles available to both local and international audiences, albeit at differential prices. Amartya Sen's influential and provocative collection of essays *The Argumentative Indian* was published in 2005 throughout the world by the Penguin Group. In London it sold for £25 while in New Delhi Penguin India released it simultaneously for 500 rupees, about a third of that price. The joint release none the less prevented it from being viewed in either milieu as primarily a cultural import. As such initiatives become increasingly sensitive to local conditions, a mainstream move to publishing in vernacular languages is an almost inevitable consequence; Penguin India has indeed already taken that step. Where commercial realities make such tactics difficult, joint publishing agreements, such as those struck in Africa for Heinemann's African Writers series in its later years or by Ayebia, publishers of the Zimbabwean novelist Tsitsi Dangaremba at the present time, often have an equivalent effect. Some writers who are anxious to avoid a segregated following have, either independently or through their agents, struck deals with both multinational and local firms: Chimamanda Ngozi Adichie, for example, is published by Fourth Estate in Britain and by Alfred A. Knopf in the United States. Throughout Nigeria she is issued and distributed by Muhtar Bakare of Kachifo, a privately owned company set up to 'Tell Our Own Stories' through an imaginative publishing list across many disciplines, an on-line bookstore, annual prizes and *Farafina*, a creative writing magazine that shares its name with a well-known musical ensemble from Burkina Faso.

The ultimate resolution of temporary disjunctions of distribution, however, lies with historical change itself, and a reforging of alliances. To allocate writers and their texts to separate geopolitical spheres is for us all to trap ourselves in ways of thinking and acting we are well on the way to transcending. At the outset of the third millennium the majority of readers do not in any case sit isolated in place, and intent before page. Self-expression, whether individual or collective, is no longer allocated, shelved or confined anywhere, but travels by a variety of means, both paperbound and electronic, to a spectrum of audiences in a multitude of overlapping languages and across a jostling plethora of genres and non-genres. The triple technologies of internet, mobile phone and texting, lying beyond the scope of this particular study but rapidly spreading across both traditional non-West and conventional West, are testimonials to this welcome fact. Mobile phones with their increasing capacities for interpersonal communication are now practically ubiquitous in Africa at every social level and in all but the most remote regions. Remoteness, in any case, is now a relative and imperilled term. Developing and diffusing, such technologies are also free from prescribed, predictable or globalised patterns of evolution. It is now far from clear, for example, that the worldwide web has conspired to privilege or bolster any one set of linguistic codes. By 2020 it is calculated that India will be texting 180 billion SMSs annually, of which 40 per cent, or 80 billion, will be in the vernacular. In Africa the desk-bound skills of the publishing sector are fast being supplemented or overtaken by the posting and downloading of digital texts or, to return to a term deployed earlier in this study, of repertoires. The book age is not over yet, and may well continue to proliferate everywhere. A growing proportion of its enabling skills – typesetting, copy-editing, collating – are, however, being performed in Asia: in southern cities such as Bangalore, in the burgeoning suburb of New Delhi's Gargaon or else in Kolkata's Salt Lake City not 30 miles from where in 1778 Halhed, Wilkins and Panchanana Karmakara set up their forge and press. Two and a bit centuries on, it is fortunately by no means clear, in the sycophantic language of Halhed's Preface, who will now 'command' or who 'obey', or indeed whether such confusing hierarchies of empire and post-empire retain any comprehensible, or barely relevant, meaning.

Bibliography

Abimbola, Wande (1976) *Ifa Divination Poetry* (Yoruba and English). Ibadan and Oxford: Oxford University Press.
—— (1997) *Ifa Will Mend Our Broken World: Thoughts on Yoruba Religion and Culture in Africa and the Diaspora*. Roxburg, Mass: Aim.
Achebe, Chinua (1958) *Things Fall Apart*. London: Heinemann.
—— (1960) *No Longer at Ease*. London: Heinemann.
—— (1966) *A Man of the People*. London: Heinemann.
—— (1975) *Morning Yet on Creation Day*. London: Heinemann.
Adichie, Chimamanda Ngozi (2006) *Half a Yellow Sun*. London: Fourth Estate.
Ajayi, J. F. Ade (1960) 'How Yoruba Was Reduced to Writing', *Odu: A Journal of Yoruba, Edo and Related Studies*, 8, 49–58.
—— (1999) 'Crowther and Language in the Yoruba Mission', Henry Martyn Lecture no. 2, University of Cambridge, Faculty of Divinity, 26 October.
—— (2002) *A Patriot to the Core: Bishop Ajayi Crowther*. Ibadan: Spectrum.
Allen, Graham and Jannaa Jessee (2007) 'An Economic Introduction to India', London: House of Commons, Research Paper 07/40.
Amaduzzi, Giovanni Christofano (ed.) (1772) *Alphabeticum grandonico-malabaricum*. Rome: Congregatio de Propaganda Fide.
Anand, Mulk Raj (1935) *Untouchable*. London: Wishart.
—— (1981) *Conversations in Bloomsbury*. New Delhi: Arnold-Heinemann.
Anderson, Benedict (1983, rev. edn 1991) *Imagined Communities: Reflections on the Origin and Spread of Nationalism*. London and New York: Verso.
Anyidoho, Kofi (1984) *A Harvest of Our Dreams*. London: Heinemann
Armah, Ayi Kwei (1968) *The Beautyful Ones Are Not Yet Born*. London: Heinemann.
—— (1973) *Two Thousand Seasons*. London: Heinemann.
—— (1995) *Osiris Rising*. Popenguine, Senegal: Per Ankh.
Aryabhata (1976) *Aryabhatiya of Aryabhata*, ed., trans. and with an introduction by Kripa Shakar Shukla and S. V. Sharma (Sanskrit and English). New Delhi: Indian National Science Academy.
Ashcroft, Bill, Gareth Griffiths and Helen Tiffin (1989) *The Empire Writes Back*. London: Routledge.
Askew, Kelly Michelle (2002) *Performing the Nation: Swahili Music and Cultural Politics in Tanzania*. Chicago University Press.

Asma'u Dan Fodio, Nana (1997) *Collected Works*, ed. Jean Boyd and Beverley B. Mack. East Lansing: University of Michigan Press.

Assumpção, Manuel de (1743) *Vocabolario em Idioma Bengalla e Portuguez, Dividado em duas partes*. Lisbon: Francisco da Silva.

Awoonor, Kofi (1973) *Ride Me, Memory*. New York: Greenfield Review Press.

Babalola, S. A. (1966) *The Content and Form of Yoruba Ijala*. Oxford University Press.

Bahura, G. N (ed.) (1971) *Catalogue of Manuscripts in the Maharaja of Jaipur Museum*. Jaipur: Maharaja of Jaipur Museum.

Bailey, Benjamin (trans.) (1829) *The New Testament of Our Lord and Saviour Jesus Christ Translated into the Malayalam Language*. Cottayam: Church Mission Press for the Madras Bible Society.

Balmer, William Turnbull (1925) *A History of the Akan Peoples of the Gold Coast*. London: Atlantis Press.

Banerjee, R. D (1980) *A History of Orissa from the Earliest Times to the British Period*. Delhi and Varanasi: Bharatiya Publishing House.

Banerjee, Sumanta (1989) *The Parlour and the Streets: Elite and Popular Culture in Nineteenth-Century Calcutta*. Kolkata: Seagull Books.

The Baptist Magazine and Literary Review. London: The Baptist Press, 1809–1904.

Baptist Mission, Serampore (1815) *Seventh Memoir Relative to the Progress of the Translation of the Sacred Scriptures Addressed to the Society at Serampore*. Serampore: The Mission Press.

—— (1816) *Memoir Relative to the Progress of the Translations of the Sacred Scriptures in the Year 1816, Addressed to the Society, Serampore*. Serampore: The Mission Press.

Barber, Karin (1984) 'Yoruba *oriki* and deconstructive criticism', *Research in African Literatures*, 15:4, 497–518.

—— (1991) *'I Could Speak until Tomorrow': Oriki, Women and the Past in a Yoruba Town*. Edinburgh University Press for the International African Institute.

Barrier, Gerald (1974) *Banned: Controversial Literature and Political Control in British India, 1907–1947*. Columbia: University of Missouri Press.

Bartels, F. L (1965) *The Roots of Ghana Methodism*. London: Cambridge University Press in association with the Methodist Book Depot, Ghana.

Baudhyana (2003) *The Baudhyana 'Srautasutra*, ed. and trans. C. G. Kashikar, 4 vols. New Delhi: Indira Gandhi Centre for the Arts in association with Motilal Banarsidass.

Bayly, Chris (1996) *Empire and Information: Intelligence Gathering and Social Communication in India, 1780–1870*. Cambridge University Press.

Bernal, Martin (1987–2006) *Black Athena: The Afroasiatic Roots of Classical Civilization*. New Brunswick, NJ: Rutgers University Press.

Bhabha, Homi K. (1994) *The Location of Culture*. London and New York: Routledge.

Bhattacharya, Prodosh (2007) 'The Reception of Marie Corelli in India', in Shafquat Towheed (ed.) *New Readings in the Literature of British India, c. 1780–1947*. Stuttgart: ibidem-Verlag, 219–44.

Bilgrami, Abdullah Husain (1871) *Dastan-e Amir Hamzah*. Lucknow: Matba Munshi Naval Kishore.

—— (1991) *The Romance Tradition in Urdu: Adventures from the Dastan of Amir Hamzah*, ed., trans. and with an introduction by Frances W. Pritchett. New York: Columbia University Press.

Bilhana (1919) *Black Marigolds*. Being a Rendering into English of the 'Panchasika of Chauras' by E. Powys Mathers. Oxford: Blackwell.

Blackburn, Stuart (1988) *Singing of Birth and Death: Texts in Performance*. University of Philadelphia Press.

—— (2003) *Print, Folklore and Nationalism in Colonial South India*. New Delhi: Permanent Black.

Blurton, T. Richard (2006) *Bengali Myths*. London: The British Museum.

Boehmer, Elleke (2002) *Empire, the National and the Postcolonial, 1890–1920. Resistance in Interaction*. Oxford University Press.

Bourdieu, Pierre (1993) *The Field of Cultural Production*, ed. and trans. Randal Johnson. Cambridge: Polity.

Bovill, E. W. (ed.) (1964–6), *Missions to the Niger*, 4 vols. London: The Hakluyt Society.

Brouillette, Sarah (2007) *Postcolonial Writers in the Global Marketplace*. Basingstoke and New York: Palgrave.

Brown, John (1985) *Secwana Dictionary*. London: London Missionary Society.

Brown, Judith M. (1985) *Modern India: The Origins of an Asian Democracy*. New Delhi and Oxford: Oxford University Press.

Browne, Edward G. (1914) *The Press and Poetry of Modern Persia*. Cambridge University Press.

Buitenen, J. A. B. van (ed. and trans.) (1975) *The Mahabharata*. Chicago and London: University of Chicago Press.

Burgess, J. (ed.) (1888–92) *Epigraphia Indica: A Collection of Inscriptions supplementary to the Corpus Inscriptionum Indicarum of the Archaeological Survey (Pali and English)*. Calcutta: Thacker, Spink and Co.; London: Kegan Paul; Leipzig: O. Harrossowitz.

Carey, William (1999) *The Journal and Selected Letters of William Carey*, ed. Terry G. Carter. Macon, Ga: Smyth and Helwys.

Carter, Thomas Francis (1955) *The Invention of the Printing Press in China and Its Spread Westward*. New York: Ronald Press.

Casely-Hayford, Joseph Ephraim (1911) *Ethiopia Unbound: Studies in Race Emancipation*. London: C. M. Phillips.

Centre National de la Recherche Scientifique and Musée de l'Homme (1996) *Voices of the World: An Anthology of Vocal Expression*. Paris: CNRS. Sound recording, catalogue number CMX 3741010 12.

Chakava, Henry (1995) 'Publishing Ngugi: The Challenge, the Risk and the Reward', in Charles Cantalupo (ed.) *Ngugi wa Thiong'o: Texts and Contexts*. Trenton, NJ: Africa World Press.

—— (1996) *Publishing in Africa: One Man's Perspective*. Nairobi: Bellagio Studies in Publishing no. 6, in association with East African Educational Publishers.

Chakravorty, Swapan (2006) 'Grantha, path, shilpakarma: Rabindranath o rachanar drishyapat', *Ababhas*, 5:4, 124–41.

Chambers, Robert (1832–5) *A Biographical Dictionary of Eminent Scotsmen*. Glasgow: Blackie and Son.

Chandumenon, Oyyarattu (2005) *Indulekha*, trans. from the Malayalam by Anitha Devasia. New Delhi: Oxford University Press.

Chatterjee, Partha (2003) *The Nation and Its Fragments: Colonial and Postcolonial Histories*.

Princeton University Press.

Chatterjee, Rimi B. (2006) *Empires of the Mind: A History of the Oxford University Press in India under the Raj*. New Delhi: Oxford University Press.

Chaudhuri, Nirad C. (1996) *Scholar Extraordinary: The Life of Friedrich Max Müller*. New Delhi: Orient Paperbacks.

Chrisman, Laura (2000) *Re-reading the Imperial Romance: British Imperialism and South African Resistance in Haggard, Schreiner and Plaatje*. Oxford University Press.

Christaller, J. G. (1875) *Dictionary of the Asante and Fante Language Called Tshi*. Basel: Evangelical Missionary Society.

Clapperton, Hugh, Dixon Denham and W. Oudney (1826) *Narratives of Travels and Discoveries in Northern and Central Africa in the Years 1822, 1823 and 1824*. London: John Murray.

Clapperton, Hugh, Richard Lander and John Barrow (1829) *Journal of a Second Expedition into the Interior of Africa from the Bight of Benin to Soccatou, to which is added the Journal of Richard Lander*. London: John Murray.

Clapperton, Hugh and Richard Lander (1830) *Records of Captain Clapperton's Last Expedition to Africa by His Faithful Attendant*, 2 vols. London: H. Coburn and R. Bentley.

Clark, John Pepper (1966) *Oxidi: A Play*. Oxford University Press.

—— (1977) *The Ozidi Saga*, trans. from the Ijo of Okabou Ojobolo. Ibadan University Press.

Clarke, Becky Ayebia (2003) 'The African Writers Series – Celebrating Forty Years of Publishing Distinction', *Research in African Literatures*, 34:2, 163–74.

Coetzee, J. M. (1974) *Dusklands*. Johannesburg: Ravan Press.

—— (1977) *In the Heart of the Country*. London: Secker and Warburg.

—— (1996) *Giving Offence: Essays on Censorship*. University of Chicago Press.

Couzens, Tim and Stephen Gray (1978) 'Printers' and Other Devils: The Texts of Sol Plaatje's *Mhudi*', *Research in African Literatures*, 9:2, 198–215.

Crowther, Samuel Ajayi (1852) *A Grammar of the Yoruba Language*. London: Seeleys.

—— (1857) *Isoamo-Ibo Primer*. London: Church Missionary Society.

—— (1864) *A Grammar and Vocabulary of the Nupe Language*. London: Church Missionary Society.

—— (1867–84) *Bibeli mimo evi ni oro Olorun ti Testmenti Lailai ali ti Titan*. London: British and Foreign Bible Society.

—— (1882) *Vocabulary of the Ibo Language*. London: Society for the Propagation of Christian Knowledge.

Currey, James (2003) 'Chinua Achebe, the African Writers Series and the Establishment of African Literature', *African Affairs*, 102, 575–85.

Dalby, David (1967) 'A Survey of the Indigenous Scripts of Liberia and Sierra Leone: Vai, Mende, Loma, Kpelle and Bassa', *African Language Studies*, 8, 1–51.

—— (1977) *A Provisional Language Map of Africa and the Adjacent Islands*. London: International African Institute.

Dalrymple, William (2006) *The Last Mughal: The Fall of a Dynasty*. London: Bloomsbury.

Darlow, Thomas Herbert and Horace Frederick Moule (1903–11) *Historical Catalogue of Printed Editions of Holy Scripture in the Library of the British and Foreign Bible Society*, 4 vols. London: Bible House.

Darnton, Robert (2001) 'Literary Surveillance in the British Raj: The Contradictions of Liberal Imperialism', *Book History*, 4, 133–76.

—— (2002) 'Book Production in British India, 1850–1900', *Book History*, 5, 239–62.

Dasa, Sudramuni Sarala (1898–9) *The Mahabharata* (Oriya). Cuttack: Orissa.

Datta, Kitty Scoular (2008) 'Publishing and Translating Hafez under Empire', in Robert Fraser and Mary Hammond (eds) *Books without Borders*, vol. 2 *Perspectives from South Asia*. Basingstoke and New York: Palgrave, 58–70.

De Lange, Margreet (1997) *The Muzzled Muse: Literature and Censorship in South Africa*. Amsterdam and Philadelphia: John Benjamins.

Derrida, Jacques (1976) *Of Grammatology*, trans. Gayatri Chakrovarty Spivak. London: Johns Hopkins University Press.

Desani, G. V. (1972) *All About H. Hatterr*, introduction by Anthony Burgess. Harmondsworth: Penguin Books.

Diouf, Mamadou (2002) 'The Senegalese Murid Trade Diaspora and the Making of Vernacular Cosmopolitanism', trans. Steven Rendall, in Carol A. Breckenridge, Sheldon Pollock, Homi K. Bhabha and Dipesh Chakrabarty (eds) *Cosmopolitanism*. Duke University Press, 111–37.

Diringer, David (1953) *The Alphabet* (second edn). New York: Philosophical Library.

—— (1982) *The Book before Printing: Ancient, Medieval, Oriental*. New York: Dover.

Edgerton, Franklin (1938) 'Rome and Antioch in the Mahabharata', *Journal of the American Oriental Society*, 58:2, 262–5.

Eisenstein, Elizabeth (1979) *The Printing Press As an Agent of Change: Communication and Cultural Transformation in Early Modern Europe*, 2 vols. Cambridge University Press.

—— (1983) *The Printing Revolution in Early Modern Europe*. Cambridge University Press.

Equiano, Olaudah (1789) *The Interesting Narrative of the Life of Equiano, or G. Vassa*, the African, 2 vols. London: T. Wilkins.

Fagborun, J. Gbanya (1994) *The Yoruba Koiné: Its History and Linguistic Innovations*. Munich and Newcastle: LINCOM.

Fagunwa, Daniel (1949) *Igbo Olodumare, apa keji Ogboju Ode ninu Igbo Irunmale*. Edinburgh: Thomas Nelson and Sons.

—— (1968) *The Forest of a Thousand Demons*, trans. Wole Soyinka. Walton-on-Thames: Thomas Nelson and Sons.

Faulkner, R. O. (trans.) (1989) *The Ancient Egyptian Book of the Dead*, ed. Carol Andrews. London: The British Museum.

Finkelstein, David and Alistair McCleery (2005) *Introduction to Book History*. London and New York: Routledge.

Finnegan, Ruth (1970) *Oral Literature in Africa*. London: Oxford University Press.

—— (1977) *Oral Poetry: Its Nature, Significance and Social Context*. Cambridge University Press.

Finnegan, Ruth (2007) *The 'Oral' and Beyond: Doing Things with Words in Africa*. Oxford: James Currey; University of Chicago Press; Pietermaritzburg: University of KwaZulu-Natal Press.

Fraser, Robert (1986) *West African Poetry: A Critical History*. Cambridge University Press.

—— (2007a) 'Half the World is Not So Narrow: Feminist Publishing in India: An

Interview with Ritu Menon', *Wasafiri*, 52, 11–17.

—— (2007b) 'Press, Partition and Famine: Benedict Anderson and the Bengal Emergency of 1905–6', in Alistair McCleery and Benjamin A. Brabon (eds) *The Influence of Benedict Anderson*. Edinburgh: Merchiston, 59–92.

Freeman, I. I. and D. Johns (1840) *A Narrative of the Persecution of the Christians in Madagascar with Details of the Escape of the Six Christian Refugees Now in England*. London: John Snow.

Fritschi, Gerhard (1983) *Africa and Gutenberg: Exploring Oral Structures in the Modern African Novel*. Berne, Frankfurt and New York: Peter Lang.

Furniss, Graham (1996) *Poetry, Prose and Popular Culture in Hausa*. Edinburgh University Press for the International Africa Institute.

Ghosh, Anindita (2006) *Power in Print: Popular Publishing and the Politics of Language and Culture in a Colonial Society, 1778–1905*. Delhi: Oxford University Press.

Gilchrist, John Borthwick (1787–90) *A Dictionary: English and Hindoostanee*. Calcutta: Stuart and Cooper.

—— (1796) *A Grammar, of the Hindoostanee Language, or Part Third of Volume First, of a System of Hindoostanee Philology*. Calcutta: Chronicle Press.

Girta, Kuman (1990) *Censorship in India*. New Delhi: Har-Anand.

Gonsalve, J. M. (1826) *Lithographic Views of Bombay, with 6 Leaves of Plates*. Bombay: General Lithographic Press.

Goodrich, Luther Carrington (1935) *The Literary Inquisition of Ch'ien Lung*. Baltimore: Waverley Press.

Goody, Jack (ed.) (1968) *Literacy in Traditional Societies*. Cambridge University Press.

—— (1977) *The Domestication of the Savage Mind*. Cambridge University Press.

Gopal, Privamvad (2005) *Literary Radicalism in India: Gender, Nation and the Transition to Independence*. London and New York: Routledge.

Government of the Gold Coast (1919–57) *Gold Coast Legislative Debates*. Accra: Government Printer.

—— (1931a) Director of Education. *The New Script and Its Relation to the Languages of the Gold Coast*. Accra: Government Printer.

—— (1931b) *Memoir of the Textual Committee*. Accra: Government Printer.

Government of India, Legislative Department (1915) *The Indian Penal Code* (Act XLV of 1860). As Amended up to June 1, 1910. Calcutta: Superintendent of Government Printers.

Grierson, George (1903) 'The Early Publications of the Serampore Missionaries: A Contribution to Bibliography', *Indian Antiquary*, XXXII, 241–54.

—— (1903–22) *Linguistic Survey of India*, 9 vols. Calcutta: Office of the Superintendent of Government Printing, India.

Griswold, Wendy (2000) *Bearing Witness: Readers, Writers and the Novel in Nigeria*. Princeton University Press.

—— (2002) 'Number Magic in Nigeria', *Book History*, 5, 275–82.

Gundert, Hermann (1871–2) *A Malayalam–English Dictionary*. Mangalore: C. Stolz.

Guy, R. Kent (1987) *The Emperor's Four Treasuries: Scholars and State in the Late Ch'ien-Lung Era*. Cambridge: Council on East Asian Studies.

Haffez (1791) *Diwan-i-Khwajah Hafez-i Shirazi. The Works of Dewan Hafez: with an account of his life and writings*. Calcutta: A. Upjohn.

Haggard, H. Rider (1929) *Mashimo ya Mfalme Sulemani (King Solomon's Mines)*, trans. into Swahili, F. Johnson. London: Longman, 1929.

—— (1938) *Koning Salomo se myne (King Solomon's Mines)*, trans. into Afrikaans from the abridgement of Michael West. London: Longman.

—— (1958a) *Imigodi kakumhani u-Solomon (King Solomon's Mines)*, trans. into Zulu, J. J. R. Jolobe. Johannesburg: A. P. B.

—— (1958b) *Imigodi yenkosi uSolomoni (King Solomon's Mines)*, trans. into Zulu, J. F. Cele. King William's Town: Afrikaanse Pers-Boekhandel.

—— (1959) *Uzibaningashekazi (She)*, trans. into Xhosa, Guybon Bualwana Sinxo. Johannesburg: Die Bantoe Se Boeke-Tuiste.

—— (1963) *Merafo ya Morena Salemone (King Solomon's Mines)* (Zulu translation). King William's Town: Afrikaanse Pers-Boekhandel.

Hair, P. E. H. (1967) *The Early Study of Nigerian Languages.* Cambridge University Press.

Halhed, Nathaniel Brassey (1778) *A Grammar of the Bengal Language* (Bengali and English). Hoogly, Calcutta.

Haq, Mahabubul (1991) *Bamla bananer niyam* [The Rules of Bengali Spelling]. Dhaka: Jitio Shahitja Prakashani.

Hawking, Stephen (1988) *A Brief History of Time.* London: Bantam.

Hill, Alan (1975) *In Pursuit of Publishing*, foreword by Chinua Achebe. London: John Murray.

Hodza, A. C. (1979). *Shona Praise Poetry.* Oxford University Press.

Hofmeyr, Isabel (2004) *The Portable Bunyan: A Transnational History of* The Pilgrim's Progress. Princeton University Press.

Huggan, Graham (2001) *The Postcolonial Exotic: Marketing the Margins.* London and New York: Routledge.

Hunwick, J. O. (1964) 'A New Source for the Biography of Ahmad Baba al-Tinbuki', *Bulletin of the School of Oriental and African Studies*, 27:3, 568–93.

Jacquemont, Victor (1933) *Etat Politique et Social de l'Inde du Sud: Extraits de Son Journal de Voyage.* Paris: E. Leroux.

Johanson, Graham (2000) *Colonial Editions in Australia.* Wellington: Elibank Press.

Jones, Daniel (1916) *A Sechuana Reader*, preface by Sol Plaatje. London University Phonetic Readers.

Jones, Derek (ed.) (2001) *Censorship: A World Encyclopaedia of Censorship.* London: Fitzroy Dearborne.

Jones, William (1807) *The Works of Sir William Jones*, 13 vols, ed. Anna Maria Jones. London: G. and G. Robinson, R. H. Evans and John Hatchard.

Joshi, Priya (2002a) *In Another Country: Colonialism, Culture, and the English Novel in India.* Columbia University Press.

Joshi, Priya (2002b) 'Quantitative Method: Literary History', *Book History*, 5, 263–74.

Julien, Eileen (1992) *African Novels and the Question of Orality.* Bloomington and Indianapolis: Indiana University Press, 1992.

Kalango, Koko (2006) *Get Nigeria Reading Again.* Port Harcourt: The Rainbow Club.

Kanda, K. C. (1995) *Urdu Ghazals: An Anthology from the Sixteenth to the Twentieth Century.* Delhi: Sterling Paperbacks.

Kesavan, B. S., *et al*. (1985) *Printing and Publishing in India: A Story of Cultural Awakening*, 2 vols. New Delhi: National Book Trust.

Koelle, Sigismund Wilhelm (1849) *Narrative of an Expedition into the Vy Country of West Africa and the Discovery of a System of Syllabic Writing Recently Invented by the Vy Tribe*. London: Seeley's, Hatchards and Nisbet.

Kramrisch, Stella (1981) *The Presence of Siva*. Princeton University Press.

Kunene, Daniel P. (1971). *Heroic Poetry of the BaSotho*. Oxford University Press.

Kunene, Mazisi (1970). *Zulu Poems*. London: Heinemann

—— (1979*) Emperor Shaka the Great: A Zulu Epic*. London: Heinemann.

Lal, Ananda and Sukanta Chaudhuri (eds) (2001) *Shakespeare on the Calcutta Stage: A Checklist*. Kolkata: Papyrus.

Laubach, Frank (1948) *Teaching the World to Read: A Handbook for Literary Campaigns*. London: United Society for Christian Literature.

Lepsius, Karl Richard (1842) *Das Todtenbuch der Ägypter nach dem hieroglyphischen Papyrus in Turin. Mit einem Vorworte zum ersten Male herausgegeben*. Leipzig: G. Wigand.

—— (1855) *Das allgemeine Linguistische Alphabet: Grundsätze der Übertragung fremder Schriftsysteme und bisher noch ungeschriebener Sprachen in Europäische Buchstaben*. Berlin: Verlag von Wilhelm Hertz.

Lizarribar, Camille (1998) *Something Else Will Stand Beside It: The African Writers Series and the Development of African Literature*. Ann Arbor: University of Michigan Press.

Long, James (1861) *Bishop Cotton's View of the 'Nil Darpan' Question*. Calcutta: privately printed.

Low, Gail (2002) 'In Pursuit of Publishing: Heinemann's African Writers Series', *Wasafiri*, 37, 31–6.

McCleery, Alistair (2007) '"Sophisticated Smut": The Penguin Edition of *Lady Chatterley's Lover* in New Zealand', *Paradise: Script and Print (The Bulletin of the Bibliographical Society of Australia and New Zealand)*, 129, 192–204.

McLuhan, Marshall (1962) *The Gutenberg Galaxy: The Making of Typographic Man*. London: Routledge with the University of Toronto Press.

Majeed, Javed (1992) *Ungoverned Imaginings: James Mill's* The History of British India *and Orientalism*. Oxford: The Clarendon Press.

Mamoon, Muntassiir (2006) 'Textbooks in Nineteenth-Century Bengal', paper delivered to the conference 'New Word Order: Emerging Histories of the Book', Jadavpur University, Kolkata, February.

Marshman, J. C. (1859) *The Life and Times of Carey, Marshman and Ward, Embracing the History of the Serampore Mission*, 2 vols. London: Longman.

Maupoil, Bernard (1943) *La géomancie à l'ancienne Côte des Esclaves*. Paris: Travaux et mémoires de l'Institut d'ethnologie, no. 42.

Mehdi, Hemjyoti (2008) 'Missionary Writing and the Self-fashioning of Assamese Cultural Nationalism in Colonial India: Revising the Past, Understanding the Present', in Robert Fraser and Mary Hammond (eds) *Books without Borders*, vol. 2 *Perspectives from South Asia*. Basingstoke: Palgrave, 71–84.

Midgely, Henry Peter (1993) 'Author, Identity and Publisher: A Symbiotic Relationship; Lovedale Missionary Press and Early Black Writing in South Africa', unpublished MA thesis, Rhodes University, Grahamstown, South Africa.

Mill, James Stuart (1817) *A History of British India*, 3 vols. London: Baldwin, Cradock and Joy.

Mintra, Dinabandhu (1861) *Nil Darpan or The Indigo Planting Mirror*, translated by 'a native'. Calcutta: G. H. Manuel.

Moffat, Robert (1826) *Bechuana Spelling Book*. London: London Missionary Society.

—— (1846) *Missionary Labours and Scenes in South Africa*. London: John Snow.

—— (trans.) (1848) *Loeto loa ga Mokeresete* [*The Pilgrim's Progress* in Setswana]. Kuruman: The Mission Press.

—— *et al.* (1851) *Bibela ea Boitsepho ee Cutsen Kholagano mo puon ea Secuana* [The Bible in seTswana]. Kuruman: The Mission Press for the British and Foreign Bible Society.

Monotype Corporation (n.d.) *Specimen Book of 'Monotype' Non-Latin Typefaces*. Redhill: The Monotype Corporation.

Morgan, Charles (1944) *The House of Macmillan, 1843–1943*. London: Macmillan.

Moss, Charles Frederick (1875) *The Late Mr James Cameron of Madagascar*. Antananarivo.

Müller, Jan-Dirk (1994) 'The Body of a Book: The Media Transition from Manuscript to Print', in Hans Ulrich Gumbrecht and Karl Ludwig Pfeiffer (eds) *Materialities of Communication*. Stanford University Press.

Mullins, J. D. (1904) *The Wonderful Story of Uganda*. London: Church Missionary Society.

Mutesa II, Kabaka of Buganda (1967) *Desecration of My Kingdom*. London: Constable.

Naim, C. M. (1984) 'Prize-Winning *Adab*: A Study of Five Urdu Books Written in Response to the Allahabad Government Gazette Notification', in Barbara Daly Metcalf (ed.) *Moral Conduct and Authority: The Place of* Adab *in South Asian Islam*. Berkeley: University of California Press, 290–314.

Naipaul, V. S (1981) *Among the Believers: An Islamic Journey*. London: André Deutsch.

—— (2007) *A Writer's People: Ways of Looking and Feeling*. London: Picador.

Nair, P. Thankappan (ed.) (1995–2000) *Proceedings of the Asiatic Society*, 4 vols. Kolkata: The Asiatic Society.

Nasrin, Taslima (1994) *Lajja = Shame*,trans. Tutul Gupta. New Delhi: Penguin India.

Newell, Stephanie (2000) *Ghanaian Popular Fiction*. Oxford: James Currey.

—— (2002) *Literary Culture in Colonial Ghana: How to Play the Game of Life*. Manchester University Press.

—— (2006) *West African Literature*. Oxford University Press.

Ngugi wa Thiong'o (1967) *A Grain of Wheat*. London: Heinemann Educational Books.

—— (1980) *Caitaani Mutharaba-Ini*. Nairobi: Heinemann East Africa.

—— (1986) *Decolonising the Mind: The Politics of Language in African Literature*. Oxford: James Currey.

Ngugi wa Thiong'o (1987) *Devil on the Cross*. London: HEB.

NOP Market Research Ltd (2005) *World Culture Score Index*. New York: NOP.

Obiechina, Emmanuel (1973) *An African Popular Literature: A Study of Onitsha Market Pamphlets*. Cambridge University Press.

—— (1975) *Culture, Tradition and Society in the West African Novel*. Cambridge University Press.

Ogden, C. K (1932) *Basic English: A General Introduction with Rules and Grammar*. London: Kegan Paul.

Okigbo, Christopher (1962) *Heavensgate*. Ibadan, Mbari.

—— (1971) *Labyrinths with Path of Thunder*. London: Heinemann.

Okpewho, Isidore (1990) 'The Oral Performer and His Audience: A Case Study of the *Ozidi Saga*', in Isidore Okpewho (ed.) *The Oral Performance in Africa*. Ibadan, Owerri and Kaduna: Spectrum Books.

Ong, Walter J. (1982) *Orality and Literacy: The Technologizing of the West*. London and New York: Methuen.

Oraka, Louis Nnamdi (1983) *The Foundations of Igbo Studies*. Onitsha: University Publishing Company.

Orsini, Francesca (2002) *The Hindi Public Sphere 1920–40: Language and Literature in the Age of Nationalism*. New Delhi: Oxford University Press.

Page, Ivan (2008) 'The Origin and Growth of the "White Fathers" Press in Bukalasa, Uganda', in Robert Fraser and Mary Hammond (eds) *Books without Borders*, vol. 1 *The Cross-National Dimension in Print Culture*. Basingstoke: Palgrave, 107–29.

Pal, Bipinchandra (1973) *Memories of My Life and Times*. Calcutta: Bipinchandra Pal Institute.

Parry, Jonathan (1985) 'A Brahminical Tradition and the Technology of the Intellect', in Joanna Overing (ed.) *Reason and Morality*. London: Tavistock Publications, 200–25.

Parry, Milman (1971) *The Making of Homeric Verse*. Oxford: Clarendon Press.

P'Bitek, Okot (1966) *Song of Lawino*. Nairobi: East African Publishing House.

—— (1969) *Wer pa Lawino*. Nairobi: East African Publishing House.

—— (2001) *The Defence of Lawino*, trans. Taban lo Liyong. Kampala: Fountain.

Peires, Jeffrey (1975) 'The Lovedale Press: Literature for the Bantu Revisited', *History in Africa*, 6, 155–75.

Plaatje, Solomon T. (1930) *Mhudi: An Epic of South African Native Life a Hundred Years Ago*. Lovedale: The Lovedale Press.

Pollock, Sheldon (1996) 'The Sanskrit Cosmopolis AD 300–1300: Transculturation, Vernacularization and the Question of Ideology', in Jan. E. Houben (ed.) *The Ideology and Status of Sanskrit in South and East Asia*. Leiden: E. J. Brill, 197–247.

—— (1999) 'India in the Vernacular Millennium', in *Early Modernities: Daedalus*, 127:3, 41–74.

—— (2002) 'Cosmopolitanism and Vernaculars in History', in Carol A. Breckenridge, Sheldon Pollock, Homi K. Bhabha and Dipesh Chakrabarty (eds) *Cosmopolitanism*. Duke University Press, 15–53.

—— (ed.) (2003) *Literary Cultures in History: Reconstructions from South Asia*. Berkeley: University of California Press.

—— (2006) *The Language of the Gods in the World of Men: Sanskrit, Culture and Power in Pre-modern India*. Berkeley: University of California Press.

—— (2007) 'Literary Culture and Manuscript Culture in Precolonial India', in Simon J. Eliot, Andrew Nash and Ian Willison (eds) *Literary Cultures and the Material Book*. London: The British Library, 77–94.

Pongweni, Alec J. C. (1997) 'The Chimurenga Songs of the Zimbabwe War of Liberation', in Karin Barber (ed.) *Readings in Popular African Culture*. Oxford and Bloomington, Ind.: James Currey and Indiana University Press, 63–72.

Pringle, Eric (ed.) (1973) *The Letters of Thomas Pringle*, 2 vols. Glen Thorn, Adelaide: privately mimeographed.

Priolkar, Anant Kakba (1958) *The Printing Press in India: Its Beginnings and Early Development*. Bombay: Marathi Samshodham Mandala.

Pritchett, Frances W. (2003), 'A Long History of Urdu Literary Culture Part 2', in Sheldon Pollock (ed.) *Literary Cultures in History: Reconstructions from South Asia*. Berkeley: University of California Press, 864–91.

Qureshi, R. E. (1995) *Sufi Music of India and Pakistan: Sound, Context and Meaning in Qawwali*. University of Chicago Press.

Rabéarivello, Jean-Joseph (1939) *Vieilles chansons de pays d'Imerina, précedées d'une biographie du poète Malgache par Robert Boudry*. Antananarivo: Imprimerie Nationale.

Report of the Governor, Brigadier-General Sir Frederick Gordon Guggisberg to the Honourable Members of the Legislative Council, Gold Coast Colony, Legislative Council Debates Session 1927–8, 3rd March, 1927. Accra: Government Printer, 29.

Reports on Native Papers for the Province of Bengal, issued fortnightly, marked confidential. Calcutta: Bengali Secretariat/Bengali Translations Office, 1876–1916.

Reports on Publications Issued and Registered in the Several Provinces of British India. Calcutta: Government Press, 1867–.

Richards, Charles Granston (ed.) (1957) *Helps and Explanations for African Authors: Some Forms of Writing*. Nairobi: East African Literature Bureau.

Richman, Paula (1991) *Many Ramayanas: The Diversity of a Narrative Tradition in South Asia*. Berkeley: University of California Press.

Rocher, Rosanne (1983) *Orientalism, Poetry and the Millennium: The Chequered Life of Nathaniel Brassey Halhed, 1751–1830*. New Delhi: Motilal Banarsidass.

Ross, Fiona G. E. (1999) *The Bengali Printed Character and Its Development*. London: Curzon.

Rushdie, Salman (1981) *Midnight's Children*. London: Jonathan Cape.

—— (1983) *Shame*. London: Jonathan Cape.

—— (1988) *The Satanic Verses*. London: Viking.

Russell, Ralph (1970) 'The Development of the Modern Novel in Urdu', in T. W. Clark (ed.) *The Novel in India: Its Birth and Development*. London: Allen and Unwin, 102–41.

—— (1992) *The Pursuit of Urdu Literature: A Select History*. London: Zed Books.

—— and Khurshidul Islam (ed. and trans.) (1969) *Ghalib (1797–1869)*, vol. 1 *Life and Letters*. London: Allen and Unwin.

Said, Edward (1993) *Culture and Imperialism*. London: Chatto and Windus.

St Clair, William (2006) *The Grand Slave Emporium: Cape Coast Castle and the British Slave Trade*. London: Profile.

St John, John (1990) *William Heinemann: A Century of Publishing 1890–1990*. London: Heinemann.

Sander, Reinhardt and Bernth Linfords (eds) (2006) *Ngugi wa Thiong'o Speaks: Interviews with the Kenyan Writer*. Oxford: James Currey.

Sarkar, Jadunath (1984) *A History of Jaipur*, rev. and ed. Raghubir Singh. Hyderabad: Orient Longman.

Satpathy, Sumanyu (2005) 'Sarala Das and the Bhaki Tradition', unpublished paper delivered at Sahitya Academi of India, 22–23 April.

Sax, William S. (2002) *Personhood and Performance in the Padav Lila of Garkwal*. New York: Oxford University Press.

Schapera, I. (1951) *Apprenticeship at Kuruman, being the journals and letters of Robert and*

Mary Moffat, 1820–1828. London: Chatto and Windus.

Schön, James Frederick and Samuel Crowther (1842) *Journals of the Rev. James Frederick Schön and Mr Samuel Crowther*, etc. London: Church Missionary Society.

Sekyi, Kobina (1974) *The Blinkards*, introduction by J. Ajo Langley. London: Heinemann.

Sembene, Ousman (1960) *Les Bouts de bois de dieu*. Paris: Livre Contemporain.

Sen, Amartya (2005) *The Argumentative Indian: Writings on Indian History, Culture and Identity*. London and New Delhi: Penguin.

Senefelder, Johann Nepomuk Franz Aloys (1819) *A Complete Course of Lithography, Accompanied by Specimens of Drawings*, trans. A. Schlichtegroll. London: Robert Ackermann.

Senghor, Léopold Sédar (1948) *Anthologie de la nouvelle poésie nègre et malgache de langue française*. Paris: Presses Universitaires de France.

Sharma, Virenda Nath (1995) *Sawai Jai Singh and His Astronomy*. Delhi: Motilal Banarsidass.

Shaw, Graham W. (1977) 'The Cuttack Mission Press and Early Oriya Printing', *The British Library Journal*, 3:1, 29–43.

—— (ed.) (1978) *Early Printing in India* (Exhibition Catalogue, October 1978–February 1979). London: The British Library.

—— (1979) 'The First Printing Press in the Punjab', *The Library Chronicle*, 43, 159–79

—— (1981) *Printing in Calcutta to 1800: A Description and Checklist of Printing in Late Eighteenth-Century Calcutta*. London: The Bibliographical Society.

—— (1994) 'The Introduction of Lithography and Its Impact on Book Design in India', *Vihangama*, II:2 (July–September).

—— (1998) 'Calcutta: Birthplace of the Indian Lithographed Book', *Bulletin of the Print Historical Society*, 27, 89–111.

Shepherd, R. H. W. (1941) *Lovedale South Africa. The Story of a Century 1841–1941*, introduction by J. F. Hofmeyr. Cape Town: Lovedale Press.

—— (1971) *Lovedale South Africa 1824–1955*. Alice: Lovedale Press.

Shoner, Karine (1989) 'Paradigms of the Kali Yuga: The Heroes of the Alha Epic and Their Fate', in Stuart H. Blackburn, Peter J. Claus, Joyce B. Fluechiger and Susan S. Wadley (eds) *Oral Epics in India*. Berkeley: University of California Press, 140–54.

Soga, Tiyo (1983) *The Journal and Selected Writings of the Rev. Tiyo Soga*. Cape Town: Balkema.

Soyinka, Wole (1973) *Collected Plays*, 2 vols. Oxford University Press.

—— (1975) *The Man Died: Prison Notes*. London: Penguin Books.

Specimens of Printing Types in Use at the Baptist Mission Press, Circular Road, Calcutta. Calcutta: The Baptist Mission Press, 1826.

Stanley, Brian (1992) *The History of the Baptist Missionary Society*. Edinburgh: T. and T. Clark.

Stark, Ulrike (2008) *An Empire of Books: The Naval Kishore Press and the Diffusion of the Printed Word in Colonial India*. New Delhi: Permanent Black.

Streeter, Burnett Hillman (1924) *The Four Gospels: A Study of Origins*. London: Macmillan.

Sukhankhar, V. S., *et al.* (eds) (1919–66) *Mahabharata*, critical edition, 19 vols. Pune: Bhandakar Oriental Institute.

Sutcliffe, Peter (1978, rev. edn 1994) *The Oxford University Press: An Informal History*. Oxford University Press.

Sutherland, Efua (n.d.) *The Story of Bob Johnson: Ghana's Ace Comedian*. Ho, Ghana: E. P. Church Press.

Taban lo Liyong (1993) 'On Translating the "Untranslated": Chapter 14 of *Wer pa Lawino* by Okot p'Bitek', *Research in African Literatures*, 24:3, 87–92.

Tagore, Rabindranath (1927) *Lekhan* [Jottings]. Santiniketan.

—— (1995) *Poems and Songs*, trans. Sovana Dasgupta. Calcutta: The Writers Workshop.

—— (2001) *Particles, Jottings, Sparks: The Collected Brief Poems*, trans. William Radice. London: Angel.

Trevelyan, C. E., J. Prinsep, A. Duff and H. T. Prinsep (1834) *The Application of the Roman Alphabet to all the Oriental Languages*. Calcutta: The Serampore Press.

Trevelyan, G. O. (1889) *The Life and Letters of Lord Macaulay*. London: Longman.

Tutuola, Amos (1952) *The Palm Wine Drinkard*. London: Faber and Faber.

Twyman, Michael (1970) *Lithography 1800–1850: The Techniques of Drawing on Stone in England and France and Their Application in Works of Topography*. Oxford University Press.

United Nations (2006) *The United Nations Human Development Report*. London: Palgrave Macmillan for the United Nations Development Programme.

van der Vlies, Andrew (2007) 'Reading Banned Books: Apartheid Censors and Anti-apartheid Aesthetics', *Wasafiri*, 52, 55–61.

Veit-Weld, Flora (ed.) (1992) *Dambudzo Marechera: A Source Book on His Life and Work*. London and New York: Hans Zell.

Ward, G. E. (trans.) (1903) *The Bride's Mirror: A Tale of Domestic Life in Delhi Forty Years Ago*. London: Henry Frowde.

Ward, Ira C. (1941) *Ibo Dialects and the Development of a Common Language*. Cambridge: Heffers.

Westermann, Diedrich Hermann (1927) *Die westlichen Sudansprachen und ihre Beziehungen zum Bantu*. Berlin: de Gruyter.

Whitehead, Clive (2003) *Colonial Education: The British Indian and Colonial Educational Service 1858–1983*. London: I. B. Tauris.

Wilkins, Charles (1785) *The Bhagvad-Geeta, or, dialogues of Kreeshna and Arjoon, in Eighteen Lectures, with Notes*, translated from the original Sanskreet with a preliminary note by W. Hastings. London: C. Nourse.

Wolpert, Stanley (1991) *India*. Berkeley, Los Angeles and Oxford: University of California Press.

Young, R. R. (ed.) (1945) *The Development of the Protectorate Bureau, Sierra Leone. First Annual Report of the Sierra Leone Literature Bureau*. Bo: Sierra Leone: Literature Bureau.

—— (1946) *Literacy for Adults in Africa*. London: The Shelton Press.

Yule, Mary (n.d.) *Mackay of Uganda, the Missionary Engineer*. Edinburgh: Constable for Hodder and Stoughton.

Index

Abrahams, Peter 155, 181; *Mine Boy* 98; *Wild Conquest* 98

Achebe, Chinua 79, 122, 164–7; *Man of the People, A* 175; *No Longer at Ease* 78; *Things Fall Apart* 78, 86, 132, 178, 181

Acholi 99-101

Adichie, Chimamanda Ngozi 165, 187

Africa 9, 24, 79, 86, 96; censorship 127; languages 20, 127; literature 86, 97; oral tradition 121; orality 81; print culture 121; publishing 10; reading habits 166, 169; Roman type 135; textual transmission 14

African literature: internationalisation of 181, 186

African National Congress 154, 158

African Times and Oriental Review 89

African Writers Series 86, 101, 143, 173, 181–2, 187

Afrikaans: liturgical texts 123; translations 175

ajami script 36-9

Ajmer 59

Akan 124

Akwapim Twi 124, 137, 172

Ali, Chaudhri Rahmat 116

alphabet: phonetic 11; Roman 35, 108; standardisation 20

Anand, Mulk Raj 176, 183; *Untouchable* 154, 159

Anderson, Benedict 38, 128; *Imagined Communities* 14, 30–1; print culture 10; sacral languages 33

Arabic 33; typeface 109

Arabic script 20, 93; Hausa literature 86, 117; local variations 34–5; Madagascar 109; Malagasy 8; Nana Asma'u 36; Umar, al-Hajj 38

Armah, Ayi Kwei: *Beautyful Ones Are Not Yet Born, The* 173; *Osiris Rising* 173; *Two Thousand Seasons* 173

Aryabhata 44, 46

Asante Twi 137, 172

Asiatic Society of Bengal 3, 42, 65, 147; *Bhagavad Gita* 4; of London 151

Aśoka 64–5; edicts 67

Assamese 128; in Bangla type 134

Assumpcão, Fr. Manuel de 6

authors 46; freedom 81; and readers 185

autonomy: independence 157, 160; South Africa 159

Awoonor, Kofi 139; *African Predicament, The* 178

Bagh o bahar 130

Bailey, Benjamin 69; designs font 55–6

Balmer, W.T.: *History of the Akan Peoples of the Gold Coast* 90–1

Bambara: language 93

Banda, Dr Hastings: Malawi 160

Bangla [Bengali] 3; font design 4, 6; language 5-6, 47; literatures 118; liturgical texts 129; 133; *Mahabharata, The* 49; script 66; standardisation 134; syntax 15; type 3, 69, 128

Bangladesh 6; penal code 150; *Satanic Verses, The* 161

Barber, Karin 50, 80–1, 108, 124

Barthes, Roland 46, 141

Baudhayana 43-4, 45

Bayly, Sir Chris 149-50

Benares: Kashi Raj Trust 140–1; print trade 113